# Daydreaming

# Daydreaming

*Using Waking Fantasy and Imagery for Self-Knowledge and Creativity*

ERIC KLINGER, Ph.D.

JEREMY P. TARCHER, INC.
Los Angeles

Library of Congress Cataloging-in-Publication Data
Klinger, Eric, 1933–
Daydreaming.
Includes bibliographical references.
1. Fantasy. 2. Creative ability. I. Title.
BF411.K55 1990 154.3 90-10931
ISBN 0-87477-567-1



Jeremy P. Tarcher, Inc.
5858 Wilshire Blvd., Suite 200
Los Angeles, CA 90036

Distributed by St. Martin's Press, New York

Manufactured in the United States of America
10 9 8 7 6 5 4 3 2 1

First Edition

*To* the delightful people who have enriched my daydreams, chief among them Karla and our children Heather, Roderick, and Benjamin

# Contents

# Acknowledgments

First and foremost, thanks must go to the thousands of research participants, my own and others', whose day-dreams and life experiences made this book possible. I cannot thank them by name, if for no other reason than because their contributions were almost all anonymous. Many of their day-dreams and life circumstances are scattered through the book.

In all instances, I have changed the names of persons and places and have made other adjustments to protect our participants' privacy without altering the psychologically important features. Because most of the contributions were anonymous, it is possible that a fictitious name I chose happened to be the participant's real name as well, but that would be purely coincidental and highly unlikely.

I also thank the others without whom my research on fantasy would not have been possible: the scores of project coordinators, research assistants, and other staff who have worked on our Project on Fantasy since 1964. Some who made particularly distinctive contributions—in approximate chronological order—include Vernice Lehmann, Ronald Hietala, Frederick W. McNelly, Jr., Joseph Fridgen, Rachel

Froiland Quenemoen, Steven Barta (who coordinated project activities for six crucial years), Deborah Smith, Susan Stumm, Thomas Mahoney, Madeline Maxeiner, Timothy Hoelscher, Sandra R. Johnson, Tony Palmer, Heather Jill Klinger, Dana Meneghel, Jack McCullough, MaryKatherine Larson-Gutman, Michael D. Murphy, Kimberly Stark, and Jill Ostrem.

Portions of the research described here were supported by Grants GS-458 and GS-2735 from the National Science Foundation, MH24804 from the National Institute of Mental Health, and grants from the University of Minnesota.

Librarians Barbara McGinnis and Carolyn Hesler provided enormously useful reference assistance throughout this project, and the MINITEX library consortium provided access to library resources without which this project would not have been feasible.

I thank Professor Steven Gold of Western Carolina University for generously sharing the results of his research.

The book benefited from three levels of editorial help. My wife, Karla Klinger, provided consistent encouragement and took time from her busy professional life to read and comment on the entire manuscript as it unfolded, providing me with first-order feedback and guidance. My literary agent, Howard Sandum, fulfilled a role that went well beyond the bounds of agentry in providing essential encouragement and editorial support during my transition from writing for academics to writing for a wider readership. Without his efforts, I doubt that this project would have gotten off the ground. Hank Stine, my Tarcher editor, may have written almost as much commentary as I wrote manuscript. His editorial dynamism helped me to transform this book. Publisher Jeremy Tarcher's support was crucial at a number of points, and his personal encouragement and grace helped make the process of bringing this book to publication a joy.

Last but by no means least, I thank the University of Minnesota, Morris, for granting and Jeremy Tarcher for financing the leave that enabled me to spend much of my time during 1988–89 just writing.

# Preface

This is a book about daydreaming, all about it, or at least as much about it as we know with reasonable scientific confidence. It is a book for readers who want to find themselves in its pages and get an idea of what other people's daydreams are like, or who want to understand what daydreaming is, how it works, and what it does to us and for us. It provides glimpses of how we have come to know what we know, but it strips away most of the scientific scaffolding and the crosstalk among scientists—so essential to the scientific enterprise—and in plain language describes the emerging shape of our knowledge about daydreaming.

Daydreaming—if you include mindwandering and reverie—turns out to be one of the central features of human life. It is rooted in processes essential to our survival, and it is connected in one way or another to virtually everything about us.

Everything, to quote Barry Commoner's First Law of Ecology, is connected to everything else. When the path-blazing psychiatrist Sigmund Freud set out a century ago to write about the interpretation of dreams, he ended up with the elements of a nearly complete psychology. He could not write about dreams without also writing about wishes, drives, emotions, perception, thought, and, in general, the organization of the mind. Much the same is true of our daydreams: they are an entry point to understanding the human mind.

Several themes run through the book. Daydreaming is both one of the most common and one of the most private things we do. Your daydreams are intensely personal and intensely revealing, because they are you in action within the arena of your mind. They are triggered by your emotional reactions and shaped by your desires and fears. Daydreams are so much a part of you that what you experience in them affects what you do in the real world. Paradoxically, daydreaming is one of the ways in which you keep your life organized, a way to milk your experiences for the lessons they hold, and a way of rehearsing for the future. It is a natural way of improving the efficiency with which we use our brains.

These conclusions about daydreaming are mostly new or recent. The effort to provide hard evidence on daydreaming and related issues has gotten under way only in the past three decades. Before that, daydreaming was more often condemned than understood. The theories of daydreaming most bandied about during the first two-thirds of this century were poorly based, and much of what budding psychologists and schoolteachers learned from their professors about the subject ranged from the misleading to the outright false. Science was slow to take daydreaming seriously. However, enough solid findings have now come in about daydreaming and topics related to it, such as mental imagery, to give us a clearer view of our inner realities.

I myself was slow to focus my research efforts on daydreaming. Like probably all intact humans, I have been a lifelong daydreamer, but overall my daydreaming has been rather average. So it was not because of my own daydreaming that I began investigating the subject. Instead, I came to explore daydreaming through a series of sidesteps. My early specialty was personality assessment—finding ways to characterize individuals so as to be able to predict their behavior. For example, I was interested in improving our ability to predict which applicants to medical school would make the best physicians and which patients at a mental-health clinic would prove to suffer from various mental disorders. The tests then gaining in popularity, and the ones I suspected would be the most useful, were standard question-and-answer inventories such as the Minnesota Multiphasic Personality Inventory. And yet research suggested that for certain specific purposes other measures—those that depended to some extent on people's fantasies, such as inkblot and storytelling tests—were superior.

Why should fantasy-based measures be better at anything? It was this puzzle that brought me to research on fantasy and, as part of fantasy, daydreaming. Yet, I was still not overly impressed with the importance of daydreaming. I still shared the old prejudices, and, in any event, there were few systematic methods for investigating the subject.

However, that soon changed. As my colleagues elsewhere and I developed new methods and the data began to roll in, the pattern they showed pointed in an unmistakable direction: our daydreams are important, they are an essential part of normal functioning, and their role in our lives is overwhelmingly benign. Furthermore, we can harness them to make them even more useful to us than they already are.

I was hooked. Over the years I have researched and taught about daydreams and have incorporated daydreamlike methods into my psychotherapy practice. They have continued to reward and fascinate me.

Methods for investigating daydreaming fall into about five categories:

- recording daydreams
- story-writing
- administering questionnaires about a person's daydreaming patterns

- thought-sampling
- instructing people to daydream and assessing its effects

Investigators often use these methods in combination or combine them with other methods, such as measuring brain waves or social skills, to gain a broader view of what daydreams are like and how they are connected to other aspects of ourselves.

The basic problem in investigating daydreams is that no one can tell exactly what your daydreams are like. To find this out, someone would have to ask you and rely on your account of them. This is what many people do when they ask others to write down daydreams they can remember having or, as psychologist Steven Gold does, whenever they have one. It can provide interesting accounts such as Melba's, who daydreamed about "owning land, hopefully in the mountains, where I can raise organic produce and fruit—live in an easy-going, self-sustaining farm situation where *money* is by no means the greatest concern. . . ." Melba's daydream captures her yearning and instantly tells us important things about how she thinks and what affects her.

Because most natural daydreams are so fleeting and easily forgotten, depending on memories of particular daydreams is bound to produce distorted information, especially if the daydream occurred more than a few seconds before. Either you will not remember what you daydreamed about or your memory is likely to be fragmented and altered by the thoughts and events that took place afterwards.

To get around this kind of problem, it occurred to psychologists that they might learn quite a bit about your fantasy life if they were to examine stories you have made up, because having a daydream and making up a story have certain things in common. As we shall see, authors depend to a great degree on their own daydreams to compose short stories, novels, and all the other forms of creative writing. These can be analyzed to shed light on their authors' minds.

Because most of us do not routinely write stories, it was

necessary to induce the nonauthors among us to create something that could be analyzed. For this purpose, Christiana Morgan and Harvard researcher Henry A. Murray devised a standard set of pictures that could be shown to people along with instructions to write creative stories about them, called *TAT stories* (for "Thematic Apperception Test"). Although they are very different from natural daydreams, they do rely in part on images and fantasizing of the kind that go into daydreaming. They can therefore tell us some important things about the writer's inner life.

Despite the usefulness of TAT stories, they are too artificial—a test situation with instructions to tell a story about a picture—to give us valid, comprehensive information about natural daydreaming. Therefore, a number of investigators, notably psychologists Jerome L. Singer and John S. Antrobus, devised standard questionnaires about our individual daydream patterns. Singer and Antrobus' Imaginal Processes Inventory has proven valid enough to tell us something about how people experience their own daydreams in retrospect and how individuals differ in this regard. Some of the largest-scale questionnaire studies have been carried out by psychologist Leonard Giambra of the National Institute of Aging in Baltimore. In one investigation, Giambra gave the Imaginal Processes Inventory to over 1,300 adults of both sexes and all ages.

Even a questionnaire as good as this one cannot answer most of our questions about *individual* daydreams—when they occur, what triggers them, where they come from, and what they are. Psychologists Mihalyi Csikszentmihalyi, Russell Hurlburt, and I have independently devised ways to sample thoughts and feelings, including daydreams, by beeping people at irregular intervals as a signal to record and describe the last things that went through their minds. For example, one such beep caught Dan at lunch with friends during a daydream of "my hands scuttling across the underside of the table, impossibly extended, and fingering Barb across the table." This method has the virtue of not relying on memory for more than a few seconds into the past, and we can train participants to focus on selected aspects of their daydreams when they report.

Finally, we can learn a good deal about mental imagery and daydreaming by asking people to engage in it while we measure the consequences. For example, psychologist Peter Lang hooks people up to a polygraph that measures such things as heart rate and sweaty palms and instructs them to create different mental images. If you were a participant, you might be asked to imagine driving down an interstate and discovering a yellow-jacket wasp trapped inside your windshield. Then Lang could find out what elements of a daydream make you most emotional (the answer: vividly imagining your movements and body sensations). Or, as psychologist Martha Farah has done, you can record brain waves and find out what areas of the brain are most active during particular mental images. Or, as Alan Kazdin has done, you can ask people to imagine being assertive with someone and find out which kinds of imaginings help them most to become assertive in reality (answer: those that give their natural daydreaming freer play).

Methods such as these have put our beliefs about daydreaming on an ever more solid base of scientific evidence. They have told us much that is new about daydreaming, and they have helped dispel myths about it that were propagated before the evidence came in. And that is the subject of this book.

# How to Use This Book

The mission of this book is to help you understand daydreaming—your own and other people's—by providing you with solid information about it. The book provides a comprehensive, up-to-date view of daydreaming in plain language, along with enough information on how we came to know what we know to satisfy most readers' intellectual curiosity. Because you may have come to the book with concerns about your own daydreaming, it addresses issues such as the link between daydreaming and mental illness (there is little connection) and how to tell the difference between them, whether you can daydream yourself into mental disturbance (you can't), how to evaluate whether you are daydreaming too much, and what the various liabilities and benefits of daydreaming are.

This information should help you to think more clearly about your own daydreaming and to make any decisions you may feel moved to make about it. But this book does not offer you diagnostic tests or simple therapeutic formulas. These are too easily misapplied and, when they are, the result can range from the disappointing to the disastrous.

As a general rule, if after reading this book you still have a serious concern about your daydreaming, it would be a good idea to consult a qualified professional. If you discover that your concern was groundless, you will at least be able to rest easy. You may be able to make the changes you want by applying some of the principles in this book, but no book can come up with dependable prescriptions for what individuals should do about psychological problems. Individual circumstances are just too complex for that. There is also a problem in treating yourself. Even professionals are ill-advised to diagnose and treat themselves for serious psychological difficulties, because they are likely to lack objectivity.

So the best advice if you continue to have serious concerns about your daydreams remains: Seek out a qualified professional. This is most likely to be a licensed psychologist or psychiatrist, although sometimes practitioners in other areas such as counseling or psychiatric nursing are also qualified for this purpose. Whatever the practitioner's profession, it would be important to look for one who is thoroughly up-to-date on the full range of scientific developments in the psychology of daydreams and mental imagery.

CHAPTER 1

# Daydreams: Our Mental Private Lives

*I am married to Harrison Ford or William Hurt. We are both medical doctors. We have six gorgeous, talented, and well behaved children. We are filthy rich.*

—Daydream report

Our minds keep flowing. That is the central fact of human consciousness. And interspersed through it all are our daydreams, a basic and natural feature of the human condition, a part of what enables us to survive.

Daydreams are a life within. The shapes and colors, the feelings, voices, and movements of that daydream life unfold even as we grapple in reality with a different set of shapes and colors, hear a different set of voices, and steer our bodies in a different set of movements through reality. Our daydream and reality spheres are two lives, simultaneous but separate, separate and yet in continual interaction.

Both lives are, each in its way, real. Both have consequences for us. The consequences of our real-world actions are to a large extent apparent, the consequences of our daydreams much less so. And yet they, too, count, because they are real brain events in the same brain systems that govern everything we do, which means that what happens in our daydreams affects our everyday behavior. They count also because they are part of our internal information system, our internal self-housekeeping and self-management system.

Few of us can feel neutral about our daydreams. We have many more daydreams than we are likely to notice, but at least a few of them are likely to stand out, to draw our attention and to make us feel delight or guilt, exhilaration or apprehension, love or hate. The emotions we feel will vary greatly from time to time and from one individual to the next. Some of us treasure our daydream lives and consider them one of our most valued assets; others view them with trepidation or concern and may even feel perplexed and unnerved by the surprising turns they sometimes take. Most of us regard them as so private we prefer to keep them to ourselves. And most of us are also curious about them: curious to know what they are made of, where they come from, how much they help or harm us, and what they can tell us about ourselves.

Fortunately, research has begun to answer these questions. What we have learned from it and what its findings signify for us are the subject of this book. We will consider:

- how our daydreams are linked to our desires and emotions
- what our daydreams are like and how they vary
- sexual daydreaming
- how we can draw meaning from daydreams and use them as a source of self-knowledge
- how daydreams can influence our decisions and actions
- how to distinguish normal daydreaming from mental disturbance
- how much people daydream, and how much is too much
- the many myths about daydreaming
- ways for dealing with daydream patterns we dislike

- the benefits of daydreaming for self-management, growth, therapy, and creativity

## WHAT DAYDREAMS REVEAL ABOUT US

If we were to boil down to just two the ways in which daydreams are important to us, they would be that daydreams reveal a great deal about our individuality, including aspects we may not yet acknowledge to ourselves, and that they perform vital functions in the way we manage ourselves.

Our daydreams are, among other things, extensions of our personalities. We daydream about the things important to us, and we daydream about them in ways that are consistent with the kinds of persons we are. Happy people have buoyant daydreams; depressed people have depressed daydreams; neurotic individuals have daydreams filled with fear and guilt. Because daydreams are of a piece with the rest of us, they reveal us to ourselves; and to the extent that we have avoided facing up to ourselves, they can reveal things about us that we had not recognized.

The possibility of our daydreams revealing things about ourselves that we did not know calls up images of tragic flaws we have never faced up to, or perhaps seething, detestable forces in our unconscious announcing themselves in our daydreams. But the things that lie behind our daydreams typically do not seethe. Depending on your threshold for detesting things, most of what you find will be simply human hopes and yearnings, fears and anger. Granted, the prospect of finding out *anything* unexpected about yourself can be a bit unsettling!

Even the most banal daydreams reflect our personally important issues. You may have a very brief daydream—perhaps only a couple of seconds long—in which you imagine greeting a coworker in the morning. This daydream might seem pretty routine and unenlightening. But the fact that you daydreamed about someone at all, the ways in which you imagined greeting her, and the mix of feelings you experienced while imagining it all reveal something about the extent to which the relationship is important to you and the way in which it is important. And the relationship is important not just for itself but for the needs and fears into which it fits. Perhaps you imagine yourself strolling past the coworker's office, ducking your head in to say hello, and then ducking right back out. This gesture might represent all of the following: You want to become a bigger part of her life. You like her more than you care to reveal at this point. You are afraid she might reject you. You wish to avoid the appearance of sexual harassment. Of course, this daydream could represent quite different things, depending on its details and on your circumstances, but all aspects of a daydream reflect you.

All daydreams are about something that turns you on or off emotionally. Mostly, they are about something you want or fear. You might not want or fear it wholeheartedly, and just what it is that you want or fear might not be screamingly obvious from the daydream, although it often is. But whether it is staring you in the face or buried below the surface meaning of the daydream, the object of your fear or desire is there.

For example, here is a common, simple daydream that could hold many clues to your desires and attitudes. Suppose you have a bellyache and are on your way to the clinic. Rationally, you know that your pain could have any number of relatively benign causes, from mild food poisoning to anxiety. But in your daydream, your physician examines you and comes up with a diagnosis: cancer of the bowel. You imagine your feelings and thoughts, start to formulate plans for telling your family and friends, work on your life priorities.

It is unlikely that you had this daydream because you wanted to die of cancer. If your feelings about a cancer diagnosis were all negative, this would indicate that you probably want very much to live, or at least not to have cancer. The fact that you were daydreaming about it tells you that there is something important to you here; your feelings about it in the daydream tell you that you are afraid of what might happen in your examination. Most likely, you want something quite different from cancer—probably to be free of cancer, to stay intact and healthy.

These interpretations of the daydream are by no means the only possible ones. You can never take a description of a daydream and arrive at a reasonably certain interpretation without considering the daydreamer's current life, state, and history. For example, in the daydream described above you might have felt appalled and frightened by the diagnosis and yet have felt an undercurrent of relief. Relief? Yes, because a cancer diagnosis can also be a solution: an incontestable excuse for not completing something, for failure, for changing the roles you play with others. A careful examination of the daydream experience might have found that you would welcome a way out of too many commitments or too many expectations of yourself, or even a chance for a long if rather unpleasant vacation from the ongoing life pattern. This might not be the dominant wish in the daydream, but if it is an element, the daydream has told you something more about what you want—to change your lifestyle. It is information about yourself that you might not already have considered.

Beyond these kinds of deductions, the daydream can tell you a good deal more. For example, the fact that you immediately imagined breaking the news to family and friends underlines the importance you attach to those relationships and—depending on what you imagined saying to them—the extent to which you feel important to them or value their opinions of you. If in the daydream you began preparing your mind and life for death, this might suggest that you are inclined to think of bowel cancer as necessarily terminal, that you are disposed to giving up before having explored the possibilities for treatment, since otherwise your daydream would probably have turned first to a search for remedies. As you can see, a simple, not uncommon daydream can permit many possible deductions about the daydreamer.

Although daydreams are mostly about something you want or fear, the reverse does not hold true: just because you want or fear something does not necessarily mean you will daydream much about it. For example, if you are lucky enough to have a dependable, ample income that arrives in monthly checks, its continuation may be of enormous importance to you, and yet it may never crop up in a daydream. Likewise, parents and future occupations are both very important to young college students, and yet students tend to think about them less often than they think about some things of far smaller importance, such as the next test or party.

In other words, we daydream about a very limited subset of the things we know about and even a limited subset of the things we want and fear. It is because our minds are so selective in the topics we daydream about and the style we each bring to our daydreams is so very personal that our daydreams are able to reveal so much about our inner selves.

## THE IMPORTANCE OF DAYDREAMS

We spend on average about half of our mental activity on some kind of daydreaming. It stands to reason that anything that people do this much must serve some important functions. After all, one of the cardinal rules of biology is that species gradually lose those capabilities and tendencies that cease to pay off. For example, the bodies of most animal species manufacture their own Vitamin C. But some species, such as humans and guinea pigs, eat such a varied diet that most get the Vitamin C they need from their food. For them, being able to create Vitamin C became less important, and they have accordingly lost the ability to produce it internally. If daydreaming were useless, we would surely do a great deal less of it than seems to be the case.

The more that researchers investigate daydreaming, the more impressive become its probable benefits for us. As it now appears, daydreaming is rooted in psychological processes that are central to the way we function, and it is connected in one way or another to just about everything else about us. Daydreaming is generated through some of the same brain systems we would use if we were taking the actions we are daydreaming about, and it is guided by the same emotions and motives that guide our actions.

Daydreaming keeps reminding us of our current concerns, keeps them cycling through our minds, and thereby helps us keep in touch with the various aspects of our lives. The concerns it comes back to most are those emotionally most important to us. By the way it keeps reminding us of our personal agendas; it helps keep our lives organized.

Daydreaming is also a way of deepening our learning from our previous experiences by leading us to keep rehashing and replaying them, often revealing things about them we had not previously noticed or suggesting better ways of dealing with them should they recur.

Another purpose of daydreaming is to explore our options for the future. We tend to play upcoming challenges through our minds, which contributes to our planning. In this respect, daydreaming is also a form of rehearsal, in the sense that we practice in our daydreams some of the actions we may take later. Because we get better at the things we rehearse, even if the rehearsal is just mental, daydreaming can help us to improve our skills, whether physical, social, or intellectual.

Daydreaming can help us move toward making decisions. Insofar as it helps us detail the consequences of our choices, it can make us more confident about making them.

Daydreaming is a channel of information about ourselves to ourselves, and therefore it can contribute to our self-knowledge and self-understanding. It reveals some of what we want and what we fear, sometimes even when we would rather not know. Keeping tabs on our own daydreams, especially during periods of stress, can therefore help us stay in touch with our real needs, feelings, and states of mind.

Daydreams can be a medium for growth experiences and therapy, partly for all of the above reasons and partly because skilled therapists can help us harness more fully the potential of daydreaming for self-knowledge and change. They can also contribute to our creativity, both in everyday life and in the arts and sciences, and are themselves a form of creative expression.

Finally, daydreaming can serve as a way to change our moods—to relax and to entertain ourselves, providing a way to have fun with life.

## THE HISTORICAL NEGLECT AND LOW REPUTE OF DAYDREAMING

The positive view of daydreaming advanced here by no means reflects the traditional opinion. In fact, thinkers through the ages have mostly either ignored or disparaged daydreaming and daydreamers. Concordances to great sacred texts—the Bible, the Koran, and the Vedas—contain several references to dreams but none to daydreams. And the historically most notable philosophers and theologians have taken a dim view toward them.

Plato, writing in Greece in the fourth century B.C., wrote contemptuously of "daydreamers . . . feasting themselves when they are walking alone; for before they have discovered any means of effecting their wishes—that is a matter which never troubles them—they would rather not tire themselves by thinking about possibilities. . . ." Avid daydreamers, we have since learned, are on average as effective as anyone else.

Michel Montaigne, the great sixteenth-century French essayist, was impressed with the power of daydreams to mislead: "Let me think of building castles in Spain, my imagination suggests to me conveniences and pleasures with which my soul is really tickled and pleased. How often do we torment our mind with anger or sorrow by such shadows, and engage ourselves in fantastic passions that impair both soul and body?" Daydreams *can*, in fact, get us worked up over something needlessly. This is part of the price we pay for their benefits. But we now know that people who enjoy frequent elaborate daydreams tend to develop a strong ability to separate fantasy from reality, which protects them from getting unduly swept away by their daydreams.

The seventeenth-century French philosopher-scientist Blaise Pascal distrusted his imaginative inner life and tried to blot it out in favor of cold reason. He described imagination as "that deceitful part in man, that mistress of error and falsity. . . . Those who have a lively imagination are a great deal more pleased with themselves than the wise can reasonably be. . . . Imagination cannot make fools wise; but she can make them happy, the envy of reason which can only make its friends miserable. . . ." In his denunciation of "imagination," Pascal was at odds with a long series of modern scientists, including Albert Einstein, who regarded their imaginative powers as crucial to their scientific discoveries.

Sigmund Freud, the father of psychoanalysis, considered daydreaming to be focused on immediate, imaginary fulfillment of wishes and therefore inherently infantile. Freud, and especially later psychoanalysts such as Ernst Kris, saw its connections to creativity in poetry and art. But Freud's insistence that daydreaming was infantile and neurotic led his imaginative daughter Anna, herself later a major contributor to psychoanalysis, to try stamping out her own fanciful daydreams. They were one reason for her seeking psychoanalysis for herself, and the fact that they kept recurring was a source of self-doubt and disappointment for her. Freud's view, buttressed by tradition, found its way into the educational psychology taught to teachers and into the budding mental-health movement, both of which for many decades mistakenly branded daydreaming as undesirable and potentially dangerous to mental health.

## The Recent Reevaluation of Daydreaming

Modern science largely ignored daydreams until recently. Before 1966, the date of Jerome L. Singer's groundbreaking book on the subject, only two scientifically oriented books devoted specifically to daydreams had appeared in the English language. *The Psychology of Daydreams* was authored in 1921 by Dutch child psychologist Julien Varendonck, who had spent years minutely examining his own daydreams. Although he was inspired and guided by Sigmund Freud, he relied on his own observations of himself and came to his own fresh conclusions, which anticipated much of what we have since learned about daydreams through more rigorous methods. For example, he noted that our emotions instigate and help steer our daydreams. In his final conclusion, he continued the psychoanalytic tradition of seeing in daydreams elements of pathology, but he also saw the broader picture: "Daydreaming proves thus to be a mental phenomenon common to all human beings, and a modern adaptation of a primitive process that can be followed far down the psychological scale. In man this form of ideation is manifested not only through absentmindedness and distraction, but presides over verbal humour and analogous formations. It causes errors and mistakes in our daily life . . . it is predominant in hysteria and neuroses; inspiration borrows its mechanisms; it explains our behaviour whenever our emotions prove stronger than our will."

Forty-five years elapsed before the scientific book on daydreaming by Singer appeared. Since then, the scientific literature on daydreaming and related topics has grown rapidly, reporting investigations whose methods range from the use of questionnaires to the study of brain waves. We still have a great deal to learn about daydreams, but their general shape—what they are like, when and how they occur—has become much clearer. And with that clarity we are seeing increasingly their importance in everyday life and their potential for improving it.

### Likely Reasons for Prescientific Views of Daydreaming

There are a number of likely reasons that daydreaming was for so long denied appropriate recognition.

First, daydreaming is such a large part of our inner life that we take much of it for granted. Like the air we breathe, on which our lives depend but which we hardly notice until it is cut off, daydreams are so much a part of daily conscious experience that they are easily overlooked. Many of them are about such everyday things that they don't clearly stand out from our other thoughts. Unlike our experience with dreams, which occur without our feeling a sense of control over them, we generally recognize that we produce our own daydreams; and, compared to dreams, their meanings are somewhat more easily discerned. Daydreaming therefore feels a bit less mysterious than dreaming and calls less attention to itself.

Second, our daydreams are so private that we tend not to talk about them, thereby leaving each other in ignorance of one another's daydream experiences. This means that the daydreams we know are mostly limited to our own. This lack of systematic knowledge of other people's daydreams led to an incomplete view of them. Psychoanalysts such as Sigmund Freud received copious accounts of daydreams from their patients; but their patients were, by definition, troubled human beings. Having little information about the daydreaming of people who were not patients, psychoanalysts erroneously linked daydreaming to psychiatric disturbance.

There is yet a third likely reason for the traditional disparagement of daydreams: the conflict between commentators' motives and the essential nature of daydreams. Daydreams are as free as our waking minds can get. They reflect our individual desires and incipient plans, often more clearly than we are prepared to acknowledge, as well as our fears and guilts. They are under nobody else's direct control. But the people who have traditionally commented on daydreams—philosophers, theologians, meditators, and educators—are preponderantly identified with a cause. And those causes require individuals to suppress many of their longings, the kinds that our daydreams reflect and advance.

Most philosophers have come out of their societies' establishments, and most have remained loyal to their civilizations' most basic values. Much of traditional philosophy has sought ways to understand the world and society in the hope of strengthening civilization. For example, Plato's *Republic*, the first of many such attempts, lays out a blueprint for organizing politics and society in general. But insofar as people espouse civilization, they have an interest in control and find a potential opponent in individuals' daydreams. Daydreaming, as free inner living, can be taken as a nuisance by those who have designs on our energies.

All advanced civilizations impose on us a heavy degree of regimentation. Individuals are required to sacrifice their individuality—their natural biological cycles of sleeping and waking, hunger and satiety, sexual desire and sexual surfeit, and even the attitudes they dare to express—to the obligations of social integration. You are expected to get to work on time, obey military orders, serve your superiors, pay your taxes and debts, and keep your word, however long ago you gave it. Daydreams, on the other hand, reflect your unmet needs, your feelings, and your preferred plans. They remind you and can occasionally incite you to stick up for yourself against your surroundings. To people in charge of order, the defenders and apologists for the established civilization, they constitute potential resistance—collectively, at least a nuisance, and, in extreme cases, even a menace.

Job supervisors and military officers lay claim to your consciousness for your organization; religious leaders and masters, for the discipline of the faith; teachers, for imparting set lessons; and parents, for obeying them. It is therefore no wonder that employers, teachers, sergeants, and parents get upset when *your* daydreaming interferes with *their* plans for you, or that theologians disapprove when your daydreams violate their religious ideals.

But as we learn more about daydreams, we are coming to appreciate their status as a vital process and a valuable resource. Enlightened leaders, relying increasingly on psychological consultants, are already making greater allowances for the way we humans function in reality, including the way our minds work, and that includes daydreaming. The chances are good that we will gradually redesign schedules and equipment to protect and harness our daydreaming rather than to disparage and suppress it.

## DAYDREAMS ARE PART OF OUR MOST PRIVATE SELVES

The phenomena that run through our conscious minds make up the whole substance of who we are to ourselves. They are our only immediate way of knowing ourselves and, for that matter, the world beyond. And they are all ours—we share these experiences of ourselves with no one else unless we choose to.

Some of what passes through our mind is so tied to outside reality that we willingly offer it to others. That is one reason the weather is such a popular conversation piece. We tell other things only selectively, because they reveal something of our individuality. For example, there are thoughts about your best friend that you might tell only to your spouse. We keep private the material that we think could damage our standing with the person to whom we are talking or that could give the other person undue power over us.

### Reluctance to Disclose Our Daydreams

Among the things we treat as most private are our daydreams, and that is a measure of how important they are to us—and how much we think they reveal our inner selves. To test this premise, we gave a group of research volunteers a choice: they could sign up to tell about one of their daydreams or to tell about one of their real-life experiences. Their choices were remarkably one-sided. Four out of five—80 percent—signed up to tell about an actual experience, 6 percent didn't care, and only 15 percent signed up to tell about a daydream, even though both the daydream and the real-life experience were to be about the same kind of thing—an achievement, something that happened with a friend, or a situation that aroused anger.

People's reluctance to talk about their daydreams extends even to situations where not talking about them is harmful. In a group of psychiatric outpatients surveyed anonymously by Texas psychiatrist Myron Weiner and law professor Daniel Shuman, 42 percent admitted withholding information from their psychotherapists. The most frequent kind of information that the men withheld was of their violent *thoughts*, with their sexual thoughts tied for second place. Among the women, sexual thoughts were tied with sexual acts for being withheld most often. Many of those thoughts would undoubtedly qualify as daydreams.

The reason we hold back on sharing daydreams is probably the way it makes us feel. Imagine your different feelings if you were to describe one of your daydreams to a close friend or spouse, to your employer, to your employee, to a coworker, to your hairdresser, or to a stranger on an airliner. You might have no difficulty telling any of them your outlook on the weather or even your vacation plans. When you returned from vacation, you might tell any of them about an experience during your vacation. But recounting a daydream is likely to feel very different from this. Suppose that you told your coworker your daydream about sneaking into the bed of an attractive individual you had met casually and making uninhibited, anonymous love. Even though it never happened—sometimes, *because* it never happened!—sharing this daydream is likely to have some of the qualities of a confession, of exposing yourself, some embarrassment.

A group of psychology students were asked to imagine how they would feel after telling a friend about a daydream or after telling a friend about an actual experience of the same kind—an exciting achievement, an event in another relationship, or something that had evoked hurt or anger. In this experiment, performed with my students Michael D. Murphy, Jill Ostrem, and Kimberly Stark, participants felt on average slightly more upset—more fearful, sad, and bashful—when what they imagined disclosing was a daydream than when it was a real event of the same kind. In fact, 39 percent of them agreed with the statement "My daydreams are my own personal business and I would not discuss them with another person."

We also found some clues as to what it takes to feel comfortable about disclosing your daydreams: feeling psychologically extra secure. Those participants who felt the least distressed after revealing daydreams as compared with past experiences are people who generally feel less anxiety and stress. They also tend to be somewhat more assertive and confident in social situations, to get distracted less easily, and to give their own thoughts free play.

These findings underline the hesitancy we feel about disclosing our daydreams. Disclosing them is intimidating because it exposes you. If you already feel insecure, you feel more protective of yourself and therefore shield yourself more from unnecessary exposure.

When one person communicates highly personal material to another, that is a major event in their relationship. It confers a measure of power on the second person over the first, it creates vulnerability, and it implies trust. By the same token, we take it as the hallmark of intimacy between two people that they freely share their thoughts, not only the trivial and neutral ones but also their innermost desires, their dreams, and their daydreams.

### Reluctance to Face Our Own Daydreams

Sometimes our reluctance to communicate our daydreams even extends to recalling or thinking about them. One possible reason for this reluctance is that our daydreams sometimes contrast with the picture we wish to cultivate about ourselves. We are complex beings with needs that often come in conflict. We may learn the advantages of doing one thing, such as getting rich or having sexual adventures, while also learning the advantages of the opposite course, such as serving humanity or maintaining a strong marriage. If you grew up knowing that you would get the most respect from parents or friends by serving the poor, you would want to think of yourself as being the kind of person who wants and does that, and you might begin to look down on the pursuit of wealth. If you grew up knowing that wealth is power and freedom and the road to respect from family and friends, you would gravitate toward opportunities for wealth and suppress any other inclinations. But the desires that get neglected this way—desires for ease and freedom from want, for example, or for relatedness and freedom from guilt—are still likely to be there, and they may show up in your daydreams. You may be a highly responsible parent and employee but daydream about ditching job and family and starting life over in another place. You may have taken a career in human services out of social conviction but daydream about getting rich. You may be a faithful spouse but daydream about sex with others.

When you find your self-image and your daydreams disagreeing, which of them is the real you? To some extent, of course, the answer is "both." But one represents the parts of you that you are willing to own up to and the other represents parts that you are not sure you know, that may hold surprises, that feel out of your conscious control. For example, dreaming of owning a palatial home when you thought you had relinquished such thoughts for other ideals may feel like self-betrayal or sin.

Because of this potential for surprise, exploring your daydreams, like exploring your night dreams, can feel either like an exciting adventure or like the way to confirm your worst fears about yourself. Compared to your night dreams, your daydreams are likely to be more easily understood. This may actually make revealing them more threatening to you, because those intentions that you may be reluctant to acknowledge are likely to be plainer to you. But daydreams are also more controllable than night dreams, which makes them on average tamer and less mysterious.

Whichever way you feel about your daydreams, there is no way to know yourself completely without feeling at home with them along with the rest of you. To the extent that some of your daydreams still spook you, there is a part of yourself that you refuse to acknowledge. When you can accept daydreams that are inconsistent with your concept of yourself, you can also accept that you have made some difficult choices in your life—to satisfy some needs and to neglect others—and can identify with all of your desires, not only with the choice you made. You can also keep reexamining your choices and reconfirm or change them when they no longer feel right. Only under these conditions of full self-knowledge—aided by the clues in your daydreams—can you make fully informed decisions about your life.

Even if you feel a bit squeamish at first about facing your daydreams, there is no need to despair. The more intimately you know and understand them, the less threatening they are likely to become. This is true of most things we fear: facing them and discovering that they do not hurt us after all diminishes the fear, whereas avoiding them maintains or heightens fear. So if you start out somewhat afraid of your daydreams, that will subside as you get better acquainted with them. If you feel too uncomfortable to tackle this project by yourself, a competent professional can provide the support you need.

## WHAT ARE DAYDREAMS?

Daydreams take the form of thoughts and mental images. Our consciousness holds other kinds of thoughts and images besides daydreams:

- perceptions
- memories
- internal commentaries
- working thoughts, which include solving problems and making decisions

There are no clear-cut boundaries between these thoughts and images. They shade into one another, and these other things that go through our minds often connect with our daydreams.

Some of the time our minds dwell on what is out there in our surroundings to perceive—to see, hear, smell, taste, and feel. During most of that time we also engage in a running mental commentary in which we keep relating what we perceive to what we want and fear. You look at the sky and think how beautifully blue it is or that it looks like rain. You look at your lover's face and know you want to kiss it. But although this inner commentary is different from daydreaming, it often leads into daydreams. For example, you not only want to kiss your lover's face as you gaze at it, you imagine doing so, and then you imagine a lovemaking session.

Another part of the time we are working with our minds, trying deliberately to achieve some mental result. We are calculating numbers or figuring out how to cast a sales presentation or trying to write a letter. We might call such efforts "working thoughts" or "operant thoughts." Even they are likely to be interspersed with little daydreams, although they are not daydreams themselves. For example, Dan is in the middle of a tennis workout, volleying with Slim, a tough opponent. Dan is trying hard to avoid being humiliated by Slim when he remembers an earlier incident of being insulted by Rex. For a moment, he daydreams that he is clubbing Rex. But he continues to focus on besting Slim, his current opponent.

When our minds are not focused on some immediate task, we are occupied with other concerns. We review our past experiences, rehearse for the future, savor good things that have happened to us or that might, and shudder at awful ones. We relive in our minds episodes of our real lives as we remember them—or regretfully as we wish they had transpired, or gratefully as we fear they might have. And we form visions of our future: our realistic expectations, together with their implications for us, or alternative possibilities for our future lives insofar as we can conceive them. And much of that time—probably most of it—we are daydreaming.

For example, your attention wanders, and without fully realizing it you look blankly out into space and imagine explaining to your boss why you missed a deadline. Or you replay and embellish parts of the long stroll you took along the beach with a new acquaintance. You imagine disrobing and making love to the attractive stranger walking down the sidewalk. You imagine cutting your forty-minute commute to ten minutes by riding a magnetically propelled people mover. Or perhaps you imagine abolishing your commute altogether by patenting your idea for a nonfat whipped cream and becoming independently wealthy. Your mind cuts to a scene of you lolling in a deck chair next to a swimming pool, sipping something cool, surrounded by grass and shrubs and flowering trees. Those are clearly daydreams.

We spend a substantial part of our mental activity in daydreaming. It is fair to say that we daydream on the average up to about half of our waking hours, although the estimate could range from near zero to about 70 percent of the time, depending on what we include in "daydreaming."

One way working thoughts differ from daydreams is that they are mostly deliberate—we *mean* to think them. For example, when you compose a letter, you intend to have the thoughts you write down. But many of our thoughts, probably about a third, are more spontaneous than deliberate. They are thoughts you did not specifically intend to have; they just popped into your mind. Because you did not will them into being, spontaneous thoughts can also be considered involuntary.

Most daydreams are spontaneous in this way. For example, suppose you are driving down the road and begin to imagine a conference you will attend later in the day. The conference may be important to you and may entail a lot of work, but the thought about the conference while you are driving came to you spontaneously. You can "see" the other people at the meeting sitting around a large table and you can imagine snatches of conversation. In the middle of these thoughts, you may make a mental note of something you need to do before the conference. Until you started to make the mental note, your thought about the conference would qualify as a spontaneous daydream.

Not all daydreamlike thoughts are completely spontaneous. Sometimes we plunge into intentional fantasies that are nevertheless very daydreamlike, and most people would consider them daydreams. People who go to certain kinds of psychotherapists spend part of their therapy hours constructing "guided daydreams"—vivid daydreams that follow the therapist's specifications. As such a patient you might be asked to imagine yourself on a meadow and then let your daydream unfold spontaneously. You intended to have that daydream, although you may not try to control the way in which it unfolds once you have launched it. In a completely different context, most people construct fantasies in order to stimulate themselves sexually during masturbation.

The majority of daydreams are brief episodes about everyday occurrences. Others are dramatic and fanciful, although these are only a small part of most people's total daydreaming. Few of us do most of our daydreaming in the style made famous by James Thurber's "Secret Life of Walter Mitty," although nearly all of us have storylike Mitty-style daydreams at least now and then. Every so often, as I pull away from the curb in my eight-year-old Chevy on my way to the nearest highway, I am telling the cabin attendants to check seat belts, and, while pulling onto the highway and accelerating as fast as my four cylinders can manage, I am barreling down the runway for takeoff. But takeoff and the daydream generally end when the actual speedometer reaches about 55 miles per hour, and this kind of daydream takes up only a tiny percentage of the time I spend awake. Our studies of other people's thoughts indicate that elaborate, fanciful daydreams are infrequent. If we were to consider only extended Walter-Mitty-style daydreams to be "true" daydreams, then the percentage of time we have them would be on the average very small.

Those of us who enjoy engaging in a lot of dramatic, elaborate daydreaming are generally none the worse for it. As we shall see, such people are on the average about as well adjusted psychologically as those who daydream less. They may even have some special psychological strengths. At the very least, they have a reliable source of private entertainment!

But our more abbreviated daydreams are no less important or personalized for their being less fanciful, for all daydreams are highly individual productions and are revealing of the person behind them. Most of them play an important role in our mental lives, helping us to cope more effectively.

Some daydreams that are less elaborate than a Mitty daydream are still to some degree fanciful. They may be images of yourself doing things you would ordinarily not consider doing or that you would be incapable of doing. For example, you might briefly imagine yourself on your deathbed, or you might imagine flying over traffic by flapping your arms. Or the thoughts might be peculiar by dint of containing a seemingly disconnected series of images, as sometimes happens in dreams. Up to about 20 percent of people's thoughts have some such slightly peculiar element.

We can now try to estimate the average proportion of time we spend daydreaming. Let us first count as daydreams all thoughts that are more spontaneous and involuntary than they are intentional. Then let us add to those any further thoughts that are at least slightly fanciful or disorganized, as well as all intentional daydreams. *Using this formula, daydreaming includes up to about half of the average person's daily mental activity!*

**The Language of Daydreams**

The English language has developed a substantial number of words that are in one way or another related to daydreams but do not mean exactly the same thing. Following are some fairly standard terms, along with their meanings, that you will encounter throughout the book.

*Fantasy* includes both daydreams and night dreams, storytelling, some kinds of creative fiction, graphic arts, films, and music. Fantasies are productions of your imagination, regardless of the form they may take. Daydreaming is that kind of fantasizing that takes the form of waking thought, including mental imagery.

There are a number of words that describe the timing and flow of thoughts, including daydreams:

*Mindwandering* refers to veering off the subject of whatever you had intended to focus on. You may be reading a page and suddenly discover that you have not absorbed the last two paragraphs because your mind was elsewhere. Mindwandering generally leads you into daydreaming, but the word itself highlights your distraction from your task.

In *chains of thought*, each thought or daydream reminds you of something that triggers the next one.

When your thoughts about some theme, including daydreams, come tumbling out quickly, one after the other, you are experiencing an *outpouring* of thoughts. In extreme cases, if they constitute a rapidly shifting thought chain, they would be called a *flight of ideas*.

Staying absorbed in a chain of thought for a very long time is being in a state of *reverie*, which refers to being "lost in thought." If your reverie is about a single thing, or if you often revert to daydreaming or otherwise thinking about one thing, you are likely to be called *preoccupied*. And should your thoughts about that one thing seem to go in circles, repeating the same elements and getting progressively staler, psychologists would consider you to be *ruminating*—chewing your mental cud! If you daydream different versions of one basic memory or scenario, we could speak of your *replaying variations* on that theme.

Sometimes daydreams become very intense and are called *waking dreams*. This term is applied especially to guided daydreams used in psychotherapy sessions, when daydreamers become observers of their own daydreams and describe them to their therapists as they unfold.

Two other terms refer to two main constituents of consciousness: *mental imagery* and *emotional reactions*.

Mental imagery consists of the sights, sounds, smells, tastes, and bodily sensations that we experience in the absence of the things they represent. For example, without actually looking, describe your surroundings—the place in which you are reading this book. With your eyes closed, count the number of seats around you, or trees, or boats, or sunbathers.

How did you go about doing this? You probably created a scene in your head, perhaps very faint and fragmentary, that gave you a sense of the furniture or layout of those surroundings. You may have pointed to each thing you were counting, mentally or even by really moving your hand. Your eyes may have moved from side to side behind your closed lids. This movement of hands and eyes shows that your mental images had dimensions and contained objects. They had some of the properties of a real scene.

Mental imagery need not be just visual. You can probably imagine a church bell ringing or your best friend's voice speaking to you. You can imagine the smell of coffee or the texture of fur or the feel of swinging a baseball bat. If you get deeply into an image of biting into a very sour lemon, there is a good chance that your lips will begin to purse, much as they would if lemon juice were actually gushing into your mouth.

Mental imagery is the most important building block of daydreaming. Along with emotional feelings, it is the material of which daydreams are made. But daydreams go beyond imagery, giving it structure over time as your images unfold in meaningful patterns. Just as buildings may be built of bricks but are more than bricks, daydreams are made in part of images but are more than images. And daydreams are not the only things that contain mental images: so do dreams and many working thoughts.

Daydreams also include emotional reactions. Depending on what we daydream about, we may feel our hearts warmed or feel depressed or frightened, we may become angry or sexually aroused, or we may be filled with love or disgust. Sometimes the events of our daydreams stir the emotional reactions, as when we replay in our minds what someone did to us and get angry all over again. At other times, the emotional reaction ushers in the daydream. For example, you may hear a name like your lover's, feel your chest quiver and a yearning rise, and daydream about your next meeting.

**Daydreams and Night Dreams**

Our minds keep churning day and night. There may be periods during deep sleep when little occurs, but by and large our thoughts flow through the day and continue into sleep and then, with perhaps occasional breaks, through sleep and back into wakefulness.

The average qualities of our mental activity change from waking to sleeping. Our mental images become more vivid during parts of the sleep cycle than they ordinarily do when we are awake, and on the average they are likely to be organized somewhat more loosely. But waking daydreams and sleeping night dreams have a good deal in common: they have some of the same qualities of thought and imagery, are triggered by some of the same events, and follow a similar ninety-minute cycle.

Dreams and daydreams each share some of the properties that are characteristic of the other. For one thing, much of sleep is spent in the kind of mental commentary we keep up while awake, although it would likely be less comprehensible to outsiders because sleepy speech is often somewhat garbled. (One woman, still half asleep but wanting her husband to raise the window shade, instructed her to "light the towel"!) Conversely, up to a quarter of our waking thoughts, and especially daydreams, have at least traces of what dream researchers such as David Foulkes have designated as "dreamlike." For example, your daydream might make an abrupt transition from imagining working in a hospital to skiing in Oregon. Or you might be daydreaming about a meeting with a bad-tempered administrator and imagine the administrator as much larger and fiercer than life.

The factors that lead you to daydream are also at work during sleep to help steer your dreams. Cues that arouse your emotions and remind you of a current concern are likely to trigger a daydream or other thought about that concern while you are awake and a dream about it while you are asleep.

Finally, both dreams and daydreams appear to follow a single ninety-minute cycle that continues around the clock. Dream researchers long ago discovered that sleep runs in such cycles. Toward the end of each cycle our dreams become especially vivid and fanciful. More recently, San Diego psychiatrists Daniel Kripke and David Sonnenschein have shown that while we are awake our tendency to daydream also peaks about every ninety minutes.

Clearly, daydreaming and night dreaming are parts of a single flow. They are each very variable, and together they make up a single continuum of human consciousness in which one continually shades into the other—much as each day the varied world of daytime shades into the equally variable world of night.

## THE PLAN OF THE BOOK

Chapter 2 answers questions about where daydreams come from—what triggers them and what shifts them from one topic to the next. It looks at the way in which our wants and fears and the emotional reactions they entail control our attention and the things we daydream about. In turn, it shows how what we daydream about reveals what we want and fear. The chapter then considers the extent to which unconscious processes influence our daydreams. Finally, it describes circumstances that control when and how much we daydream and our rhythms of day- and night dreaming.

Chapter 3 describes what our daydreams are like—what our daydream experiences consist of, what we daydream about, how much we daydream, and how that varies according to our age and sex. It argues that daydreams are a form of constructive self-distraction that helps to remind us of our personal agendas and to keep our lives organized.

Chapter 4 describes how our daydreaming styles differ

from one individual to the next. It examines the three main kinds of individual differences and the source of our different daydreaming styles in our personalities and goals. The chapter then discusses people who enjoy especially heavy amounts of daydreaming—so-called "fantasy-prone personalities"—and the relationship between heavy daydreaming and mental health.

Chapter 5 shows how daydreams reveal the individuality of the person behind them and how to extract some of their meaning. It begins with analyzing simple, everyday daydreams and moves to the especially vivid imagery of guided daydreams and night dreams. It then shows how the same principles by which daydreams can reveal our personalities have been applied to analyzing the stories that people tellin response to standardized pictures. It discusses how well we can describe people's personalities by analyzing the stories they write and the extent to which people can manufacture stories to fool an analyst about their real personalities. The chapter shows next how we reveal ourselves and our potential selves in our creative writing, and it ends with some rules and considerations for extracting information from daydreams.

Chapter 6 examines the role of daydreaming in sexuality. It begins by describing the amount of daydreaming that is sexual, and it considers how the amount of our sexual daydreaming relates to the quality of our sex lives, our attitudes toward sex, and our psychological health. It looks closely at some particular varieties of sexual daydreaming, including rape daydreams. The chapter goes on to show that daydreams are a common part of people's sexual experiences and describes the ways in which they are beneficial or damaging.

Chapter 7 describes what mental images—a key ingredient of daydreams—are made of and why that makes them such a useful tool for learning and self-exploration. It looks at the linkages between imagining something and seeing it, hearing it, and moving our muscles—linkages both in our minds and in the brain-system overlaps that unite these activities. These linkages make daydreaming a medium for learning and self-improvement, including changing our emotional reactions and our social and physical skills.

Chapter 8 describes myths about daydreaming that hold it to be a symptom of mental immaturity and erroneously warn that too much daydreaming causes one to slide into serious psychological disturbance. The chapter reviews what we know about the relationship of daydreaming to mental illness and to our ability to distinguish fantasy from reality. It explores the question of how much daydreaming is too much and how you can tell whether you have reached that point.

Chapter 9 describes the ways in which people can get overly preoccupied with worry and obsessional thought and suggests ways in which they can free themselves from it. It discusses ways of telling the difference between healthy preoccupation and counterproductive worry, how worry comes about, and how to break into the worry cycle as well as into preoccupation with anger, sex, and fear. It ends by discussing unhappy daydreams and how daydreams can affect your ability to deal with temptation.

Chapter 10 describes the many benefits of daydreaming, such as relaxation, stimulation, self-organization, and improving your physical and social skills. It describes how these benefits are harnessed for personal growth and for psychotherapy, especially in the form of guided imagery. Also described is new evidence on the benefit of daydreaming in making decisions. The chapter discusses the role of daydreaming in the creativity of scientists, writers, and artists, and it demonstrates how children's imaginative play is linked to healthy personalities. It ends by summing up the case for daydreaming as a natural process vital to our effective human functioning. Daydreaming rests on basic biological capacities and is, ironically, a way to help us reap the maximum use of our brain power.

CHAPTER 2

# Why We Daydream: Where Daydreams Come From and What They Reveal About Us

*I was one of the top tennis players in the U.S. but was not ranked or anything. I just played for the fun of it and could beat about anybody. I lived in a big house in the mountains with my own private tennis courts beside them. I played tournaments now and then to earn money to live on but I didn't have everyone all after me to be in the papers and play for any teams. I kept going over certain plays in my mind and how good I was.*

—Daydream reported by an anonymous student

One of the age-old questions people have had about themselves is about the origin of their spontaneous daydreams and creative insights. Early religions viewed them as inspired or implanted by gods and devils. Early scientific investigators collected and classified them and tried to demonstrate their origins in our infantile wishes. But only in recent decades have scientists' outlooks and research tools become adequate for undertaking a more rigorous scientific analysis of why we daydream. As evidence on this question slowly accumulates, researchers are increasingly able to provide some reasonably well-based answers.

The question of why we daydream really breaks down into four other questions:

- What are our daydreams made of?
- Where do they come from?
- What sets them off?
- What causes us to daydream about one thing rather than another?

The next four sections of the chapter address these four questions in turn. They will show that the evidence compiled by researchers suggests some basic principles governing the way our daydreams are set in motion. In brief, these principles are that daydreams

- are a mental version of our everyday ability to see, hear, smell, taste, feel, and move, using parts of the same brain mechanisms that these activities do
- are woven around things related to our goals
- are triggered by emotional reactions
- are most often triggered automatically
- take place when circumstances preclude doing something immediate about a goal
- may be suppressed when we are busy with an emotionally more compelling activity
- may push aside something we were focusing on that is emotionally less compelling than the daydream
- are less likely to be triggered by things whose emotional impact has worn thin

## WHAT ARE DAYDREAMS MADE OF?

Daydreams come out of the very essence of your being. They seem to pop up without any effort on your part, and they unfold as spontaneously as they started. But they are produced by the same brain machinery that produces the rest of your thoughts and actions, and they occur for the same reasons. Just as everything else you think or do is a reaction to something outside you or inside you, daydreams are reactions, too.

The most obvious feature of our daydreams is the action of envisioning things happening in our "mind's eye." Humans, like other primates, rely heavily on their ability to see, and the parts of our brains devoted to seeing are very highly developed. But when we see, we are really creating—in our brains—a model of what we are looking at, and we can recreate that model long after we are no longer looking at the particular thing that gave rise to it. That is, we humans have evolved the capacity to create views in our minds—our own mental imagery.

This capacity is not limited to vision. We also have the capacity to create in our minds hearing, smell, taste, bodily feelings, and the sensation of moving. These forms of mental imagery are the basic stuff out of which daydreams are made.

No one knows at exactly what point in evolution species developed this ability to create mental imagery, but it clearly provided a major advantage for survival. The ability to think ahead by picturing our future, as we do in daydreaming, must have greatly improved our ancestors' ability to plan, to prepare, and to make intelligent choices. And it laid the necessary biological basis for daydreaming.

This capacity was not entirely new. It was an extension of our brains' already existing equipment for seeing, hearing, moving, and the like. Chapter 7 will look more closely at the way in which the brain mechanisms for mental imagery, the chief component of daydreaming, overlap the mechanisms for sensing and moving. For now, the important point is that our daydreams are part of our larger ability to sense and to act.

## WHERE DO DAYDREAMS COME FROM?

Daydreams are reactions in competition with the other ways you can react, and in some ways they are very much like those other reactions. By virtue of their being reactions, daydreams are rooted in the basic biological feature of human life: the imperative and capacity to pursue and achieve goals.

Reactivity is ultimately what distinguishes most animals from most plants. No matter how much a tree needs nutrients, holding a fistful of fertilizer under its branches will not change its behavior. But place food within scenting distance of a hungry human, rat, or amoeba and watch it locomote toward the food.

Our very existence depends on these reactions. Unlike trees, which must count on their surroundings to provide everything they need, most animals must get up and pursue what they need. In other words, if we can call all those things we go after "goals," humans survive only insofar as they achieve certain requisite goals. The struggle to achieve those goals—the objects of our strongest desires—is ultimately what we daydream about.

As we have evolved over the eons into relatively sophisticated beings, we humans have become capable of ever more complicated reaction patterns. Instead of just swimming around until we sense the presence of food, like a hungry amoeba, we make decisions to pursue a variety of goals—everything from going out for pizza to winning the Nobel prize or getting closer to God—and we sometimes keep after these goals for many years. That does not mean that we have left our more primitive reaction patterns behind; we simply have built on them. And in the process of making our goal pursuits longer and more complicated, we have paved the way for daydreaming.

When hungry human infants are touched in the right way, for instance, they are equipped from birth to root around with their faces looking for a nipple, and when they find one and get their lips around it, they suck. They get better at this as they gain experience, but the rudiments of the pattern are normally there at birth. In other words, the hungry infant sets off after a goal and then, by virtue of having begun, is set up to react in specific ways to specific sensations as they arise. In its broadest outlines, this is exactly what we continue to do about any goal that we decide to pursue, however major or trivial it may be, whether it is to buy a doughnut or to win a presidency. We do what we can to move toward each goal, and when we encounter something associated with it —or something that could lead toward it—we react: we notice, and we are likely to think or do something about it. And here, when we react by thinking, is where daydreams come in.

When we commit ourselves to pursuing a goal, we automatically program ourselves to notice things related to the goal and to take action under the right circumstances; but circumstances are often unfavorable. Then we have to hold back our actions until the time seems right, and that is a prime opening for daydreaming.

Suppose you decide to buy new hinges for a basement door. You keep running into things that make you think about hinges, but you have to wait until you find yourself in a hardware store. In the meantime, your brain is not ignoring those hinge reminders. As you walk through doors, you notice their hinges, and you spontaneously note to yourself which ones would work for you and which ones would not. Without particularly intending to, you see yourself with the hinges you would like to find, holding them up to the door and screwing them in. You remember that your favorite screwdriver is missing and entertain mental images of a family member carrying it away and not returning it. Now you are well into a daydream.

Here your brain is reacting internally, just as it was programmed to do, and it is holding you back from actually plunking down money yet, just as it was programmed to do. When you react mentally without acting physically, you have some form of thought or mental imagery, and when it is unintentional or fanciful it is a daydream.

This means that your daydream starts as an impulse to act on a goal, an impulse that stops short of turning into overt, physical movement. It roots your daydreams in your most basic tendencies to go after what you want, and it makes them first cousins to action itself.

This way of looking at daydreams has been reasonably well documented at several points in psychological experimentation. Take, for example, our internal reactions to things that remind us of goals. The famous Soviet psychologist A. R. Luria and his research collaborator O. S. Vinogradova asked people to listen to a series of words and to signal when they heard a particular word, called the "target" word, that would come up on the list. While these people were listening, Luria and Vinogradova measured their physiological reactions, changes in the amount of electrical current conducted by the palms of their hands and the amount of blood in their fingers. When people heard the target word their hands went into a brief physiological reaction: their palms conducted more current and their fingers held less blood; and, of course, they signaled that they had heard the word. But the main point of the study was what happened when they heard a *synonym* of the target word. They didn't signal, because they knew they were supposed to signal only at target words; yet they often reacted physiologically as if they had just heard the target word. The synonyms reminded them of the target word and they reacted internally.

Other research has shown that at least some internal reactions take the form of thoughts, including daydreams. For example, a golfer was sitting in our laboratory listening through a headset to two different narrations, one to each ear. On one channel, in the middle of a long passage, the narrator mentioned insects. A fraction of a minute later, the tape sounded a tone and stopped—a signal to the listener to describe his thoughts. He reported that his thoughts had been about golfing when the reference to insects drew his attention, and "that's when I noticed how bad they really were when we went golfing and how they just wouldn't leave you alone—they'd fly all around your head. . . . The last thing I was thinking about was all the bugs and ticks up north . . .

and I was just thinking about how bad the mosquitoes were and the bugs."

This was no simple word association to the tape. Out of all the things on the tape that might have triggered a train of thought, this reference to insects sent the listener into a stream of vivid images about being bothered by "bugs and ticks up north" while golfing. The golfer's report exudes life and feeling. He is obviously living through something in his mind that has some of the properties of reality, including strong feelings. It is as if the insect reference tied into a scenario in his head that was primed to roll, a concern (the inner state of having an unmet goal) about something he would have to contend with if he continued to go north to golf.

Our goals are often easily recognizable in our daydreams, but sometimes we picture them differently in our daydreams than the way we would think about them rationally or talk about them when asked. We might be tired of working or bored with our lives and want to change them, but our daydreams might be about combing beaches in Tahiti or becoming a rock star. These themes would be ways of meeting the real goal of changing our lives, even though some might be unrealistic. And they seem to be triggered by cues in the same way that more realistic daydreams are.

Blaine, another participant in the same experiment as the golfer, listened to narrations that included the words "the powers of a man of learning." When, shortly thereafter, the tape stopped, he reported: "And then I thought what it would be like if I was the only person who knew that we were actually here and had the true answer. I thought what a celebrity I'd be and how much money I could make for selling the answer, and I pictured myself with a mansion. . . . What a thrill that would be . . . !" Again, out of all the phrases Blaine could have noted, he responded to something close to his heart—something related to his concern of getting good grades and the future they might bring. Just as with the golfer, the words on the tape that triggered a daydream—even though the daydream was far less realistic—were words that bore on one of his most compelling goals.

## WHAT SETS OFF DAYDREAMS?

Judging from these laboratory experiences, cues that remind us of our goals can trigger daydreams. We have tested that possibility directly and have also looked at some further issues: how automatic this triggering is, how hard it is for us to ignore these triggers, how the triggers work—to what extent cues have first to arouse our emotions to set off daydreams—and, when there are competing triggers, which one wins out to influence our daydreams.

### Goal Reminders as Triggers

To find out what it is that sets off daydreams, we did more in our experiments than just *look at* connections between what was on the tape and what listeners reported thinking about; we also *modified* the narrations to see whether we could deliberately influence listeners' thoughts and to find out what kinds of modifications had the most impact.

Our first experiments showed that we could influence many of a listener's thoughts by inserting on the tape words that were associated with one of the listener's current concerns—that is, a concern about some unfinished business, some unmet goal to which the listener remained committed. These goals could be as varied as coping with loud neighbors, shoring up a love relationship, finding a better job, or creating a more spiritual lifestyle.

Before the day of the experiment, participants went through interviews and filled out questionnaires about their current concerns. We then doctored the scripts from which our narrators taped their narrations: at varying intervals, we modified one of the two scripts to allude to a current concern of the particular listener. We then modified the second script—the one being played into the listener's other ear—so that it simultaneously alluded to human goals that we thought were probably not of concern to that listener. At each of these intervals, we pitted two allusions against each other: into one ear, an allusion to a current concern, and into the other ear an allusion to a nonconcern.

These allusions were by no means all the influences operating on our participants' thoughts. They had to compete against a third, powerful source of stimulation: the listener's internal thought stream that continued its own course throughout the tape. And they had to compete against the parts of the script that we had not modified, which also often triggered the listener's mental associations. For example, an unmodified part of a narrative used the word *dignity*, which set one participant off into "thinking about a group meeting I was in where we were talking about prayer and the dignity of self-worth that every person has even if they seem to be in a mess."

Nevertheless, nearly a third of the listeners' thoughts were related to the modified passages that alluded to their current concerns about unmet goals, which was twice as many thoughts as were related to the passages alluding to nonconcerns. This finding strongly supports a basic conclusion: *Daydreams and other thoughts arise when we run into something—such as a word, an event, or a thought—that reminds us, consciously or unconsciously, of our unmet goals in situations that do not lend themselves to meeting those goals.*

Those daydreams are made up of mental acts—mental versions of the acts that we have learned through our past experiences for realizing those goals. They include perceptual acts, such as the golfer's hearing and feeling the mosquitoes; thoughts, such as of how much money you could make if you had a monopoly on knowledge; and imaginary actions and outcomes, such as Blaine's profiting from selling his exclusive knowledge. Other acts include memories, such as the memory of participating in the meeting of a support group or of insects buzzing around your head, and feelings, such as revulsion at "all the bugs" or the thrill of owning a mansion. In other words, our daydreams consist of the perceptual, cognitive, and action sequences that we carry around in our minds all primed to roll toward realizing the goals that the cues reminded us of. When the circumstances are unconducive to actually doing something about the goal, those actions remain mental, often in the form of daydreams.

All this means that daydreams reveal something about what daydreamers are after and something about the way they perceive, think about, and act on their world. In Blaine's case, we quickly learn that he is primed to think of ways to turn a profit and that he thinks of gaining knowledge as one of those ways. We also learn something of what he thinks his monopoly on knowledge could bring him: fame and fortune, including a mansion. Given his sense of "thrill" at having these things in his daydream, they are probably things he finds highly attractive and are very likely among his goals.

Not only are we more likely to remember and think about things related to our unmet goals, but we also have difficulty ignoring them. Psychologist Jason Young asked people to look at some letters in the middle of a video screen, decide whether the letters made up a word, and push a button as soon as they had decided, which made it possible to measure their decision speed. On the left side of the screen were a few lines of computer jargon that the participants in the experiment were instructed to ignore. Occasionally, Young buried among those apparently irrelevant lines on the left a word associated with one of the participant's concerns. For example, the participant might be a transit commuter, and the word might be *buses*. When these concern-related words appeared on the left side of the screen, the participants made their decisions about the letters in the middle more slowly. The more important the concerns to which a buried word was related, the more it slowed them down. This was true even though, as far as Young could tell, his participants were following the instructions of ignoring the lines on the left and even though they were apparently unaware that words related to their concerns had been buried there.

From results such as Young's, it looks very much as if some part of our minds is constantly on the lookout for things that bear on our concerns, and when we encounter one we react to it at some level. Even when we are not conscious of it, the reaction ties up our mental processes enough to slow down other mental activities. While we are concentrating on something else that requires our full attention, we are most likely to react subconsciously; but when our minds are free to roam, our response to a reminder of a concern is likely to make its way into our daydreams as well.

A few years ago I became curious as to just how automatically something concern-related triggers daydreams. Do daydreams really happen completely automatically, or does a person have to *want* to daydream about the concern?

We reasoned that if we could show with dreams what we had found with waking thought, this would mean that the process whereby reminders of goals trigger dreams—and, by inference, daydreams—must be completely automatic. When people are awake, it is hard to make sure that they are not making deliberate decisions about their thoughts. But when they are asleep, they are unlikely to be able to make those decisions deliberately. We decided to take advantage of the fact that night dreams are in many ways similar to daydreams. Accordingly, we ran a series of experiments with people while they were asleep.

In one of these, my then-student Timothy J. Hoelscher found out through questionnaires what the participants were currently concerned about. Next, the participants spent a few nights sleeping in our laboratory hooked up to electrodes that fed into a polygraph, which measured their brain waves and eye movements. That way we could determine when our participants were asleep and especially when they were in REM sleep (the kind of sleep that carries the most vivid dreams).

About six times each night, Tim read the sleeping participants carefully selected words or phrases. Some were associated with their own concerns about goals, while others were associated with someone else's concerns that they didn't share. A few seconds later, Tim woke the participants up and recorded their accounts of the dreams they had just had. Subsequently, assistants who knew nothing about who had what dreams or concerns judged how closely each dream was related to the words that Tim had read them just before.

As with our studies of waking thoughts, dreams were much more likely to reflect words related to the sleeper's own concerns than to reflect words related to someone else's concerns. Even through their dreaming, participants' brains had stayed alert to things related to their current concerns and reacted to many of them by changing what they were dreaming about. Since these participants were certifiably asleep, they must have reacted to the words automatically and also changed their dreams automatically.

The way our sleepers reacted to the words we read them ranged widely. In some instances, the sleeper simply reported hearing someone in the dream say the words Tim had actually read. More often, the words were worked into the ongoing dream or gave rise to a whole new elaborate dream segment.

For instance, one of our participants had expressed a concern about keeping in touch with his family. At one point during this participant's sleep, Tim used the cue word *family*. When the participant was awakened shortly thereafter, he recounted the following dream: "I was babysitting two of my cousins, Bobby and Nancy, and we were on Washington Street, uptown. And we were just in an antique store. These little kids were there touching everything so I kicked them out of the store. And we were walking across the street and those two I ran out of the store ran out into the street and they were crossing and going to a different store . . . that sold arts and crafts, stuff like that. That's about it."

The dream suggests some of what "family" means to this participant: It is an extended family, and it is associated with events that are hard to control. There are a number of other features to this dream, but the point it illustrates is that even under the greatly diminished conscious control that we exercise during sleep, our minds are capable of weaving a concern-related cue word into an elaborate scenario, one in which we see, hear, and otherwise sense certain things and in which we take action.

This evidence shows that when we commit ourselves to some goal—be it a relationship with someone or a career objective—the brain stays sensitive to signals that bear on that goal; and it reacts at a level that functions automatically even when we are paying attention to something else, or even during sleep. During sleep, those signals often trigger dreams. Most likely, those same kinds of reminders act just as automatically on the waking brain to trigger daydreams.

**Emotions as Triggers**

Of course, not everything that reminds us of an unmet goal triggers daydreams. In fact, it is hard to find something that does not have at least a distant connection to something else in our lives. We rediscovered this old truth the hard way. Early in our experimental work we tried to write passages for our tapes that would not remind our listeners of anything significant. Seeing our efforts fail, we made one last desperate try: we referred on one tape to a gray blob. When we stopped the tape a few seconds later, our listener didn't hesitate a bit in reporting her thoughts. She was thinking of her friend, who liked elephants!

This failure made us realize that we were asking the wrong question. We stopped looking for cues that were or were not associated with our participants' concerns and asked instead a different kind of question: When we encounter competing triggers at the same time—two or more cues associated with different personal concerns—what determines which one we react to?

One important rule, it now appears, is that other things being equal, *whatever arouses us most emotionally wins the com-*

*petition for our minds.* We notice it, remember it, and think about it.

The emotion could be of many kinds, such as joy, fear, love, hate, anger, or guilt. It does not have to be particularly hefty to trigger a daydream; in fact, we might not even be aware of it. It might be just a brief emotional blip; but in the absence of anything more compelling, it carries an increased chance of launching a daydream or other thought about whatever set it off.

The first firm indication that this might be true came when we asked people to fill out questionnaires about their recent thoughts. Their thoughts were about the things they wanted to have or avoid or get rid of, that they desired or feared or that made them angry. This makes perfect sense: most of our emotions are about our goals. We are happy when we reach them or when it looks as if we will. We are angry when something gets in our way, afraid when we are threatened with failure, and disappointed, depressed, or even grief-stricken when we fail. That holds true whether the goal is a career goal such as a promotion, the changing of a personal relationship, a spiritual goal, or anything else we strive for. Goals and emotions are inextricably intertwined.

As one might expect, the things our participants had thought about the most were somewhat more valuable to them, more pressing, and more attainable than the others. Thus the goals they thought most about were more closely tied to expectations of joy or relief, to all the emotions evoked when we are under pressure, and to hope. But, strikingly, the participants also thought more about goals they were having trouble securing, goals that posed unexpected difficulties or special challenges, such as keeping a job despite an unfriendly boss or winning an unusually tough tennis match. These, of course, bring with them all the irritations, disappointments, anxiety, and exhilaration that go with frustrations and challenges. And our participants also thought more about their personal relationships that were in danger of breaking up, with all of the anxiety and grief that entails. On the other hand, they were very unlikely to have thought about things that were routine parts of their lives, about which we normally experience little emotion.

*Emotions and memory: some clues to daydream triggers.* There are a number of reasons to think that emotion caused our respondents to think about some of their goals more often than others. First, emotion affects other kinds of cognitive mental processes. We know that we are much more likely to remember events if they are emotionally charged. Most of us can remember in great detail our first sexual experience, or where we were when we learned that Jack Kennedy had been shot or that the space shuttle *Challenger* had exploded. Cognitive scientists have named such recollections flashbulb memories, because they seem so bright and durable. We don't yet know just why highly emotional experiences are engraved on our minds in this way, but it happens quite regularly. A considerable number of experiments back up the idea that, other things being equal, people are more likely to remember words that carry an emotional charge for them.

This makes it likely that emotional reactions are also part of what triggers daydreams. Memory is very different from daydreaming, but they are related. In our own laboratory experiments, the taped passages that alluded to participants' concerns not only triggered more daydreams, they were also remembered much more often than the other passages and to about the same degree. Therefore, if we pinpoint what causes people to remember something—memories being much easier to work with in the laboratory than daydreams—we may have clues to what triggers daydreams.

People are more likely to remember words that arouse their emotions and words that remind them of their unmet goals. This raises a question as to which feature of something helps you to remember it: its emotional charge, its association with your goals, or both separately.

We looked into this question through laboratory studies

carried out with West German psychologist Michael Bock and our student Ulrike Bowi. In these studies, people were exposed to lists of words—simple, everyday words such as *Arbeitsplatz* (job), *Schulden* (debts), and *Mutter* (mother)—and later received a surprise test to assess how well they remembered them. They were more likely to remember the ones about which they felt the most emotion. They were also more likely to remember those words on the list that they associated with one of their own unmet goals. And in most cases, the goal-related words also aroused the person's emotions. So evoking emotion and being related to a concern generally go together.

But this is not always the case, a fact that gave us an opening for finding out which one is more immediately responsible for our remembering a word. When we could separate something's being related to a concern from its being emotionally arousing, it was the emotional charge of a word that related to its being remembered better.

It looks very much as if our emotional reaction to goal-related things helps fix them in memory. We commit ourselves to bringing about something we want, and as a result of that commitment we set ourselves up to respond with automatic bursts of emotion to our goal and to everything we associate with it. The emotion seems to be a signal to the brain to store in memory whatever set it off, and as a result we end up remembering things related to the goal.

*Triggers inside our own daydreams.* Sometimes an element of the daydream itself sets off a new emotional reaction, which is then likely to launch a new episode in the daydream. For example, something reminds you of a meeting you have to attend, and you start thinking about the last meeting of the same group. You remember feeling attracted to one of the other people there, and that sets you off into a daydream about going off with that individual after the meeting. You hadn't started to think of the meeting for that reason, but envisioning the attractive individual in your replay of the previous meeting sent a spurt of emotion through you and triggered a new episode.

In this way, one daydream can lead to another, producing long reveries. When the emotional tone of the daydream is strongly negative, we think of it as worry.

*Daydreams about past concerns.* The process whereby goal-related emotions trigger daydreams probably explains why we sometimes daydream about things that are no longer related to our goals. Emotional reactions become attached ("conditioned") to the things that evoke them, and this bond takes a while to extinguish. The emotional reactions become progressively weaker, unconsciously inhibited on each occasion before they can reach full expression. Until they are weakened to the point of being ignorable, those emotions bring daydreams along with them.

That seems to be true about both happy and tragic things. If you went to a splendid party last weekend, you are likely to replay variations of that party in your head for some days afterward, savoring the good feelings you experience during the replay. A young woman comes out of a daydream and records her thoughts: "Boy, did we have a party last night. The guys on the hockey team are good-looking. I fantasize being with one I met in particular." Eventually, those memories will wear out a bit, you will begin to react less strongly to reminders of the party, and your daydreams about it will subside. But there will have been a period of time between the end of the party and the end of the feelings and daydreams when you were able to get some good emotional mileage out of the experience.

If you have just irrevocably broken up with a loved one, the same thing holds true. A great variety of clues will remind you of your severed relationship, and they will arouse pain, anger, and pangs of grief—and most likely trigger reminiscences and other daydreams. You will daydream about what you might have said and didn't, about how things might have come out differently, about what you might do in the future. This, too, will gradually subside with time, though perhaps never completely.

Or suppose that you have done badly on an important job interview. It is over, and so are your chances of being hired by the company. Nevertheless, for a while it seems as if everything reminds you of your failure. When you do something well, you imagine how things would have gone if you could have done as well during the interview. When you do something badly, it reminds you of your failure at the interview. You look at your desk and daydream about the office you might have had at the other place. But as time passes, those kinds of things are less and less likely to set off thoughts about the interview. It takes increasingly direct reminders, such as the company's name, to set you off. Eventually, you hardly ever think about the lost opportunity.

We now have laboratory evidence that past concerns arouse less emotion than current ones. When we become emotionally aroused, the palms of our hands let electrical current pass through them more easily. West German psychologist Reiner Nikula connected some research participants to a polygraph and measured fluctuations in the electrical conductivity of their palms. During this time, he also periodically asked them what they were thinking. When he asked them just after a skin fluctuation, they were especially likely to report thinking about a current concern; but when he asked them at other times, during which they were presumably experiencing fewer surges of emotion, they were more likely to say they had been thinking about a past concern.

For a whole array of reasons, then, it appears that words and other things related to our concerns about goals automatically arouse our emotions, and through them they control our memories and thoughts, our dreams and daydreams.

*When triggers lose their power.* Sometimes things related to our concerns fail to arouse strong emotion. That is because the emotion we feel about something can easily change, either because our actual relationship to the thing changes or because we become overly accustomed to something that doesn't change.

For example, at one moment a certain string of numbers is a matter of complete indifference to you. The next moment, you learn that it is the telephone number of someone you love, and so those cold digits come alive. You remember them vividly. When you hear them later, your heart does a flip and you think of your beloved. Then you fall out of love. For a while, the series of numbers still reminds you of the person you once loved, and it evokes mixed feelings. Years pass. Now you have forgotten the numbers, and they no longer have meaning for you. Seeing them elicits at best a vague reaction.

Had the phone number belonged not to a beloved but to a routine business prospect, its hold over your emotions would never have grown so strong; and after you no longer needed the number, the emotion it could evoke would have dissipated more quickly and completely. You might have had some daydreams about this business contact while it remained an active concern, but if the contact was completely routine, it is unlikely that you would have daydreamed about it even then—that is, unless it had some meaning for you beyond that of a routine contact, such as an opportunity for something bigger, like a job offer, a club membership, or a sexual adventure. Then you might well have daydreamed about it, but the impetus for the daydream would have come from those larger concerns.

However, there are some things that are important to us about which we seldom daydream. The most likely reason is that we no longer experience strong feelings about them—because they no longer affect our daily lives or because we take them for granted.

You have probably heard the joke about the person who lived next to a boiler plant. All day and all night, he was subjected to the drumbeat of loud, regular pounding, but he became accustomed to it and learned to sleep soundly through it all. One night, the power went out and the pounding stopped, whereupon he woke up with a start and cried out, "What was that?" Most of us would continue to yearn for quiet and daydream about moving away, but there is nevertheless some real psychological truth in that joke: we become accustomed to sensations as long as they do not threaten our goals, including our comfort, and then we stop reacting to them with strong emotion.

Growing accustomed to things goes well beyond noises. We can become accustomed to positive things in our lives, and these then drop out of our daydreams. The first time a person receives a large paycheck is usually a very happy day, evoking the kind of happiness that leads entrepreneurs to frame the first dollar they earned in their new business. But as paycheck follows paycheck, especially when there is little reason to worry that the next check might not come and when the amount stays about the same, the joy wanes. The paycheck has not become unimportant—just try taking it away! But it *has* lost its emotional punch, and things related to it are unlikely to stir daydreams. In contrast, the prospect of a much *larger* paycheck is something else again—fit food for daydreams!

Unfortunately, when we live peacefully and contentedly with those we love, when there is little more to desire from the relationship, it loses some of its hold on our positive feelings. It has not become unimportant (again, try taking it away!). But in the absence of a threat to the relationship, the feelings it evokes are much paler than those it evoked at the beginning, and its hold on daydreams wanes as well.

When a relationship is threatened or disrupted, daydreams about it grow again. If it breaks apart altogether or if a partner dies, there will for a time be an outpouring of daydreams and other thoughts about the relationship until the strong, painful emotions surrounding it have had time to weaken their hold.

To pull together what we have seen thus far, our mental processes seem to follow the path laid down by our emotional reactions, and these seem closely but not completely tied to our goals, to our wants and fears. When something around us or within us sets off an emotional reaction, and when we cannot simply take action or use reasoning, the emotional reaction is likely to set off some daydreaming about it.

### Competing Triggers: Why We Daydream About One Thing and Not Another

Most of the time—even while we are engaged in conversations or listening to lectures—our minds are busy with a steady stream of observations, mental images, thoughts, and feelings. However, at any given moment, there are many more of these that could have been going through our minds instead. Beneath the surface, our minds are arenas of fierce competition for access to our consciousness, which is a very limited resource. Each time we encounter something that could evoke a reaction, that reaction comes into competition with the other reactions we might be making and with whatever we are already engaged in doing. Right now, during the time you are reading this, you could instead have fixed yourself something to eat, gone to the bathroom, telephoned a friend, gone swimming or skiing, noticed the itch on your backside, or thought about any of these things or about any number of other possible things. You are reading this sentence instead because at this moment your desire to read won out against the competition. If your mind had wandered off into a daydream, it would have meant that your daydream had defeated all of those competitors, including reading. So your daydreaming is not just a matter of a daydream happening—it is a matter of a daydream having beaten out the other things you could have been doing with your mind.

My erstwhile student West German psychologist Werner Schneider investigated how emotional reactions affect this competition. He gave his research participants a task very similar to the one used by Jason Young: pressing one button if the television screen shows an *X* and a different button if it shows a *Y*. Near the *X*s and *Y*s, but otherwise unrelated to them, the screen also carried words, which the participants were instructed to ignore. Later the participants rated each word according to how much emotion it made them feel. When the *X*s and *Y*s were accompanied on the screen by an emotionally evocative word, such as *blaze* or *wreck*, the participants were slower to press their buttons than when the distracting word was emotionally more neutral, such as *vowel* or *cable*. As in Young's experiment, the reactions to supposedly irrelevant words competed against carrying out an assignment and interfered with it. In Young's case, the words that interfered were related to participants' current concerns, but in Schneider's experiment, the interference was directly linked to emotion. In fact, those of Schneider's participants who generally react with strong emotions showed more interference from the emotionally charged words than people who usually react more coolly.

The reaction times in these experiments are rarely slowed down by very much—usually just fractions of a second—but they show that even words that people ignore register in their brains and, according to how much they arouse emotions, interfere with whatever else is going on. The reaction to the emotionally arousing word comes into conflict with the reaction to the *X* or the *Y* and slows it down. This suggests that the more something we encounter stirs our emotions, the more likely it is to win the competition for our minds and, probably, to trigger daydreams.

*Daydreaming versus concentrating.* Imagine what would happen if every encounter with something of emotional significance pushed our minds in a new direction. If you were an air traffic controller, you would look at the monitor screen, which would remind you of last night's television program, and you would start replaying that in your mind for a second or so until an interaction in the show reminded you of something your spouse said that troubled you; but just then another controller might read off coordinates that contain the number 42, which reminds you that you are having trouble fitting into your size-42 jackets and that you had better start losing weight, which might trigger a concern about losing something else, such as your spouse or your job, which would keep the string going until something on screen signaled an impending collision between the planes under your control, which might finally draw your attention back to the screen.

Under these conditions, mental life would seem even more chaotic than it already does. Attention spans would shrink to near the vanishing point. Sustaining any kind of activity, communicating in more than grunts or words of one syllable, would become next to impossible. We would never have survived as a species long enough to write about it. Fortunately, our brains have developed some delicate mechanisms to protect us from perpetual self-interruption.

One of the most important functions of the brain is to inhibit us, to keep processes from going forward to their logical conclusions. In life as in the stock market, timing is everything, and that means we must be able to delay or block our impulses to act or to say something. In fact, a substantial proportion of the nerve cells in our brain, when they become active, do not stimulate the next nerve cell but instead keep it from firing. And that is what saves our minds from chaos, from being at the mercy of every new cue that comes along. We have already seen an example of this: when we want to do something but the circumstances are not right, we postpone acting. Most of the time this does not require a conscious decision; it simply never occurs to us, consciously, to sign a contract in the swimming pool or to dive into the lawn.

This kind of inhibition seems to go on at a number of different levels. Consider what happens to you while you sleep. Each night, every normal sleeper goes through active, vivid dream episodes that put the sleeper's body under stress and evoke a great deal of incipient activity. In your dream you may be running or flying, writing or making love. Yet, if you are like most people, you do not jump out of bed and act out your dreams. Just at the point where sleep goes into its most lively dream phases, your brain sends out signals that relax your skeletal muscles—the ones that move your body around—and thereby inhibit you from carrying out the actions you are dreaming of performing. This protects your sleep and keeps you from hurting yourself.

When you are awake, your brain also protects you to some extent from interruption. It inhibits those of your reactions that would interfere with whatever you are already doing, at least until you come to a good stopping point. When you are engrossed in a demanding, important task, you daydream less. But the inhibition is not complete; an emotionally potent daydream is still likely to get through. Your brain acts like a good secretary who protects the boss from unnecessary interruptions. It subconsciously evaluates the situation, and if some new signal seems important in comparison with what is already occupying you, it distracts you at a conscious level. Otherwise, it shunts the new signal aside and leaves your conscious mind alone.

An example of a signal that gets through most of the time is your name. People notice their names under conditions when they are oblivious to everything else from that quarter. If you play two different taped channels to a person simultaneously, one to each ear, and ask the listener to repeat all the words on one tape while ignoring the other one, the person will probably notice next to nothing on the ignored channel; but if that channel includes the listener's name, she will notice that! In general, even people who are concentrating on something are likely to react to cues that evoke strong emotional responses.

So when you encounter an emotionally evocative cue, you begin to react; but that reaction has to compete against reactions triggered by other cues at about the same time *and* against the inhibition that protects your ongoing activity from disruption. The emotionally most compelling reaction will win the competition. That is why, if you are deeply engrossed in a task that you are good at and that is important to you, very few things will be able to distract you. Those that do will be reactions carrying powerful emotions. The most committed executive will have to fight being distracted from work by strongly emotional daydreams when deeply in love. The most engrossed scientist is likely to experience breaks in concentration from distracting daydreams and other thoughts when faced with a divorce or a diagnosis of cancer. Cues in these people's own thought streams, as well as the many external reminders of their current concerns, will keep triggering daydream reactions about their love, their loss, their tumors. The less engrossing the ongoing activity, the less you have at stake in it, or the less good you are at it, the more vulnerable you are to those distracting cues, and the more likely you are to plunge into a daydream.

As the evidence stands now, this appears to represent a fundamental principle of daydreaming. It is very likely a principle that applies to all kinds of daydreams and, for that matter, all kinds of thoughts, including the ones that people find distressing and the ones that go into thinking creatively.

## DAYDREAMS AND THE UNCONSCIOUS

Imagine that you daydream about spending a weekend with someone you love or about outmaneuvering a rival at work. You think you know what you want in these situations. But a psychoanalyst is likely to argue that your daydream was really set off by an unconscious wish—to reunite with your mother, drawing on her strength as you did in infancy, or to continue your unconscious feud with your father or sister. In your daydream, your lover has taken the place of your mother, your rival the place of your father or sister; but you are conscious of none of this. Much of what has been written by nonscientists about daydreams has emphasized this idea that they are set off by unconscious mental processes, especially by unconscious wishes and expectations.

Daydreams are indeed clearly subject to unconscious influences by some definition of *unconscious*, but different people mean different things by the term. To Sigmund

Freud, who first popularized it, the unconscious meant mental processes—wishes, feelings, ideas, memories—that we cannot freely bring into consciousness. Moreover, we don't realize we ever knew they are there or that we are doing anything to keep from remembering them. To others, *unconscious* might mean simply something of which we are not aware at a given moment in time but that we could easily bring into our consciousness. (Freud called this *preconscious.*) To some nonpsychologists, *unconscious* means spontaneous, or nondeliberate.

There is no hard evidence that our daydreams are set off by unconscious wishes or ideas in Freud's sense. It seems that they may be, although the size of the unconscious influence, relative to influences of which we daydreamers are aware, is probably not overwhelming. How large it is cannot be estimated with the evidence now available. But modern research is producing new concepts of what goes on outside our conscious awareness, and it is clear that it must also influence our daydreaming.

Actually, most of what makes us tick psychologically goes on below the surface of consciousness, just as most of the processes in a hand calculator or a computer go on off-screen. But the results of our unconscious mental processes eventually leave marks on the screen of our consciousness. You meet a friend and say, "Linda, good to see you!" In that situation you have no idea of what went on in your brain to make the connection between the person you were looking at and the name "Linda." You felt as if you "just knew," but your brain had to go through many steps to make the connection, steps you are unable to bring to consciousness. They are among the many unconscious goings-on that affect our conscious thoughts, including daydreams.

There are a number of other ways that forces outside our consciousness can influence our daydreams. (1) Through "subliminal perception," we can see and hear things, and be affected by them, without knowing it. (2) Our intentions may start up before we are aware of them. (3) We lose track of our own developmental histories—how we came to be the adults we are—and yet elements of those histories can continue to affect the way we behave, feel, and think; and (4) we may pattern our thoughts and actions on those of other people without realizing what we are doing.

**Subliminal Influences**

We may believe that we react to the world only in terms of what we consciously see, hear, smell, taste, and touch, but people are quite capable of making decisions or reacting emotionally on the basis of things they were not aware of seeing. In a study by Oxford psychologist Anthony Marcel, people could pick the one of two words that was related to a previous word—even though that one had been on the screen so briefly that research participants were unaware they had seen anything at all. In fact, they were so sure they had not seen the first word that some of them walked out in a huff, angry that these psychologists would press questions about something they clearly had not seen! This demonstration of subliminal perception means that our brains receive and analyze information below the level of consciousness. And this information affects our decisions, emotions, and, most likely, our daydreams.

New York psychologist Lloyd Silverman showed that subliminal cues can change people's responses to inkblots, which draw on our imaginations much as our daydreams do. Just before research participants told him what the inkblots reminded them of, he very briefly projected in front of them pictures such as a drawing of a nude or of a fierce-looking man wielding a knife, or statements such as "MOMMY AND I ARE ONE" accompanied by a picture. For purposes of comparison, he also projected more neutral pictures or statements, such as "MEN ARE THINKING." He projected these for only four milliseconds—four-thousandths of a second—which is too fast for most people to recognize or even to detect a difference between different stimuli. Nevertheless, his stimuli had systematic effects on participants' inkblot responses. Compared with the neutral pictures or statements, subliminal nude drawings led participants to form more sexual images from the inkblots, such as "a woman's skirt you can see through" or "sex gods." Subliminal aggressive pictures led them to have more aggressive images, such as "two men fighting" or "a knife."

Inkblot images have enough in common with daydream images that the effects Silverman found probably apply to daydreams as well. Projecting "MOMMY AND I ARE ONE" lowered participants' anxiety levels and had other positive effects, which would have at least indirect effects on their daydreams. This suggests that our daydreams can be influenced and perhaps triggered by very low-level cues of which we may be unaware.

**Unconscious Intentions**

It is not only information from outside that can affect our daydreams without our knowing it. Our own impulses and intentions begin below the surface of consciousness and are under way before we become aware of them. In order to explore the timing of intentions and our awareness of them, San Francisco psychologist Benjamin Libet and his colleagues studied brain-wave components that signal our intentions to move a finger. They showed that those brain signals go off before we are even aware that we decided to move. In other words, we can become conscious of making a decision *after* the brain has already begun preparing to carry it out. This is a clear case of an unconscious process affecting our behavior. If it is true of moving muscles, it is most likely also true of imagining moving them and of the "action" in our daydreams in general.

**Our Past Selves Within Us**

There is yet another sense in which our daydreams are subject to unconscious influences: we often lose touch with our own earlier, cruder ways of dealing with life, which continue to exist as part of our more refined adult ways. We start as helpless infants with a primitive inborn capacity to relate to our caregivers and end up, in most instances, as reasonably sophisticated adults able to do complex things to communicate and to manage our relationships. But those sophisticated social skills do not wipe away the more primitive ones. They are an extension of the more primitive skills, an elaboration and refinement—in some ways an overlay. In the process, we forget much of what it was like to live more primitively and much of the long developmental process that led from infancy to adulthood. By the time we are twenty years old, we consult books and lectures to find out what infancy was like, because we have only scattered, dim memories; and most of what we knew as young adults about infants we gathered by watching infants, not by remembering our personal histories.

But our old, primitive selves are still there, buried within our craniums under the layers of sophistication. And just as glittering office towers buckle and move with the earth under them in an earthquake, our polished ways give way to cruder ones when circumstances summon our older yearnings and fears. For example, disputes between diplomats are couched in elaborate reasoning and fancy language, but it is easy to discern below the surface exchanges recognizable on any playground: "Did not." "Did too." And when face-to-face disputes between adults deteriorate, the parties often start acting more and more primitively, even until one starts hitting the other.

We generally try not to act on our cruder impulses. Most of us have spent many years furbishing our images of ourselves to fit what those around us consider good and proper. We may not recognize our own more primitive urges; we may have become so used to thinking in enlightened terms that we cannot see the love-hunger, the exploitativeness, or the vindictiveness in our actions, and if we do recognize them we may wonder where they came from. And we will continue—so far as we can—to act the way we think we should.

But in our daydreams we can often dare to be freer with ourselves. We are not completely free, as we are still capable of feeling guilty for violating our own standards even in daydreams, but most of us are more permissive with ourselves in daydreams than we are in real life. And therefore our daydreams are more likely to reflect urges we screen out of our rational behavior, urges we may no longer understand because we think we have outgrown them. In that sense, they are unconscious urges, but integral parts of us nonetheless.

Monica is in her thirties, an educated woman who has drifted in and out of public-sector jobs. She grew up with a judgmental, hard-driving father, a highly successful attorney. He acts and speaks with a tone of authority so great as to intimidate all but the most self-confident people around him. He applies the highest professional and moral standards to everyone, including himself. Few people consistently meet his standards. He drinks heavily. Monica sought to please him, adopted the same judgmental attitude as his, and worked hard. She recognized during her teens that if she was to have a life of her own, she somehow had to separate her goals from his; but there was a certain comfort in being guided and loved by someone so strong and good, a certain security. She rebelled against his demands that she achieve for herself his own highest professional goals, and she even rejected many of his moral values. But she daydreams about herself in relationships with men who, like him, radiate a sense of utter moral authority, who are equally judgmental and exacting, and who also drink heavily. Eventually, without realizing the connection to her past, she finds Don, a man of those specifications but with a saving touch of supportive kindness, and she marries him.

If daydreams reflect our goals, as they do, those goals are not always exactly the way we describe them to ourselves. Monica knew that she was interested in men and that she wanted an enduring relationship, a marriage. She knew that she wanted someone as smart as she who was able to share some of her interests and happy to support her in her career.

But many men could have filled those specifications as well as the man she married. She daydreamed about a certain kind of man, one with particular qualities that went well beyond her rational, thought-out specifications—one with the qualities that the child Monica learned to love in her father. A careful look at her daydreams would have told her more than she was otherwise telling herself.

Monica might not have found someone like Don. She might have remained single or, more likely, married a good companion—someone who met her rational specifications and with whom she could be content, but one without that special cast of personality that marked her father. However, she would very likely find herself daydreaming about making love to men like Don. And she would wonder why, and what it meant regarding her love for her husband.

### The Images Behind Our Daydreams

*A dream is always simmering below the conventional surface of speech and reflection.*

—George Santayana

There is at least one more sense in which our daydreams reflect unconscious influences. Our daydreams sometimes come in flashes so fast that we hardly know they were there. Sometimes they merge with our seemingly rational thinking in ways that make them hard to recognize, and then their influence is for practical purposes unconscious. Film artist Woody Allen—a master at dissecting the human psyche—dramatized those connections in his film *Play It Again, Sam.* As he is imagining telling his best friend about his affair with the friend's wife, the camera cuts away to two stolid, courtly Britons having a gentlemanly conversation of exactly the same kind. In his planning for his future conversation with his old friend, he has adopted his concept of British manners—he has merged his daydream of two civilized men in British accents with his rehearsal for his own future. And throughout the film, as he defends his actions and bucks up his courage, the camera cuts to side interchanges with his idol Humphrey Bogart and his own former wife—daydreamed conversations that get woven into his decision making. He is living simultaneously on three levels: the real-life level he must come to terms with, the realistic daydream level of which he is fully aware, and a more fanciful daydream level that serves as the pattern-maker for the other two.

In real life, we may not realize which images lie behind the ones we know about—we might not actually visualize the British gentlemen as we create a daydream of civil conversation with a lover's husband. The British-gentleman daydream may be completely fused with the daydream of talking to our friend the husband, lending it its courtly, proper, self-contained tone but remaining otherwise imperceptible. And the conversations with Humphrey Bogart might carry Bogart's manner and meaning without revealing his face and identity. People not accustomed to introspection—not sensitized to the minutiae of their own inner experiences—might miss these daydreams-behind-the-daydreams altogether. For practical purposes, they would be unconscious.

## WHEN DO WE DAYDREAM?

What we daydream about and how much we daydream depend to some extent on the settings we find ourselves in. Our surroundings, which include the physical setting and the people and conversations around us, influence the content of our daydreams. That is because, as we have seen, our surroundings may remind us of particular concerns or cue off emotional reactions that trigger daydreams about them. But the sheer amount that we daydream also depends on our surroundings, as well as on our biological rhythms. Specifically, we daydream most when:

- we have little to do
- what we have to do requires little concentration
- there is little at stake in how well we perform

- we are not very interested in what we are doing
- we are at a certain point in our ninety-minute brain cycles

**Daydreaming and the Demands of Mental Work**

Most of us spend very little time just lying around musing. Instead, we spend much of our time carrying out some kind of activity. It might be a work task such as making a sale or a piece of furniture; an act of movement such as walking or driving somewhere; a household task such as cooking, cleaning, or washing dishes; a social activity such as holding a conversation; or a recreational activity such as playing ball, dancing, light reading, or watching television. Each kind of activity exacts a certain price in attention, and in return it offers the possibility of feeling better, or at least less bad—however fleeting or far in the future that might be. We tend to work our daydreaming into the interstices of these other activities, into the attentional spaces they leave unused.

The amount of attention required by some activities, such as watching television or driving down a North Dakota freeway, may be minimal. During such activities, we tend to daydream a lot. Other activities, such as playing basketball or driving in Manhattan traffic during rush hour, require close attention. If the rewards are sufficient, we pay as much attention as we have to, and we daydream correspondingly less; but—as psychologists Edwin Locke of Wisconsin and Klaus Schneider of West Germany have shown—we rarely exert ourselves much more than the minimum needed to succeed. If the stakes are very high, we may throw in some extra exertion as insurance, but that doesn't happen very often. Consequently, we are able to daydream a considerable share of the time.

But besides taking place in the left-over spaces, daydreaming competes with the demands of whatever tasks we are involved in. Which wins the competition depends on which one evokes the strongest emotions. If the task is reasonably important and nothing stirs strong feelings about some other matter, we daydream in mind-spaces during the task. If the task is trivial and boring, such as washing dishes, daydreams are likely to crop up and interrupt thoughts about the task even if nothing very pressing is going on in our life. And if we are in the midst of some personal crisis, the strong emotions it unleashes and the spontaneous thoughts they carry with them may intrude on the attention we need to carry out almost any task.

Because demanding tasks require more attention, they leave less room for daydreaming, and daydreaming occurs less often. Psychologists John Antrobus and Jerome L. Singer showed the truth of this by bringing people into the laboratory and giving them various tasks to perform. Some tasks required more attention than others, either because they were more complicated or because they required a faster pace; and those tasks reduced the number of extraneous thoughts.

People also let their minds wander less when they have a lot at stake in what they are doing. For example, when Antrobus and Singer's participants stood to lose more money by making mistakes, they had fewer extraneous thoughts than when they had less to lose.

Finally, daydreaming also depends on the interest value of the activities we engage in. For example, Leonard Giambra showed experimentally that readers experience less mind-wandering while they are reading more interesting material than when they find the material is duller. Presumably, what makes material interesting is that it stirs our emotions, which means that it competes better with the emotional twinges that divert our minds to daydreaming.

So compelling, interesting, and high-stakes activities can reduce our extraneous thoughts, including daydreams, but they probably cannot suppress them completely. Reflecting on a series of experiments, Jerome L. Singer concluded in 1975 that there may be a "relatively irreducible minimum of about 10 percent" of extraneous thoughts. Our minds may be constructed to resist total concentration. After all, *complete* concentration on something means being oblivious to everything else, which in a hazardous world can endanger our survival.

**Daydream Rhythms**

There is yet one more factor that determines how much we daydream, one beyond our surroundings and tasks, beyond even our crises and emotional states: a natural, biological *rhythm*, one that continues around the clock to shape both our waking and our sleeping dreams. On the average of every ninety waking minutes, our tendency to daydream peaks; and every ninety minutes while we are asleep, our dreams become especially vivid and fanciful.

San Diego psychiatrists Daniel Kripke and David Sonnenschein showed this to be true both in the laboratory and in natural settings. One group of participants spent ten hours in the laboratory wired up to physiological recording devices. They were beeped every five minutes, at which point they summarized their thoughts since the last beep. Another group spent twelve hours of unrestricted activities outside the laboratory carrying timers that beeped every ten minutes, at which point they narrated their thoughts into dictaphones. In both groups, daydreaming peaked on the average about every ninety minutes.

The group in the laboratory showed the same kind of rhythm in their brain waves. Their so-called alpha waves, which have a frequency of about eight to twelve waves per second, peaked on the average at the same times as their daydreaming. Alpha waves have often before been found associated with mindwandering periods or periods of mental relaxation. The fact that they fluctuated along with daydreaming in Kripke's and Sonnenschein's investigation strengthens the conclusion that there is a natural daydreaming rhythm of, on the average, ninety-minute intervals.

This does not mean that we daydream every ninety minutes and only then; it means that the state of our brains is particularly favorable to daydreaming at those times. It probably also means that at those times our brain states are less suited to heavy concentration.

These ninety-minute cycles are probably superimposed on a still longer daily cycle. Judging from Leonard Giambra's laboratory evidence, we experience a relatively large amount of mindwandering during the late morning and early afternoon and much less from late evening to early morning. These times parallel the usual fluctuations in our body temperatures through the day, leading to the possibility that our minds wander the most when we are physically the most activated and energetic. At those times, our minds may be most inclined to dart from subject to subject, testing everything for relevance to our various personal concerns.

These daydream rhythms open up possibilities for managing our time so as to improve our performance at whatever we might wish to do at work, in school, or at play. If we could somehow fit the tasks we work on to our daydream rhythms, we might be able to improve efficiency. For example, if we sat down to concentrate when our daydreaming is lightest and took our coffee breaks at our daydream peaks, we might get more mileage out of our mental working time. In some occupations, such as air traffic control, plans such as this might actually save lives. Furthermore, our daydream peaks are probably particularly conducive for creative thinking. Taking breaks to give our daydreaming freer rein might increase our output of creative ideas. Although I am not aware that anyone has tried systematically to harness daydream rhythms in this way, theoretically it should enhance our performance.

You might think that there is one time when we definitely do not daydream: when we are asleep. Technically, of course, that is by definition true. But the presence of ninety-minute daydream rhythms underscores another, more profound truth: waking thought and daydreaming are continuous with sleeping thought and night dreaming. Our minds remain active around the clock, fluctuating from speechlike and realistic thought to more pictorial and fanciful thought, whether we are awake or asleep. Daydreaming and sleep-dreaming may even be partly interchangeable. Massachusetts psychologist Robert Kunzendorf and his colleagues have found that people who report daydreaming more than others report sleeping less.

As we go to sleep, the activity of our minds gradually becomes more dreamlike. It goes through a transition period called the "hypnagogic" state, during which many people are still conscious enough to observe their mental activity changing. Eventually we sink into sleep itself, go through the same ninety-minute rhythms in which we alternate between mostly self-talk and mostly vivid dreaming, and then—in the absence of disturbances such as alarm clocks—gradually emerge into waking. Again, we come out through a transitional period, this one called the "hypnopompic" state, which like the hypnagogic state falls in between sleeping and waking thought.

Just as in daydreams, in our night dreams we also work over our current concerns, our unfinished business, especially if they evoke strong emotions. Just as in daydreams, we respond at night to words that trigger those emotions, and the words then often send our dreams off in new directions. The style in which we daydream, which reflects our individuality as daydreamers, extends to the style in which we dream at night. True, dreams are on average looser, wilder, and more vivid. And during most dreams—excepting only the occasional "lucid" dream, when we know we are dreaming—we become totally immersed, and dream feels like reality. Yet daydreams sometimes take on some of that feeling of reality as well. This makes the conclusion that daydreams are on a continuum with night dreams, rather than sharply different phenomena, hard to dodge.

CHAPTER 3

# What Our Daydreams Are Like and What They Are About

*Life is full of internal dramas, instantaneous and sensational, played to an audience of one.*

—Anthony Powell

We humans are forever comparing ourselves with other people, wanting to know whether we fit in, whether we are better or worse than the others, whether we are normal. Among the most pressing questions many of us have —and are afraid to ask—is how our own minds compare to the minds of others.

We know how the others look to us from the outside: generally self-possessed, organized, and rational. We are less sure how we look to them, but we know that our own minds seem to ourselves more chaotic than those of others appear to be. We know about our own mental foibles and lapses—about the things we confuse, about forgetting the names of acquaintances and forgetting what it was we went into the next room to get, often because a brief daydream or other thought intervened. We become aware, on occasion painfully so, that we sometimes have great difficulty keeping our minds on some task we are supposedly performing because our minds keep wandering off into daydream reveries. We also know that some of our own daydreams are such that we would be embarrassed to disclose them to family and friends. Still, most of us get by, and, knowing what our minds are like inside, many of us wonder how we have managed to keep the others fooled into thinking that we, too, are as organized and smart as they.

Therefore, we tend to be very curious about how other people's minds work and how they compare with ours. But most of us are hesitant to ask our acquaintances—we may not even know how to ask—and so we are left alone with our own uncertainty, wondering about the others.

Of course, no one can know for sure what is in anyone else's mind. At this stage of the science we still have to depend mostly on what the other person tells us. But many people are willing to tell us quite a bit, and through careful questioning psychologists have gleaned considerable information from them about their inner experiences. We have learned something about how long daydreams last; how much we talk to ourselves under our breaths; how much of the time our daydreams are movielike, with picturelike elements and sounds; how much we daydream, and how many of our thoughts are fanciful, spontaneous, and away from the here and now; how our daydreams change as we get older; the amount of our daydreaming that is about the past and the future, and how that changes with age; and what people daydream about, and how men and women differ in that regard.

In this way we have gained a reasonably detailed picture of daydreaming: our daydreams, like our other thoughts, are surprisingly short, and they make up about half of all our thoughts. Most of us silently talk to ourselves a majority of the time. Our daydreams generally sport a video track of pictures and often a soundtrack as well. Up to a quarter of the time our daydreams are a lot like night dreams—vivid, fanciful, or disjointed. As we get older, we probably daydream slightly less, but daydreaming remains a part of us throughout life. We daydream more about what we are doing at the moment and about our immediate surroundings than anything else, but many of our daydreams are about our past experiences and our hopes or fears for the future, and this changes only slightly as we age. We all daydream about the things we are concerned about, that turn us on emotionally, that we want to have or to try out, to leave behind or attack.

## SOME FEATURES OF DAYDREAMING

Although daydreams are all *about* something—they have a cast of characters, props, and often a plot and a setting—they also have other features:

- they occur over a certain amount of time
- we may be talking to ourselves during them
- they may be more or less picturelike
- they may contain sounds other than our own self-talk
- they may be realistic or to some extent fanciful

These features make up, in a sense, the medium for our daydreams, just as film and soundtracks provide the medium for films and printed words provide the medium for books. Because of that, these daydream features contain important information about us. The rate at which we shift from daydream to daydream and thought to thought determines the number of thoughts we have per day and the extent to which we elaborate them. Given that we keep talking to ourselves, we reveal ourselves in what we say to ourselves and how we say it. The picture, sound, and other sensorylike features of our daydreams contain important clues to the way we approach ourselves and the world, and our flights of fancy often contain the seeds of our greatest creativity.

### Length of Daydreams

If you have worried that your mind keeps jumping erratically from one thing to the next, you are quite right, and you are not alone. All this jumping about also means that we each have an enormous number of thoughts per day.

This information is based on my studies of college students, whom we trained to estimate the length of their thoughts whenever we beeped them. They carried their beepers through most of their normal daily activities for a day at a time.

Judging from their reports, about half of all our thoughts last only about five seconds or less. The thoughts that last longer sometimes last much longer, going on for a minute or more, but even so, the average thought is only about fourteen seconds long. Furthermore, daydreams and other thoughts have about the same average length, whether they are spontaneous or intentional, focused on the here and now or on other things, straightlaced or fanciful. This means that our minds commonly dart around quickly in different directions, averaging about four distinct thoughts per minute, or nearly 4,000 distinct thoughts during a sixteen-hour day!

**Self-Talk: The "Interior Monologue"**

We talk to ourselves continually, even when we seem to be quiet. Even the reputedly taciturn Scandinavian-American Minnesotans who made up a large part of our beeper sample chattered away to themselves most of the time.

The single most common feature of daydreams and other thoughts is self-talk. We hear an unexpected sound and say to ourselves, "What the heck was that?" We walk along, appreciating the nice weather, and comment to ourselves, "What a nice day!" We play through our minds the image of a friend. We see him in our daydream smiling and talking, and we may think in nearly so many words, "I wonder if he'll visit. I wonder if he really cares about me."

Judging from the reports by the research participants we beeped—who rated their thoughts on many other qualities besides length—our inner voices are completely quiet in only about a quarter of our thoughts. In another quarter, we say one or a few words to ourselves. Half the time, we say more than just a few words—either fairly complete statements or running commentaries. This internal chatter cuts across all types of thoughts.

So if you sometimes feel self-conscious about conversing with yourself, even though you are doing it safely under your breath, relax. It is probably a natural part of being human.

**Visual Imagery**

Humans are very visual creatures, and this quality shows up in the picturelike features of most daydreams. As a species we have excellent eyes—eyes that give us good resolution, full color, and 3-D—and large portions of our brains are organized around processing their input. Correspondingly, our imaginations are loaded with visual representations of whatever we might be thinking about, so that even most of our brief, spontaneous thoughts carry visual images.

Sarah is sitting in a restaurant, joking with a man about having an affair with him. Behind her joking, she is also daydreaming—imagining making love to him, picturing him in vivid color: his skin tones, his hair, his lips. She vaguely imagines the setting, romantic and far away. To herself, she says, "I'd like it!" Then, "Maybe not with him, though!"

As we muse about this or that, we act out in our minds not only words and movements but also the activities of our eyes and the visual perceptions that go along with them, so completely are we present in our mental imagery. In fact, about two-thirds of our daydreams have some visual components, one-half have distinctly picturelike qualities, and up to one-third feature prominent color and movement.

Two-thirds of our research participants' daydreams and other thoughts contained a mental picture of something such as a person, car, house, or scene. Sometimes this was no more than a flash or a very muted suggestion, such as when, in a kind of cameo, you see yourself hugging your lover and quickly turn your mind to something else. But about half the time there was more than just a touch of visual imagery. Then the thought had the qualities of a picture as a prominent part of the experience. These pictures generally contained some color and movement, prominently so in a quarter to a third of the thoughts.

In this regard, our daydreams show themselves to be first cousins to our night dreams. Like waking thought, not all of our mental activity during sleep contains visual imagery. Some of it is almost pure self-talk that we almost always forget by the time we wake up, but the most vivid parts, which we sometimes remember as dreams, are full of visual experiences, usually in color and with a considerable amount of movement. And so are many of our daydreams.

## Sound Imagery

Humans are also auditory creatures. One of the qualities that makes our species unique is our highly developed capacity for language. Most people acquire language by hearing it spoken and cultivate it further in conversation. Apart from language, we use sounds to locate things that we have not yet fixed our gaze on. In a dangerous world of hungry predators or speeding automobiles, this capacity has great survival value. And just as sound is part of life in the external world, it is also carried into our thoughts.

About half of our daydreams and other thoughts include some sound apart from our own voices. In most of these we imagine other people's talk, and in about a third we include sounds other than talk. We imagine our spouses, parents, friends, roommates, employers, coworkers, and many others talking. We also imagine music, traffic sounds, bells, noisy parties, the wind and surf, and all the other kinds of sounds that go with living.

Even so, for most of us vision plays a larger part in our images than does hearing. About 90 percent of the people in our studies rated their thoughts, including daydreams, as being on the average more visual than auditory.

**Daydreaming: A Multimedia Slice of Life**

Daydreams often contain most of the features of a real experience: sights, sounds, action, emotion, and outcomes. Ned, one of our beeper-toting research participants, provided an example of a daydream that contains self-talk, visualization, and sound as well as a good deal more: self-affirmation, pride, irritation, and finally angry defiance. Ned has been sitting at his desk at home figuring out his taxes and has come to a place that causes him difficulty. But just then, as the beeper sounds, he realizes that his mind has been elsewhere. He was seeing himself sitting at his harpsichord playing music he had written himself. He could see and feel his movements, and he could hear the music. At the same time, he was thinking, "I could maybe expand the ones I did already. My recital is the best to hit Minneapolis! Fuck you all!"

Actually, Ned had no recital scheduled and did not own his own harpsichord, but he was feeling frustrated and angry. He needed the tax refund that his return could bring him. He also needed some recognition, some sense of personal power and affirmation. His daydream built on his love and knack for music, projecting his playing ability into a future in which he would be wildly successful—and in which he could declare a contemptuous independence from the rest of humankind.

Ned's daydream is a very common kind of experience, but it passes through our minds quickly and is soon forgotten. Had you telephoned Ned ten minutes later and asked what he was doing, he would have told you he was figuring out his tax return. If you had asked him what he had been thinking about, he most likely would have reported thinking about taxes—period. Through catching himself in the middle of this thought stream, he became fully aware of his multimedia inner life.

Even without beepers, many participants in other research projects also report very vivid and complete daydreams. National Institute of Aging psychologist Leonard

Giambra gave a questionnaire, the Imaginal Processes Inventory, to hundreds of research participants of varying ages. More than half reported that they had experienced daydreams "so clear that I often believe the people in them are in the room."

For most, this was a rare experience, but 7 percent reported that it was "usually true" of their daydreams. It was most common among college students: 62 percent reported that they had at some time had that kind of experience. It was less common for older age groups; but even among the few respondents between 75 and 92 years old, a third reported having daydreams that vivid, and one out of twenty reported it as "usual."

## Fanciful, Dreamlike Features of Daydreaming

It is significant that we speak of day*dreams*. Not only are they often—like night dreams—vivid visual and other sensory experiences, they can take us through flights of fancy that turn the real world on its head.

Imagination grants us a luxury for which the world outside exacts a high price: the luxury of denying and defying reality. The real world can disapprove of us and humiliate us when we violate society's expectations, and it can break our bones or our immune systems if we violate its natural laws. But safe in our imaginations, we can act as we please and no one is the wiser. Undisciplined by harsh external reality, our daydreams often help us do just that.

One prominent dream researcher, psychologist David Foulkes, along with his colleague S. Fleisher, asked some volunteers to relax in a comfortable setting and periodically had them describe their thoughts. Using the same measures they had applied to dreams, the researchers found that under these relaxed conditions their volunteers' thoughts were dreamlike fully a quarter of the time. That is, a quarter of the thoughts contained the kinds of improbable activities or distorted images that characterize many of our dreams.

*Defying social expectations and natural laws.* The dreamlike thoughts that Foulkes and Fleisher's participants reported are more than just laboratory events. In a third of their thoughts, our own beeper-carrying research participants imagined doing something that they believed others would consider at least rather unusual for them. Moreover, they believed that 6 percent of their thoughts—one out of seventeen—would shock or dumbfound their acquaintances.

For example, Ray had been listening to a discussion of social issues and began thinking about prostitution. He began to envision setting up an operation on his campus, planning out its details, imagining women he knew being drawn into it. Finally, "I was thinking of having a cathouse in one of the dorm rooms in Notting Hall, and I was kinda picturing myself as the campus pimp."

This plot was far from plausible. Had he tried to act on it, he certainly would have shocked his friends. The daydream probably ended up shocking Ray himself, because a few thoughts later he expressed his distaste for prostitution, describing it as "nauseating." But in his daydream he had mapped out for himself what prostitution might entail on his campus, and he probably identified some elements of it that he would find gratifying.

As many as 21 percent of our participants' thoughts—one out of five—included some action that, from a physical standpoint, was probably or clearly impossible. As Ned was sorting his laundry one evening with the stereo and television both on, he began to imagine a car speeding down a highway, going out of control, and crashing into a tree. In his daydream, the police arrived along with an ambulance, but the driver stepped out uninjured.

Sometimes fanciful daydreams are simply creative ways to defuse anxiety or to produce some self-amusement. Max was new to our research and found the laboratory situation unsettling. He had met only my research assistants and had never seen me. One beep in our laboratory caught him "thinking about what Klinger looks like . . . imagining . . . all the different things. He would have to be in a really dark—sort of like two candles lighting a fairly large room and have really frizzed-out hair like sort of a mad scientist, real small and sitting at a desk filled with dusty books, with piles and piles of books in back of him . . . and sort of chuckling now and then." (The part about my desk was accurate! As for the rest. . . .)

Sometimes fanciful daydreams are part of a desperate search for a way out of a predicament. Alice is at a party where she is playing Risk and is losing. As she runs out of obvious moves, she imagines moves that violate the rules. She dismisses them, but she is unable to think of brilliant legal moves, and so the illegal ones keep occurring to her.

Some fanciful daydreams simply explore our options, even though we might never actually undertake some of them. For example, Lila, overstressed by her workload, is lying on the sofa, listening to music and imagining herself floating down the Mississippi on a raft—something she is very unlikely to do.

Looking back over their daydreaming patterns, most of Leonard Giambra's questionnaire respondents agree with our beeper subjects. Although the majority of their daydreams lack these kinds of bizarre and improbable elements, most participants reportedly experience them sometimes. They occur especially often among college students and other younger adults up to about age forty; and at most ages men report slightly more of these elements than do women.

Apparently, our imaginations often experiment with the socially daring and the physically disastrous. It is a natural part of playing with ideas, and now and then it leads to major discoveries; for what we may soberly dismiss as unrealistic or irrelevant occasionally turns out to be the creative solution to a problem. There are many well-known examples of this. In Albert Einstein's "thought experiments," which took place before the age of aviation, he fantasized himself passing another observer, each of them in a spaceship traveling close to the speed of light. Those fantasies were directly responsible for his theories of relativity, which changed the course of history.

*Disconnected thoughts.* Another way in which normal waking thought can be dreamlike is that dreams are often rather disconnected, jumping inexplicably from one thing to another. Our research participants' waking thoughts seemed to them at least somewhat disconnected nearly half the time. One out of five thoughts seemed significantly disconnected, and one out of twelve was completely fragmented.

This means that about half the time our daydreams and other thoughts flit around more or less erratically. They do not flow in a logical progression; their images may provide just fragments of pictures; and if we become aware of this we may think we are unusually disorganized. But the advantage of this fragmentation is that we consider many different facets of our surroundings and our lives in rapid succession. This is seemingly part of a monitoring process that helps keep us aware of the many things of which we need to keep track.

In any event, as our minds flit around they keep coming back to the important issues. For example, as we listen to someone give a speech, we actually spend only a small portion of the time simply absorbing it. The rest of the time, as psychologist Paul Cameron once showed, we are thinking and daydreaming about the speech, about other people in the room, and about matters related to the speech only distantly or not at all. But unless we have stopped caring about the speech, we keep coming back to it and end up with a reasonable idea of what the speaker said.

Like everything human, some people experience more mental discontinuity of this kind than others do; but unless it gets out of control to the point of seriously impeding daily living, it is still just the normal condition of the healthy human mind.

## DISTRACTIBILITY HELPS KEEP US ORGANIZED

Our minds seem to resist staying with a single topic. When we are doing something important, we keep returning to it; and the reason we have to keep coming back is that our attention to the activity is typically interrupted by the steady cropping up of daydreams and other new thoughts. Research shows that about one-third of our thoughts are largely spontaneous ones we had no intention of having, and another third—mostly a different third—are about something other than what we are doing and other than our immediate surroundings, occurring when our minds drift off and break our concentration.

But this distractibility of ours, nuisance that it can sometimes seem, performs a function. It helps us keep track of our commitments and our personal agendas.

### Spontaneous Versus Deliberate Thoughts

The fact that our thoughts do not flow in a logical progression does not mean they occur randomly. What gives us the impression of randomness is that thoughts often occur *spontaneously*—that is, without our having particularly intended to have them. Most daydreams are spontaneous in this way; instead of being deliberate, they just pop into our minds. But their timing and substance—when they show up and what they are about—are definitely not random. As we have seen, new thoughts are triggered by events that touch on our concerns and arouse our emotions; and the new thoughts—prominently including our daydreams—are about those concerns.

Deliberate and spontaneous thoughts alike are about the goals we try to reach, but in other ways they differ. For one thing, they feel different, in that spontaneous thoughts lack the act-of-will quality that accompanies deliberate thought. Also, deliberate thoughts are tools we use to accomplish specific ends. When you are reading a road map to discover the best route for a trip, you have a goal in mind and a criterion for success: whether you end up identifying that route. Until you finish, you try to keep at the task and you evaluate each step of the process. This means that, as psychologist Carlton Parks and I found in laboratory studies, deliberate thoughts are peppered with evaluations of how well you are doing: "OK"; "No, that won't work"; "This looks promising"; "I think I've got it." They are also studded with attempts to control your own attention: "Let's see, where was I?"; "What do I need to do next?"; and they use various non-verbal ways of yanking your attention back to what you had set out to do.

These qualities—undergoing continual evaluation, continually bringing attention back—are largely missing from spontaneous daydreams and other spontaneous thoughts. These come into being unbidden, have no apparent purpose in arising at that moment, are therefore seldom evaluated for where they get you, and are mostly forgotten seconds or minutes later. But often enough they also arouse emotions, remind us of something we might have overlooked, let us relive and perhaps revise an earlier experience, and take us through a rehearsal for something coming up. When that happens, they sometimes grab our attention and concern enough to trigger deliberate thoughts.

This kind of self-distractibility through spontaneous thoughts is an important asset, because it keeps us monitoring our environments for features that we may need to react to, just as it keeps us monitoring our thoughts for implications we may not have recognized at first. For example, you are rushing past a store window and suddenly remember that you are late in getting a friend a birthday present. Or you are planning a party, and as you daydream about talking to your guests and the image of one friend's face comes up, you remember that the friend is a teetotaler and that you had better stock up on nonalcoholic beverages. This kind of reminding-through-distraction happens often, and—

paradoxically, for a distraction—it helps us keep our lives organized.

The cost of this distractibility is normally slight. Most of the time, if the thing that distracted us turned out not to require urgent attention, we readily return to whatever task we happened to be working on at the time. The disruption to whatever we might have been doing is therefore short-lived. We need the capacity for distraction, but we also need the power to limit it when necessary through concentration. The important factor for good functioning is to keep distractibility and concentration in reasonable balance.

Because our daydreams and other thoughts are triggered by our emotional reactions, and because these are largely geared to our goals, we normally achieve this balance automatically. Our emotional reactions send us back to the important tasks and goals often enough to give us an effective level of concentration. However, circumstances or mental illness sometimes conspire to keep us from achieving the necessary balance. What we can do then is addressed in a later chapter.

We can get an idea of just how distractible we are by looking at how many of our thoughts just pop into our heads spontaneously and how many are deliberate thoughts about something we are working on. On the average, our sample of college students rated just under a third of their thoughts as mainly spontaneous, a little under a half as mainly deliberate, and the rest about equally spontaneous and deliberate. This indicates that the majority of our thoughts are more deliberate than spontaneous and therefore are under our organizational control. But it is not a large majority. Evidently, we experience on the average a considerable amount of distraction.

People vary rather widely in this regard. About two-thirds of our students rated a majority of their thoughts as mostly deliberate, but nearly a third rated a majority of their thoughts as mostly spontaneous. This suggests that a third of us daydream and think spontaneously more often than we think deliberately—a remarkably high degree of self-distraction. And yet that, according to our initial research, does not seem to hurt our ability to cope. Looking at a group of psychology students, the amount of their spontaneous daydreaming and other thinking was virtually unrelated to measures of psychological adjustment, such as their anxiety levels or feelings of well-being. Nor was it related to their grades on the examinations in one of their courses.

We still do not know why having more of this inner distractibility does not hurt us. Perhaps the automatic way our spontaneous thoughts deal with what is important to us compensates for giving our thoughts less deliberate direction. Or perhaps the extra boost spontaneous thoughts give to our creativity compensates for our thoughts being less orderly. As the great seventeenth-century philosopher John Locke noted, "The thoughts that come often unsought, and, as it were, drop into the mind, are commonly the most valuable of any we have."

**Drifting Off Versus Concentrating**

Yet another way of assessing how distractible we are is by examining the proportion of time our minds drift away from what is going on around us. By that criterion, judging from our students, one could say that we are distracted about a third of the time. Our students claimed to spend less than two-thirds of the time paying a fair amount of attention to what was going on around them. They were rather inattentive a little more than one-third of the time, with their minds absorbed in daydreams or other thoughts removed from the here and now. For example, Amelia was reading a book on mythology and had come to a section on Hercules. The beeper caught her deeply engrossed in thinking "what it would be like to be the strongest man in the world."

Here you may have detected a coincidence—first we saw that our thoughts are spontaneous a third of the time, and now it turns out that we are inattentive to our environments a third of the time—and you may be wondering whether we are talking about the same one-third of thoughts; but we are not. About a third of the thoughts that are focused on the here and now are spontaneous, and so are about a third of the thoughts focused on another place or on the past or future.

Young or old, male or female, we report experiencing mindwandering and distraction, and quite often we consider them to be nuisances. Leonard Giambra's respondents reported in their questionnaires that mindwandering and distraction are on the average "usually true" of them. But age seemed to make a difference here. Mindwandering was worst for the college students and somewhat less troublesome for people ages fifty and over.

Giambra's laboratory studies have confirmed this trend: older men and women experienced fewer thoughts that were unrelated to their laboratory tasks than younger people did. Men at older ages also reported being slightly less distracted by external things such as loud music and talking than are younger men, whereas older women reported about the same amount of distractibility as at younger ages.

The reason older people average less mindwandering may be related to two other laboratory findings from recent research with psychologists Carlton Parks and Marion Perlmutter. First, older people report fewer current concerns than young adults. There may therefore be fewer different concerns for their minds to wander off to. Second, when they are trying to work on a task, more of their thoughts are aimed at evaluating how well they are doing or at refocusing their attention on the task. The things they say to themselves, therefore, may help keep their minds from wandering as much.

So you can expect that, as you age, your thoughts will perhaps drift somewhat less, and if you are male you will perhaps become somewhat less distractible by commotion around you. Why this happens and what its consequences may be are still a mystery.

## HOW MUCH DO WE DAYDREAM?

The question of just how much we *do* daydream is for daydream researchers, oddly enough, an embarrassing one. To answer it requires that we be able to define daydreaming, and the fact is that there is no generally agreed-upon definition. If anything, there are at least three different definitions.

Some people, including Sigmund Freud, considered daydreams to be above all fanciful—that is, to violate the rules that reality normally imposes on us. This might mean breaking social conventions, or it might mean violating natural laws. Daydreams were for Freud about fulfilling the daydreamer's wishes in ways that got ahead of reality and were often downright unrealistic. For that reason, he judged them to be an eruption of our primitive, infantile ways of dealing with life; and he thus associated daydreaming with neurosis. As we shall see in a later chapter, this association with psychological inadequacy was a mistaken view. But because Freud's influence was so enormous, his view of daydreaming became generally accepted by educators and mental-health professionals until recent times, when systematic research refuted it.

A second group of scientists, including the first pioneer of modern daydreaming research, Yale psychologist Jerome L. Singer, distinguished daydreams primarily by the fact that they took the daydreamer away from the here and now into some other time or place.

A third group saw the essence of daydreams in their spontaneity. This was the view taken by William James, Julien Varendonck, and, to a degree, Carl Jung. It was adopted by an authoritative dictionary of psychological terms, and it was my own view until the mid-1970s. I subsequently realized that each of these three features—fancifulness, drifting, and spontaneity—expressed a legitimate perspective on daydreaming; and, even more persuasive, that each of these features was largely independent of the others.

The three perspectives correspond closely to the different

ways that most people use the word *daydream.* For example, you start your car, begin tooling down the street, and catch yourself in a Walter Mitty kind of reverie: you are at the controls of a jumbo jet, you have instructed cabin attendants to check seat belts, you are rumbling down the runway; now the rumbling gives way to smooth flight as the great ship lifts off. . . . You know you are daydreaming because you have constructed a different reality from what you know exists—your reverie is *fanciful.* But suppose you are a teacher, and you notice one of your pupils gazing out into space, obviously not paying attention to you. You would be very likely to ask him to "stop daydreaming and pay attention." And the student would understand you to mean simply that *his mind was elsewhere.* Later, as you are reading a book, you suddenly realize that you have stopped following the text—even as your eyes continued to move along—because your attention strayed to something of which the text reminded you, and that in turn reminded you of something else, and so on. You were mindwandering, which most people would also call daydreaming; and what makes it mind*wandering* is that your mind slipped the leash of your intentions and went in its own direction *spontaneously.*

It might seem as if these three definitions are just different sides of the same thing. After all, your Walter Mitty fantasy also took you away from the here and now and was probably spontaneous. But our research shows that each of these three facets of daydreaming more often than not occurs without either of the others. The student's attention may have been elsewhere, but he might have been trying to figure out what to say to his parents about his bad report card, a thought neither completely spontaneous nor fanciful. Your mind-wandering while reading may have been spontaneous, but it might have included the thought that the book was a good bargain, an unfanciful thought focused on the here and now.

Rather than worry about reconciling these three definitions of daydreaming, it is probably better to think of them as different *forms* of daydreaming. Another alternative—my favorite solution—is simply to think about thoughts as more or less fanciful, more or less spontaneous, and more or less removed from the here and now. That way, one can skate around the problem of precisely how to define a daydream! And the answer to the question "How much do we daydream?" then boils down to questions we have already answered about proportions of thought that are fanciful (about a fifth to a third), spontaneous (about a third), and away from the here and now (again, roughly a third).

We can also consider how often we engage in various combinations of these daydream features. Which combination we consider to define daydreaming determines the answer to the question of "how much"—and the differences are enormous:

- at least slightly fanciful *or* spontaneous *or* away from the here and now: about 70 percent—over two-thirds of the time
- spontaneous *or* away from the here and now: about 50 percent
- at least slightly fanciful *or* spontaneous: about 50 percent
- at least slightly fanciful *or* away from the here and now: about 50 percent
- spontaneous *and* away from the here and now: about 10 percent
- at least slightly fanciful *and* spontaneous: about 10 percent
- at least slightly fanciful *and* away from the here and now: about 10 percent
- at least slightly fanciful *and* spontaneous *and* away from the here and now: only about 3 percent

That is quite a range, with the largest estimate twenty-three times the smallest. Furthermore, the extremely fanciful, Walter Mitty kind of daydream is much less frequent than any of these. Most of us have some fanciful daydreams, but for the majority of us the extremely fanciful ones occupy only a tiny fraction of our thoughts. Of course, most people define daydreaming much more broadly.

Leonard Giambra's 1,300 respondents largely confirm this picture. Asked how often they daydream—largely by their own individual definitions of "daydream"—94 percent of the college students reported daydreaming at least once a day, most of them several or many times a day.

Giambra also asked older age groups and thereby made an interesting discovery: older people claim to daydream less often. As the ages of his respondents rose, the amount of daydreaming they reported declined. The percentage of daily daydreamers at about age sixty dropped to 76 percent. At about age seventy it dropped to 71 percent, and for the small group between seventy-five and ninety-two years old it dropped precipitously to 27 percent. Before age forty-five, not one person reported never daydreaming; but 15 percent of the seventy-five-to-ninety-two-year-olds reported never daydreaming. It appears that, with increasing age, we think more realistic thoughts and focus more completely on whatever we are trying to do at the moment.

## WHAT WE DAYDREAM ABOUT

When we describe our daydreams, it is usually in terms of what they are about: the characters, settings, time, action, and feelings. Research is beginning to give us some concrete information about what takes place in our daydreams. Our findings from college students suggest that on the average, approximately:

- one-third of the time we are mainly paying attention to what we are doing at the moment or to what is going on around us
- one-third of the time we are daydreaming and otherwise thinking *about* what we are doing at the moment or what is going on around us
- one-third of our daydreams are divided about equally among the past, the future, and no particular time

- one-quarter of the time or more, we are thinking about other people and relationships
- 3 percent of the time we focus on anxiety-provoking or worrisome thoughts
- less than 1 percent of our thoughts—but up to perhaps 5 percent of the daydreams we notice—are about sexual activity, with much the same statistic holding for violence

Other findings indicate that, as we get older, we daydream slightly less and our daydreams are taken up less with sex and heroics. In other words, our daydreams work over the whole range of matters that are at issue in our lives.

**Daydreams About the Past, Present, and Future**

Overall, our daydreams focus most often on the present, with the past about as prominent as the future. The college students whose thoughts we sampled with beepers spent two-thirds of their time thinking about the present—reacting to what was going on then and there and how it might progress over the next few minutes. Many of these reactions are wishes and judgments. For example, Lila is listening to a lecture and wishing the lecturer would finish, or she is in the bathroom and reflecting on how dirty it has gotten. But other thoughts about the present constitute short daydreams. For example, Lila has had trouble relating to her apartment-mate, Midge. In one conversation, Midge is telling Lila what an awful person she is. Lila begins to imagine herself acting more and more defensive, denying this and explaining that, as she fantasizes about the minutes ahead of her. In a later conversation, as they are talking, Lila imagines telling Midge why she is upset, and in her mind she sees Midge begin to cry. These are mostly short flashes of imagery, but they are true little daydreams in that they are spontaneous reactions and contain imaginary actions.

Our participants divided the other third of their time

equally among thoughts about the past, about the future, and about no particular time. These percentages are about the same for daydreams as for other kinds of thoughts. That is, the thoughts about any given time period were about as likely to be fanciful, spontaneous, or situational as those about any other time period.

The thoughts about the past and future are probably on the average more emotional—and therefore more memorable—than those about the present. At least, Leonard Giambra's college students judged on their questionnaires that the present, past, and future are all represented about equally often in their daydreams, which means that they remembered fewer thoughts about the present than our beeper participants recorded thinking about.

It makes sense that thoughts about the past and future would carry more average emotion. Thoughts about the past contemplate events that have left us with some kind of unresolved emotion. Sometimes we are uncomfortable with what happened, or not satisfied that we took the best possible action, and then the daydream activates a critical review of the situation and how we reacted. We find something we could have done better, or we draw a conclusion we might not have drawn before.

For example, Lila is replaying being kissed by Rick. As if surprised by her insight, she remarks to herself that he must like her; after all, he did kiss her. On another occasion, she replayed a visit with her grandfather. He did not look or feel well, and she became afraid for him. Brad thinks disapprovingly about a friend who became drunk the night before and wonders how closely to relate to him in the future. Hugh goes over and over in his mind an unsuccessful job interview. It keeps returning to his mind, quite spontaneously. In his imagination, he sometimes sees it from the viewpoint of his interviewers as well as from his own. He sometimes imagines doing it differently and how others would have reacted if he had done it that way. In a sense, he has yet to let the experience go; it is as if he is trying to undo the damage. Yet his coming back to it over and over is anything but deliberate: he would just as soon forget the experience.

In this way, daydreams about the past are learning occasions that spontaneously mine our past experiences for lessons left to draw. In a fast-paced life, we often zip through events so quickly that there is too little time to reflect on them. Our thoughts about the past, often unbidden, bring us back to those experiences that we have not worked through and let us come closer to mastering them. On his next interview, Hugh knew much more precisely what to do and what not to do. His ruminating about the previous experience had helped make him a much more capable applicant.

Sometimes, we savor a thought about the past for mainly the positive emotion it brings. The beeper caught Clyde, for instance, recalling very vividly his girlfriend giving him flowers and how good he felt. It caught Ned in the kitchen ostensibly reading but actually daydreaming pleasantly about aspects of an earlier visit to an English pub: the smoky atmosphere and "joking with the guys, having a pint." He treasured the memory and hoped that those pubs had not changed during the intervening years.

These pleasant memories can provide important sources of satisfaction. When life hands us disappointments and failures, they can serve as solace and as correctives to despair by reminding us that we have had pleasures before, have been liked and loved, or have succeeded at one thing or another —and probably will again.

Thoughts about the future play a somewhat different role, but a no less important one. They generally take the form of rehearsals, playing out scenarios—sometimes several alternative scenarios—for upcoming events. These previews enable us to modify our plans, to confirm or contradict the amount of pleasure or distress we expect to reap from future activities, and to strengthen our motivation to prepare for them.

For example, Nora has guests but is immersed in some reading that she must finish. In the midst of her reading, she daydreams about afterwards "getting high" with her guests. That sets her to wondering whether getting high is really what she wants to do. On a later day, she daydreams about her mother's coming to dinner the following week and reaches the realization that the visit will have to be short because of all the work she is committed to finishing. Lila is daydreaming about going out that evening, enjoying "visions of us all dancing and having a good time." On a subsequent afternoon, she daydreams about the next day's course examination—and imagines herself doing badly because she is poorly prepared. The thought motivates her to keep studying. But by mid-evening the beeper catches her daydreaming about camping and enjoying the outdoors.

This forward-looking function of daydreams seems to apply especially to dealings with other people. College students daydream more about future personal contacts than about past ones, and, as discovered by Edwards, Honeycutt, and Zagacki, five out of six imaginary personal interactions helped the daydreamer plan for some future interaction, even if the daydream was mostly about the past.

Younger people often think that older people—especially the very old—have written off the future and spend their time reminiscing about the past. That clearly is not the case. The balance of time frames does seem to shift slightly with age: Leonard Giambra's older age groups judged themselves to think slightly more about the past and slightly less about the future than the younger age groups did. But the more striking finding is that this shift is tiny. Even the oldest respondents, who were from seventy-five to ninety-two years old, reported a balance between past and future thoughts that was very similar to that of the college-student group.

Overall, women reported daydreaming about the past more than did men. That was especially true from the mid-twenties to the mid-thirties and again from the mid-forties to the mid-fifties. These are traditionally "crisis" periods in many women's lives: the decade beginning with their mid-twenties as they typically adjust to the rigors of marriage and motherhood, and the decade beginning with their mid-forties as they face menopause, the departure of children, and changes in the rhythms of their daily lives.

The peaks for men in daydreaming about the past came in their early forties and late sixties, which are likewise for many men critical age periods. As they enter their forties, they are more likely to review their life goals and achievements, confront their mortality, and reconsider their whole attitude toward life. During their late sixties, many of them are adjusting to retirement and making their peace with their life's achievements.

During these times of difficult transition, both sexes are more inclined to look back, to reassess and savor our life experiences to date. For example, Eldred often recalls the times he helped his company set policies that improved the business. He imagines the people he mentored and the warm feelings he experienced in seeing them grow in professional stature. He replays the family outings when his children were young, and he imagines himself doing some things he had neglected in reality, things that he ruefully thinks might have headed off his son's chemical dependency. In this way, Eldred takes stock of his life's achievements and failures and draws a positive net balance. But Eldred continues to live for his future as well, and therefore he also daydreams about his retirement home, his upcoming travels with his wife, his volunteer activities, and his possible future role as a part-time professional consultant. He has reached a time in his life when he needs to focus more heavily on his past than usual, but his daydreaming continues to include a healthy component of an imagined future.

So thoughts about the past and future remind us, teach us, enrich our experiences, gratify us, prod us to reconsider, help us plan, and help motivate us. These are obviously very constructive uses of thought; and yet, remarkably, the thoughts are often largely spontaneous, as were the daydream examples drawn from Ned, Lila, Nora, and Hugh. They are, as it were, a free benefit of the way our psyches are organized, a benefit born of orderly distractibility. They are more likely to happen when our minds are not fully occupied with something before us, at times when we have mental capacity to spare. Then these thoughts pop up unbidden and expand our utilization of our brain power.

**People, Places, and Things**

Apart from time perspective, the things we think about are as varied and scattered as the things we are concerned with. Because concerns vary so much from one person to the next, we vary greatly in the proportion of time we spend thinking about particular categories.

These large differences between individuals make it hard to generalize about the topics of people's thoughts; most people will turn out to be exceptions to the generalizations. Nevertheless, there are some items worth reporting, in order to provide some general sense of what people do think about and, perhaps unexpectedly, do not spend much time thinking about.

Using beepers, we have so far analyzed what forty-four individuals thought about in their natural, everyday settings, each participant reporting on the average about three days' worth of thoughts. These days were separated by several days or several weeks and represented different days of the week. The participants included both men and women and were disproportionately but not exclusively young college students.

About a third of the time, the participants reported attending simply to what they were doing or to their surroundings without much other thought. The remaining two-thirds of the time, they reported some kind of thought, even if it was about the present.

More than a quarter of the time, like Lila's daydreams about Rick or Clyde's about the girlfriend who brought him flowers, they were thinking about other people or about interpersonal relationships. The most common thoughts about other people were restricted to contemplating others and, as in Brad's reassessment of his drunk friend, to evaluating them.

The beeper caught our participants only 6 percent of the time in active, focused problem-solving thought, such as figuring out how to fix a car or how best to write a report. By definition, this is not daydreaming, but the figure is surprisingly low.

Beyond that, the participants spent 3 percent of the time praising or criticizing themselves; another 3 percent on anxiety-related thoughts, some of which included daydreams; and 2 percent giving themselves instructions on doing something. The remaining thoughts were scattered across many different domains or contained no describable content.

*Anxiety*. Anxiety-related thoughts include daydreams of failing in some life area, such as being fired for incompetence, failing a test, or being rejected by a lover. They also include events taking some kind of horrible turn. We have quite a few of them, because the things they are about carry a strong emotional charge. Therefore, anything that reminds us of something we fear is likely to trigger a daydream about it.

For example, those of us afraid of flying often have flashes of daydreams in which our plane blows up or runs out of control and crashes.

Frederika, who is afraid of heights, daydreamed about hiking in the mountains, which she felt under pressure to do to please her friend. Her daydream ended with the ground crumbling under her feet, sending her falling down a sheer drop to the rocks below.

Max recalled working on some wiring at home and holding an electric cord in his mouth. He had a sudden vision of his little daughter imitating him and electrocuting herself. He immediately resolved to stop setting that bad example.

Hugh had had a brief affair with his boss' wife, after which their relationship soured. He sometimes daydreams that she spites him by telling her husband, and he plays through the scenes of his boss's angry reactions, which mortify Hugh, turn his boss' friends in the company against him, and end with his losing his job.

Unpleasant as these daydreams can be, they keep our minds on dangers in our lives, whether real or imaginary. Sometimes, as in Max's case, they prompt us to take action to avert the danger.

*Sex and violence.* When we think of daydreams, we commonly think of sex and aggression as being prominent among them. For example, Madge, a middle-aged, married professional woman, daydreams that "I am with a man I am attracted to. I am in another city in a hotel for a convention. He goes to my room. We embrace, get undressed, make love. The lovemaking is conventional, but he is entranced. We make arrangements for a repeat."

Madge also has violent daydreams. Bothered by her husband's snoring, she daydreams: "I have a hammer and awl. I hammer the awl into the base of his skull. He quiets down."

Not all angry daydreams are this bloody. For example, Lila is a little on the shy side in public, but one afternoon, during a boring lecture, she daydreams about rising from her seat and starting to speak. In vituperative detail, she berates and attacks the lecturer.

Other violent daydreams are defensive. For example, Hugh is driving down a highway, but in his mind's eye he sees himself being attacked by a street gang. With the resourcefulness and skill of a James Bond, he manages to wreak havoc on the gang. He imagines kicking one assailant in the groin and, as he is doubled over, smashing the assailant's face with his knee. As the others hesitate and come to the aid of their casualties, Hugh escapes.

Most of us spend some of our time in daydreams such as these. But, among the many thoughts of our beeper participants, only 1 percent were primarily angry thoughts and fewer than 1 percent were openly sexual thoughts. The small proportion of thoughts that are hostile or sexual has come as something of a surprise because of a common belief that daydreams are often romantic, sexual, and violent. Yet, even if all of the sexual and hostile thoughts we found in our beeper reports were daydreams, the proportions of daydreams in these two categories would still only be about 2 percent sexual and 2 percent angry.

You might wonder whether our sample was atypical, but it was probably not. University of Nevada psychologist Russell Hurlburt sampled the thoughts of ten students at a different college—again with beepers during everyday activities from waking to bedtime—and obtained the same results. Psychologists Ruth and Steven Gold at Western Carolina University asked students to write out any "daydreams" they noticed having. Only 5 percent of those daydreams were explicitly sexual and 9 percent were angry or violent. Because the Golds' students reported only the daydreams that struck them as reportable, their percentages probably include only the more memorable, emotionally arousing daydreams and thereby overestimate the proportion of sexual and aggressive daydreaming. Therefore, it seems safe to say that although most people have sexual and violent daydreams, these daydreams make up a very small proportion of the total.

Obviously, we think about sex most heavily while we are engaged in it, a time when research participants set aside their beepers; but those thoughts are not just realistic ones about sex here and now. A variety of research reports have documented that during sexual activity, people engage in a high rate of sexual daydreaming as well—not only during masturbation, but also during foreplay and copulation. And these daydreams mostly feature sex with someone other than the current sex partner. We will look at sexual daydreaming and fantasy during sex more closely in a later chapter.

*Why we may think we have more daydreams about sex and violence than we do.* Some of us think we have more daydreams about sex, violence, and other emotion-arousing matters than our research findings suggest. Of course, some of us really do; there is tremendous individual variation in what we daydream about. But there is another reason that our memories may not accord with research findings: we tend to remember things that rouse our emotions and to forget the others. That has been shown to be true for night dreams and for words we have seen: we are much more likely to recall the emotional dreams and the words that evoke the most emotion.

This principle most likely also applies to daydreams. If so, we are more likely to remember a daydream about a sexual encounter, attacking someone, or winning the lottery and moving to the Bahamas—if that really turns us on—than a routine reverie about public transportation while waiting for a bus. In this way, the memories of our emotionally laden daydreams would be prominent enough to distort our judgments about how often we have a certain kind of daydream.

**How Our Daydreams Change as We Age**

Judging from Leonard Giambra's questionnaire studies, daydreaming of most kinds occurs somewhat less often in older age groups, but it declines more for some kinds of daydreaming than for others. For example, problem-solving daydreams decline very little with age, but sexual daydreaming drops precipitously, especially for women. So do hostile and heroic daydreaming.

Because Giambra was dealing with different age groups, rather than with the same group at different ages, his findings lump together the effects of age and the effects of being born into different historical periods and cultures. Therefore, it is impossible to know with certainty whether people in general daydream about sex less as they age or whether, irrespective of age, people born about 1950 have more sexual daydreams than do people born about 1900.

But Giambra also asked his respondents about their actual sex lives. The more sexually active they had been, the more they had daydreamed about sex. Their sexual daydreaming therefore seemed to go along with a sexually active lifestyle, and it dropped off along with a decline in sexual activity.

And drop off it did. His college-student respondents, both

men and women, considered that sexual daydreaming was on the average "usually true" of them. For his fifty-year-old women and sixty-five-year-old men, sexual daydreaming had become "usually not true" of them. That is where it stayed for the men over age seventy-five, but for the women over age seventy-five it had become "definitely not true."

Most likely, we do not daydream much about doing things that we have no further prospect of doing in reality. Healthy people are capable of experiencing rewarding romance and sex at any time of life; but as we age, more and more of us give up goals of new sexual experiences, especially goals for sexual adventures, and we correspondingly stop daydreaming about them. This is not to say that these daydreams stop altogether, especially in the form of reminiscence, and we continue to experience occasional yearnings. But even very fanciful daydreams are generally woven around themes that are still live for the daydreamer. The young or even not-so-young adult who still has romance on the agenda may daydream about some fairly unrealistic experiences with love and sex; but these express a more realistic set of unmet goals for personal fulfillment that the person has not yet given up as hopeless. When the person gives up on these goals on a deep emotional level, the daydreams about them largely stop as well.

This also applies to topics other than sex. As we age, we become physically more fragile and security-conscious. As a result, we become less able and willing to extend ourselves physically in risky situations; and this shows up in our daydreams. Additionally, psychological and physical changes probably dispose us to become less physically combative. Just as sexual daydreams decline sharply with age, so do daydreams of heroism—on themes such as "saving a drowning child," "putting myself in danger to save my family," rescuing people from fires or airplane hijackings, and so on. Giambra's college women and especially men considered these kinds of heroic daydreams to be "usually true" of themselves, but most women over age sixty-five considered them to be "definitely not true," with older men averaging "usually not true." Hostile daydreams declined to just about the same extent, daydreams such as imagining "physically hurting someone I hate," "telling off my parents," and "seeking revenge on those I dislike." The trend, then, is for daydreaming to become more peaceable.

## DAYDREAMING AS A POWERFUL RESOURCE

Step back for a moment, away from the daydream canvas, and consider all that we have discovered about daydreaming. It is born of our capacity for distraction, which turns out to be essential for anyone's survival. The things that distract us do so because they remind us of something important to us; and then, if we have the opportunity, we think about that thing—spontaneously, usually without interfering very much with what we are doing at the moment. We daydream most when what we are doing is less than crucial for us and when it is not too demanding of our attention.

This means that we daydream when we have mental capacity to spare, when we have brain power that would be wasted if we were not daydreaming. Our daydreams make use of all our capacities—all of our senses and our abilities to act, think, and speak. They dwell on our unmet goals, on our fears and hopes. They help us to absorb more fully the lessons of the past and to plan for the future. They keep working over our concerns, mostly realistically but sometimes also playfully, fancifully, and creatively—mostly leaving alone that which we deem utterly hopeless, but otherwise probing the limits of our possibilities. In this light, daydreaming helps us to maximize the use we make of our brain power: while riding piggyback on our other activities, it keeps us working on our most compelling concerns.

CHAPTER 4

# What Our Daydream Styles Say About Our Personalities

*I was on a game show and won a trip. I don't know where to, but it was far away. Some guy was with me and no one else was around. I felt cold and a little frightened. We went sight-seeing, but there were no sights to see. It was as though the world was empty.*

—Anonymous daydream

Our daydreams reveal a great deal about us, and they do it on two levels: a level of specific details about us and a level of our broadest personal styles. At the detailed level daydreams reflect such things as our current concerns, our emotional reactions to specific events, our coping styles, and what we expect from life. Chapter 5 describes the way our daydreams reveal this more detailed kind of information about us. The present chapter looks at how the broad outlines of our daydreaming styles reflect the broad sweep—the most basic traits—of our personalities. We will look at the basic ways we daydreamers differ in our daydreaming styles; how our daydreaming styles reflect our personality traits; how those of us who enjoy engaging in frequent imaginative daydreaming compare with the rest of us in personality, background, and mental health; and differences in the daydream styles and patterns of different social groups.

## BASIC DIFFERENCES IN DAYDREAMING STYLES

Before we can show how our daydream styles relate to our personalities, we need ways of describing those styles. Arriving at them is no easy matter. There are innumerable kinds of daydreamers, probably as many as there are humans, which makes it hard to find a manageable number of ways to describe them all.

But as researchers looked into the problem, they discovered that important features of daydream patterns could be reduced to three dimensions:

- how vivid, upbeat, constructive, and enjoyable the daydreams are
- how laden with unpleasant feelings they are—feelings such as guilt, depression, and fear of failure, which make our inner lives gloomy and anguished
- how much our attention jumps around from one thing to the next, which makes us distracted and nervous

These three dimensions refer to typical qualities of our overall daydream experience rather than to specific daydream themes. They by no means capture all the fine grain of our daydreams any more than height, length, and width capture the tones of a music box or the smell of a cedar chest. What they do is to provide some broad outlines for an individual's inner life—a very general characterization. In the process, they manage to reveal a remarkable amount of what our individual inner lives are like.

The dimensions represent key qualities of our daydreaming in the sense that each one subsumes many more specific qualities. If you are high on the first dimension, it means that you take real delight in many of your daydreams, you tend to experience them as vivid mental pictures and sounds, and you get deeply absorbed in them. They also help you find solutions to your problems more often than for the average individual. You tend to experience more daydreams altogether than most people, and more of your daydreams are likely to be about sex.

If you are high on the second dimension, many of your daydreams have a very negative cast. They often tend to be about your fears, your regrets, and things you feel guilty about. They will be hostile more often than average, but they will also feature you performing more acts of heroism, such as saving your family from a fire or winning a dangerous political campaign. Some of them will be so vivid they will seem almost real.

If you are high on the third dimension, you suffer from a high degree of inner distraction, have trouble concentrating, and become easily bored. You become deeply engrossed in some of your daydreams and are more likely than average to experience strong, unpleasant emotions during them. But you also experience your share of good feelings in daydreams and, on the whole, you take an average amount of pleasure from them.

Psychologists arrived at these three key qualities of our daydream lives by means of a long daydream questionnaire, the Imaginal Processes Inventory (IPI). The creators of the IPI, psychologists Jerome L. Singer and John S. Antrobus, in addition to several other investigators have by now given the IPI to thousands of adults of all ages, and they have put the results through intricate mathematical analyses.

These investigators also established that how high you score on one of the qualities says little about your score on the others. In other words, your individual daydreaming style falls into some combination of those qualities, and there is probably someone out there for every possible combination.

You could typically have many vivid, enjoyable daydreams and score high on the first dimension, while also scoring high on the second one because you also have many gloomy and unpleasant daydreams; you could score low on the second because you have few unpleasant daydreams; or you could score in between. Regardless of how you score on the first two dimensions, you can also score high, medium, or low on the third dimension, inner distractibility.

But other researchers have for several decades looked for broad dimensions of personality in general. Several kinds of personality qualities have repeatedly emerged from enough different studies that many psychologists are coming to regard them as true basic dimensions of personality. As it turns out, the general dimensions of daydreaming styles strongly resemble these broad dimensions of personality. In fact, it is beginning to look as if our daydreaming styles may be merely extensions of personality. That is, the way we daydream is one more expression of our personalities.

For example, Minnesota psychologist Auke Tellegen has found that a large portion of the differences among different people's personalities can be boiled down to three dimensions:

- *positive affectivity*—the average amount of good feeling we experience
- *negative affectivity*—the amount of our anxiety, tension, and other such feelings
- *constraint*—the extent to which we exercise self-control or self-discipline

These three look a lot like the main dimensions of daydream patterns. There is a positive (upbeat, constructive) daydreaming dimension and a good-feeling personality dimension; a daydreaming dimension and a personality dimension both involving negative feelings; and a daydreaming dimension of erratic attention at one extreme (and highly consistent and controlled attention at the other) and a personality dimension of self-discipline and self-control at one extreme (and of impulsiveness and lack of discipline on the other). This last pair may appear to be opposites, but they are probably just the same dimension labeled in two different ways (erratic versus controlled), just as saying that a glass of water is mostly full means the same as saying that it is only slightly empty.

In fact, research by a number of psychologists—Bernard Segal of the University of Alaska, Jacqueline Golding and George Huba of UCLA, Jerome L. Singer of Yale, John Antrobus of the City College of New York, and my own research group—has now shown that our daydreaming styles are consistent parts of our personalities. Those of us who enjoy various kinds of excitement and are on the lookout for personal enrichment through stimulation also enjoy more frequent and more vivid daydreaming. Those who tend to be generally unhappy people have unhappy daydreams. Those of us who feel bored and aimless, hostile and depressed, with little interest in achieving, little endurance when challenged, and a sense of having little control over what happens to us also tend to have a very erratic daydream life, our attention yanked from one thing to the next, our concentration easily broken. *How much* we daydream has no bearing on how happy or unhappy we are, or on how well or poorly adjusted we are; but *the particular style* of our daydreaming is related to these factors, because daydreams reflect our overall personality.

There is no one life course by which we develop a particular kind of daydreaming pattern. Conversely, there is no way to deduce people's life histories or the specific experiences that molded their personalities from the daydreams and thoughts they tell us about. Our daydreaming patterns are the end result of our whole complicated life experience and heredity; and many different life paths can lead to the same general daydreaming pattern. But whatever our daydream patterns, they fit in with the rest of our personalities because they are integral parts of those personalities.

## HOW OUR MAIN DAYDREAMING STYLES RELATE TO OUR PERSONALITIES

The main daydreaming styles of our fellow daydreamers shine through even the transcripts of their thought samples. This becomes very apparent in the cases of the three research participants, Rudy, Vanessa, and Lucy, whom I chose on the basis of their IPI scores. The flavor of their daydreams that arises from their transcripts corresponds nicely to what the IPI scores say about them and is echoed by their scores on other personality tests.

### The Happy Daydreamer

Rudy's scores on the IPI indicated that he enjoyed daydreaming and did it often. They also indicated that he had no more unpleasant emotions than average in his daydreams and about average amounts of mindwandering and concentration. His thought samples are completely consistent with that profile.

When we stopped Rudy one day with a signal tone, he reported, "I was thinking about this weekend when I was to go home and see a friend. It's homecoming and I was thinking about some of the things that would be happening, like going to the football game. And then I remembered something about last year when I went to the game, . . . that they got beat at the football game. Then after that was the homecoming dance. . . . The last thing I remember, I was wondering how the coronation was going. I'm going to go tonight before homecoming starts. . . ."

These were pleasant thoughts about a pleasant topic. Rudy was reminiscing about a memorable weekend and looking ahead to another one, confirming and reinforcing his plans. But this sample of Rudy's thoughts was not unusual for him. Most of his thoughts turn into something pleasant and interesting. For example, he starts out a thought with a memory of standing in a long line, and then, suddenly and spontaneously, he fantasizes a comical situation in which "everybody wants to go someplace and there is a big, mad rush; I just remember that feeling." Rudy savors those feelings and the humorous situations into which his imagination takes him.

Rudy's thoughts regularly radiate that kind of exuberance. Once, in a more serious vein, he contemplated how he was doing as a research participant and what he would do when he was done with his participation, but his mind quickly jumped to remembering a pair of friends, high on marijuana, laughing uncontrollably in a cafeteria.

Those people, like Rudy, who enjoy their daydreams may not be systematically happier than others, but they tend to be on the lookout for mental stimulation, whether in their daydreams or in the outside world. They are more likely to seek and welcome excitement and—probably as part of that quest—to favor sexual daydreams and to be interested in other people's thoughts and feelings. As New York psychologist J. S. Tanaka has shown, they also enjoy mental challenges more and have greater confidence in their insights.

**An Emotionally Up-and-Down Daydreamer**

Independent, calculating Vanessa takes control of her life but is also consistently serious and often worried, having a very different inner world from that of Rudy. Unlike him, her thoughts and daydreams often focus on what is wrong with the world, on dangers and problems that might lie ahead for her, and on weighty decisions. She is thoughtful and observant, and her thinking style helps her to plan ahead; but her mood is often rather downcast and discontent.

All these aspects of her personality are reflected in a sample of Vanessa's thoughts while listening to a tape recording of a literary passage: "I was thinking about the small amount of power that the powerless have and the elite's control over them. . . . [Then about] the biographers presenting all the vile things about the men they wrote about and that that was their duty." Of all the reactions she might have had to that tape, hers was critical and gloomy.

Like many people with her daydreaming pattern, her daydreams contain more animosity than do those of most other people. Upon thinking about her noisy neighbors' stereo, she launches into a daydream in which she files a complaint with the police. Vanessa also daydreams more often than average about doing something heroic, such as saving a political candidate from an assassination plot, rescuing someone she loves from dying in a fire, or being a diplomat who negotiates the end of a war.

This penchant for daydreaming about anger and heroism probably arises out of two of Vanessa's qualities: first, she pictures many dangers and challenges, both for herself individually in daily life and for the society around her; and second, she grapples with problems rather than caving in to them. Her daydreams express both qualities: Vanessa dwells on the obstacles, challenges, and hazards in life, and she daydreams about herself taking up the challenge and performing sometimes heroic deeds in response to them.

People who have many unpleasant daydreams often daydream about failing, doing something embarrassing, or feeling afraid and guilty. Correspondingly, on personality tests they tend to score as more anxious, bored, emotionally volatile, and generally unhappy than other people. They criticize themselves more and feel mentally less efficient. As Oregon psychologist Steven Starker has shown, they have more trouble with insomnia and nightmares.

**An Erratic Daydreamer**

Unlike Rudy and Vanessa, Lucy is exceptionally distractible. Although a certain amount of mindwandering is normal and healthy, her mind wanders more than she would like. She complains that she has trouble keeping her mind on the things she sets out to do.

Distractibility is harder to detect in a transcript of a thought sample than ebullience and gloom are. Nonetheless, when we beep Lucy, she reports fewer thoughts than Rudy and Vanessa—probably because in her distractible state of mind she has more trouble remembering thoughts beyond the last one. With her short attention span, her reports are also much less detailed, and they focus more often on the distractions created by her immediate surroundings. For example: "I was thinking about this weekend and looking forward to seeing my cousins, and before that I was thinking about going home and eating." Or, one of her longer thought chains: "I thought about a basement of a church [and then] . . . about a hayride that my cousin and her boyfriend had been at [and then] . . . about my cousin's art history class." There clearly are internal linkages for her between those different thoughts, but moving from a church basement to a hayride to an art history class involves a considerable range of material and suggests a mind that readily shoots off onto new tangents.

Like her daydreaming style, Lucy is something of a free spirit. She often indulges her impulses—for example, by deciding on the spur of the moment to take in a movie even though it will put her behind in her work—and she is unwilling to get ahead by conforming to other people's expectations. This does not mean that she thinks especially well of herself—in fact, she tends toward feeling downcast and self-critical—but she prefers to make her own decisions and do her own criticizing. Just as her daydreaming style is relatively unconstrained and erratic, so too is the way she runs her life. As with Rudy and Vanessa, Lucy's daydreaming style fits the rest of her personality.

Excessive distractibility such as Lucy's generally accompanies certain personality traits. People who have trouble focusing their thoughts also tend to have less focused lives. They are chronically more likely to feel bored and unhappy. Just as they feel less in control of their thoughts, they tend to feel less in control of their lives—as if what they do for themselves may be less important than the lucky breaks or disasters imposed on them by other people or by fate. Perhaps as a result, they feel more dependent on other people. And just as they scatter their attention, they scatter their energies: they tend to aspire to more modest goals than other people do, they give up more easily, and they feel more hostile.

All three of these daydreamers, then, demonstrate their daydream styles in the thoughts our beepers caught them in, and both their daydream styles and thought samples reflect their personalities.

## DAYDREAMS AND THE GOALS WE PURSUE

Apart from what the three daydream dimensions reveal about our personalities, our daydreaming also reveals a great deal about the goals we pursue. A very large part of personality is revealed by the kinds of major choices we make—about careers, friends and lovers, religion and recreation, the pace of life, size and kind of responsibilities, and how to structure our time. These choices determine the goals we strive for—career goals, particular relationships we want to pursue or keep, lifestyles we want to maintain—and, as with other aspects of personality, our concerns about the goals are reflected in our daydreams.

### The Kinds of Goals We Pursue

In one investigation, NYU psychologist Loriann Roberson asked a group of office workers to list their concerns about their jobs—things they hoped to do or to avoid. The participants listed such things as improving their service to a client, reducing the number of clients they see per week, or changing their supervisors. Roberson then beeped them at unexpected intervals over the following week. At each beep, they jotted down their latest thoughts. Fully two-thirds of the participants' thoughts turned out to correspond to one or another of the work issues they had written down on their original list. This is a very large proportion, and it is all the more remarkable for the fact that in making up their lists they had been instructed to concentrate on work-related matters. This, of course, discouraged them from listing a great many other concerns—about their homes and love lives, children and hobbies—which would have intruded into some of their thoughts at work. Yet two-thirds of the time they were thinking about the mostly work-related concerns they had put down on the list. Therefore, the true proportion of daydreams and other thoughts that reflect our current concerns must be considerably higher than two-thirds. This suggests that virtually all of our daydreams and other thoughts revolve around the kinds of goals we have set for ourselves, including the issues they raise in our lives.

This factor is also illustrated by a group of students whom North Carolina psychologists Steven Gold and John Reilly instructed to list ten of their concerns and then, over the next two weeks, write down all the daydreams they experienced. One student, Henry, wrote: "I imagined selling at a convention I am going to this summer. I am a salesman and I imagined going to Phoenix the week before the convention and getting my room reserved early, paying for it then, getting the phone number and then seeing people in my room from all over the southwest, selling them hundreds of dollars' worth of my products." Henry's daydream clearly sprang from his business goals and had him succeeding to a possibly unrealistic extent. Other daydreams were more whimsical: "Today I have to get my hair cut. I was just imagining this girl cutting it shorter and shorter till I had bald spots. I would have to wear a hat to all my classes." This daydream might seem to have little to do with goals, and yet it clearly reflects a minor goal—getting a haircut—as well as Henry's broader concern for his appearance.

Even though these students had been permitted to list only ten concerns, those ten were again reflected in two-thirds of their daydreams. But many of the remaining daydreams were probably related to the concerns they had been prevented from listing. Had they been allowed to write down all of these, the number of daydreams related to their lists would surely have been much larger. Here, too, the results suggest that most, if not all, of our daydreams revolve around the goals we are concerned about.

*Masculine and feminine goals.* Our daydreams also reflect a personality dimension that affects our goal choices: some men are extremely masculine and some women are extremely feminine in the way they act and the goals they pursue. Very masculine men are much more concerned with succeeding in their careers and much less concerned with their appearance than are feminine women. Other people of both sexes combine within themselves both traditionally masculine and traditionally feminine traits in a fairly equal balance. They might, for example, both like to play a spirited game of basketball (traditionally masculine) and also be a sympathetic, sensitive listener (traditionally feminine), and their concerns about success and appearance will differ much less than between the more sex-typed men and women. The daydreams of people with this balance of characteristics differ from more traditionally sex-typed individuals in at least two ways: what they spend their time thinking about and the feelings that accompany their thoughts.

According to Cincinnati psychologists Margaret Crastnopol and William Seeman, the more balanced men and women daydream to nearly the same extent about succeeding in their careers and about being physically attractive. In sharp contrast, women who are psychologically very feminine spend much more time thinking about being attractive than very masculine men do, and very masculine men report daydreaming much more about success. In other words, our choices of goals—as part of our personalities—is reflected in our daydreams.

More balanced individuals also report more positive, enjoyable daydreams. In a study of Puerto Rican New Yorkers, psychologist Jose Del Pilar found that being more balanced means, among other things, entertaining a wider range of possibilities for oneself—a wider range of possible jobs, recreational activities, and personal relationships—as well as expressing a greater variety of emotions. Apparently, this greater freedom to explore and enjoy life translates into a larger variety of possibilities that we can enjoy in daydreams.

### Our Success in Pursuing Goals

Our daydreams also reflect how successfully we are pursuing our various goals. Those of Gold and Reilly's students who generally maintained good grades daydreamed somewhat differently about school than the less successful students. The school daydreams of the better students ended more happily on the average and conveyed a more positive mood than did the daydreams of the poorer students. This means that our daydreams reflect not only which goals we have but also our hopes and discouragements regarding them.

### Deliberating About Goals Versus Pursuing Them

Our daydreams also probably reflect the mindsets we are in as a result of pursuing our goals. West German psychologists Peter Gollwitzer, Heinz Heckhausen, and Birgit Steller asked their research participants to think of a personal issue that might lead them toward a significant change in their lives, issues such as whether to move to a new residence, switch careers, or break up with a partner. One group was put into a "deliberative mindset" through instructions to think about their gain in deciding to make the change. In other words, they were to deliberate whether the change would be worthwhile. The other group was put into an "implemental mindset" through instructions to list steps they would need to take in order to make the change, and they were requested to specify when, where, and how they would take these steps. The participants were then given the beginnings of three fairy tales and asked to make up endings for them. This is an exercise that draws on their imaginations in a way not too unlike the process of daydreams.

The stories the participants composed reflected the kind of thinking they had been doing regarding their personal issue. When participants were in deliberative mindsets, their fairytale characters were more deliberative ("the king racked his brain"), and when they were in implemental mindsets their characters took more action ("the king ordered a trusted officer to stay at home at the castle and protect his daughter"). These findings make it seem likely that our daydreams, too, reflect the mindsets we are in with regard to our goals.

**Night Dreams and Goals**

Research has also shown that our night dreams, like our daydreams, reflect our waking personality traits and current concerns. As Arizona psychologist George Domino found, people who claim to value achievement on personality inventories dream more about achievement, those who score as more dominant than others—for example, more powerful and influential—act more dominant in their dreams, and so on. California psychologist Veronica Tonay recently added to this list. She found that the better-adjusted people in her study had less fearful dreams and the active people had more active dreams. This means that night dreams and daydreams alike explore the issues we are concerned about, the unfinished business of our lives.

These findings turn on their head views that had once been regarded as accepted truth. Before the days of systematic research on daydreams and night dreams, many psychiatrists and psychologists suspected that the way we act in them is opposite the way we normally act in real life. They thought that because our psychological defenses are weakened during sleep and to some extent during daydreaming, dreams represent feelings and desires that we are too frightened or embarrassed to acknowledge consciously. Dreams probably do reflect these at times, but primarily dreams are about the same largely conscious concerns we grapple with in daydreams.

Overall, then, both our daydreams and night dreams reflect quite directly the kinds of people we are. The same personalities and the same goals we carry around in waking life shine through our thoughts and dreams, day and night.

## PERSONALITIES OF HEAVY DAYDREAMERS

Some of us spend much more time in imaginative daydreams than others. In fact, daydreaming is one of some people's main pleasures, something that they try to squeeze into their round of daily business and draw on gladly while they are commuting, doing routine chores, or spending time in a waiting room. There has been a lot of general interest in what heavy daydreamers are like. Writers from Plato on have noted their existence, often scornfully. We have been told erroneously that they are ineffectual, infantile, or psychologically afflicted. Yet, until recently, very little was known about heavy daydreamers. Not surprisingly, people were reluctant to admit to heavy daydreaming, with the result that we couldn't know who daydreamed heavily and therefore could not—even through casual observation of our acquaintances—test the largely false beliefs that we were taught. As a result, we were all abandoned to our preconceptions about heavy daydreamers, which were often incorrect.

### Hypnosis and Fantasy-prone Personalities

Ironically, the first solid information we gained about heavy daydreamers was roundabout—through the study of outstanding hypnotic subjects. The trail begins with Massachusetts psychologist Theodore X. Barber, the researcher who has most successfully demystified hypnosis through a step-by-step analysis of what makes it work. By the early 1970s, he and his coworkers, especially the Canadian psychologist Nicholas Spanos, had arrived at a startling conclusion: the active ingredient in hypnosis consists of the hypnotic subject's imagination.

In standard hypnosis, a hypnotist helps you to relax deeply and to concentrate your attention on his or her voice. After you have attained this state, the "trance," the hypnotist provides you with instructions—"suggestions"—regarding what you should be experiencing. The hypnotist might suggest that your arm has become so light that it will float up and rise into the air by itself, without your deliberately making it move. And a good many hypnotic subjects indeed discover that their arm is rising—more tremulously and uncertainly than if they had simply raised it intentionally, but definitely in the way the hypnotist suggested. Many others find their arm going nowhere. They wait for something to happen, perhaps focusing hard on their arm, but there it stays, as heavy as ever. One question that Barber and Spanos sought to answer was what made the difference between the subject whose arm floated right up and the one whose arm sat there like a lead weight.

They discovered that the crucial difference was in the subjects' ability to conjure vivid mental imagery. Insofar as the person being hypnotized follows the hypnotist's suggestions in imagination—for example, by actively and vividly imagining the arm rising—she finds herself carrying them out. If the hypnotist suggests that the subject's arm is rising as if pulled up by a balloon, a good hypnotic subject will imagine it being pulled up by a balloon. By concentrating on that image, the subject's arm is likely to "levitate"—to rise as if by itself. People who do not focus on some such image are likely to find nothing happening in their arm.

This conclusion was startling mainly because it departed from the then-current wisdom about hypnosis. Benjamin Franklin had arrived at the same conclusion 200 years ago, though on the basis of much poorer evidence, and by the 1960s California psychologist Josephine Hilgard had noted that good hypnotic subjects seemed more drawn to what she called "imaginative involvements"—such as absorption in reading and the arts—than other people.

Therefore, Barber and his colleague Sheryl Wilson next

gathered a group of twenty-seven women who were among their best hypnotic subjects, together with twenty-five other women for comparison, and studied them in detail. Wilson and Barber expected the first group to be good at imagining things, and they were. But the group went far beyond just being good at imagining: all but one also *loved* to daydream—vividly and fancifully—and did so a large part of the time. Their daydream lives were an extremely important part of their overall lives. They used their daydreams to entertain themselves, to blot out unpleasantness around them, to try out being other people, and to picture—or hear, feel, smell, and taste—whatever they might be reading about or hearing someone tell them. Furthermore, they had done this since early childhood, when most of them at one time or another had made up imaginary playmates for themselves.

Wilson and Barber dubbed these people "fantasy-prone"—heavy daydreamers. Therefore their study of good hypnotic subjects turned out to be an inadvertent study of heavy daydreamers.

**Personalities of Especially Heavy Daydreamers**

The fantasy-prone group also showed a number of other characteristics. For one thing, they feel more strongly affected by their mental images than most people. Their images often affect them physically. For example, they might experience orgasms during purely imaginary sex, or they might become sick to their stomachs over televised violence or when they were afraid they had eaten spoiled food. Most of them experience their mental images as very vivid, often "as real as real," and so they sometimes confuse memories of things they imagined happening with things that really happened.

Given their very vivid daydreaming, many of these women believe that their inner experiences represent realities that most others reject. Most of the heavy daydreamers believe in mental telepathy and precognition and regard themselves as occasionally receiving telepathic messages or foreseeing the future. Most also have had "out-of-body" experiences while they were dreaming, daydreaming, or meditating—experiences in which they had the sensation that their spirits were outside their bodies. Half of them have experienced automatic writing, in which the words they wrote or the song they made up seemed to come from a source outside them. All of these phenomena involve powerful mental images that arise in the mind spontaneously. Heavy daydreamers experience them with such force that many consider them to be more than pure imagination.

However, most of the heavy-daydreaming subjects are well-adjusted, productive women with successful educations, careers, and marriages or serious relationships. To the outside observer, there would be little to distinguish them from any other group of socially and professionally active women. They are also socially astute enough to know that many people would fail to understand their extensive enjoyment of daydreaming, and they therefore keep this part of their lives secret, often even from their husbands.

**How We Become Heavy Daydreamers**

Investigators quickly became curious about the life experiences that might nudge us into becoming heavy daydreamers. The childhood experiences of the women studied by Wilson and Barber were distinctive in two ways. First, most of the women reported that at least one significant adult had encouraged their imaginativeness—often a parent, but sometimes a teacher or relative. Second, most of them also reported unusual hardships during childhood. In particular, several were isolated and lonely as children, and a third of them had been severely beaten.

Psychologists Steven Gold, Christopher Sheaffer, and Bruce Henderson showed that children who daydream most or play in a very fanciful way tend to have parents who themselves daydream a lot and support it in their children. Additionally, their parents provide a more stimulating environment—they were themselves better educated than other parents, and their homes offer more reading material and stimulating toys. Accordingly, these youngsters both learn that it is fine to give their daydreams full rein and are surrounded by the kinds of books and toys that can enrich their daydreams.

Children who are relatively isolated also end up day-dreaming more. Jerome L. Singer has shown that people who were only children average more daydreaming than people who grew up with brothers or sisters. Only children spend more time alone and therefore have more opportunity and more need to develop skills for entertaining themselves.

*Discipline, abuse, and heavy daydreaming.* That fantasy-prone adults have had harsher discipline as children has been found repeatedly. The parents of the imaginative preschoolers studied by Gold, Sheaffer, and Henderson tried more than the other children's parents to control their children's lives by setting limits, controlling their television viewing, or spanking them as a means of discipline. Assuming that highly imaginative children grow up to be fantasy-prone adults, this study confirms that they encountered harsher discipline as children.

The hardships these children experienced did not seem to spill over into the amount of fear or anger they daydreamed about. In fact, they had on the average *fewer* scary and aggressive daydreams than other children. Their home environments, harsh as they may have been, seemed very selectively to produce children who daydreamed more often and fancifully and were more absorbed in their daydreams.

These findings about childhood influences that produce heavy daydreaming are echoed in studies of adults. In a group of college students who—beyond just strict discipline—had been abused physically as children, psychologists Michael Nash and Steven Lynn found that two-thirds of them turned out to be excellent hypnotic subjects, who are usually fantasy-prone. This is twice as many as they found in groups that had not been abused, of which only about one-third were excellent hypnotic subjects.

*Can your child-rearing cause heavy daydreaming?* In thinking about these findings, one needs to be careful about drawing conclusions regarding cause and effect. We cannot be sure to what extent it was the parents' child-rearing practices that produced more imaginative children. Instead, they may have passed on a biological disposition to daydream heavily, regardless of environment. Their own imaginativeness and their disciplinary practices might then have been reactions to having this particular kind of child.

Recent evidence from studies of twins who have been reared apart since early infancy has shown that our personalities are heavily determined by our genes and surprisingly little by our home environments. The same is very likely true of our disposition to daydream. In the studies, pairs of twins had been separated on the average only a few weeks after birth and reared by different families, typically without knowing each other during childhood and even through part of adulthood. Yet, Minnesota psychologists Auke Tellegen, Thomas Bouchard, and David Lykken found that twins tended to resemble their co-twins on most of the personality traits they assessed, such as their amount of negative emotions, of self-control, and even of holding traditional values.

Among the things that genes strongly influence is the disposition to get deeply absorbed in things, whether in something we are reading or in our own thoughts. The disposition to become absorbed has been found closely related to being fantasy-prone; and this makes sense, because being fantasy-prone means getting deeply absorbed in daydreams. Therefore, people probably become heavy daydreamers in substantial part because of the genes they have inherited.

If we inherit the predisposition toward heavy daydreaming through our genes, the differences in the home environments of heavy daydreamers might be due to parents' reactions to their children. For example, parents of a very imaginative child—like Calvin's parents in the comic strip *Calvin and Hobbes*—might end up imposing tighter discipline out of self-defense; or a very imaginative child might draw her parents into her fantasy play and thereby stimulate parents' own daydream lives.

There many be yet other factors that produce heavy daydreaming. The investigators say nothing about whether the more fanciful children came from more affluent homes or whether they were on the average a more intelligent group, which might have something to do with becoming imaginative. But because research on heavy daydreaming is fairly new, we do not yet know the answers to these questions.

**Heavy Daydreaming and Psychological Health**

One erroneous belief propagated before the beginning of careful research was that heavy daydreamers are psychologically disturbed, or at least immature. We now have evidence that refutes this view.

Based on what Wilson and Barber learned about their fantasy-prone women, they composed a questionnaire that could be used to identify other fantasy-prone individuals. Two Ohio psychologists, Steven Lynn and Judith Rhue, used Wilson and Barber's questionnaire to select a new group for study. Over a series of studies, they gave their questionnaire to more than 3,000 college students, both men and women, and considered the top 4 percent fantasy-prone. These they compared to the bottom 4 percent and to a group drawn from the middle. They wanted to find out whether a more representative group of fantasy-prone individuals behaved like Wilson and Barber's women, and whether being fantasy-prone was related to psychological health.

Using a series of standard psychological procedures, Lynn and Rhue found that their fantasy-prone group was very much like Wilson and Barber's women. For example, four out of five people in the fantasy-prone group were excellent hypnotic subjects, as compared with about two out of five in the other groups. Their mental images were on the average much more vivid to them than was the case in the other groups. The fantasy-prone group felt lonelier as children, and they also preferred to play alone rather than with friends.

They reported more encouragement from their parents to read, but they were also punished on the average more often and more severely. Furthermore, they often began to use fantasy as a way to blot out the pain of being punished, something that was rather unusual in the other groups.

The picture that emerges here is of children who received some encouragement to develop their imaginations—which may have been lively to begin with—but who then actively employed their imaginations to cope with the problems of growing up. They plunged into fantasy to cover the pain of being beaten, and they invented imaginary companions to make up for the missing real ones. In the process, they even came to enjoy playing alone.

The vast majority of Rhue and Lynn's fantasy-prone participants turned out mentally healthy. On most measures, they did not differ significantly from the less fantasy-prone. For example, they did not seek help for psychological problems more often, they had about the same number of friends, and they thought they came up to their own ideals as much on the average as the others did.

On one measure, the fantasy-prone group outscored the others: on how much they prefer complex to simple drawings. Because this last measure has been shown to be associated with creativity, the finding suggests that the fantasy-prone group—the heavy daydreamers—may have a creative edge over the others.

A small proportion of the fantasy-prone group did give evidence of psychological disturbance. Of fifty fantasy-prone participants, three individuals reported having been hospitalized once or twice for psychological problems, whereas none of the participants drawn from the middle or the bottom 4 percent had. Furthermore, the fantasy-prone group averaged higher on some measures of mental disorder than the other groups did.

The difference between three individuals hospitalized and none might have been due to chance; however, the fantasy-

d themselves on the average as
ed than the other groups rated
ed somewhat more difficulty in
asy and reality.

the psychological health of the
ynn also administered two stan-
earch participants, the Minnesota
entory (MMPI), the most widely
r psychological disorder, and the
in ways that are known to relate
nkblots, the fantasy-prone group
er groups. But on a number of
rone group had significantly ele-
ight average tendencies toward
ior, and paranoia. The elevations
ew extreme individuals; they reflect
tendencies for the group as a whole.

However, these MMPI scales do not necessarily indicate just what their labels suggest. For example, very creative people may score higher on the schizophrenia score, very energetic and optimistic people may score higher on manic behavior, and so on.

The slight association between fantasy-prone scores and MMPI scales might also have to do with problems in Rhue and Lynn's measures. Those MMPI scales include some questions that can be interpreted in a variety of different ways. Some answers that might indicate schizophrenic symptoms could also be given by a fantasy-prone person with no hint of schizophrenia. Both might admit to having odd thoughts, for example, but the fantasy-prone individual might be referring to wildly fanciful daydreams, whereas the schizophrenic might be referring to thoughts that stick in the mind and, for a time, keep him from getting beyond them. Both might confess to time periods when they were oblivious to what was going on around them, but the fantasy-prone individual may have been oblivious because of a vivid daydream, whereas the schizophrenic might have been preoccupied by hallucinated voices. However, their responses to such questions would look identical on the MMPI answer blank. When such answers are added into fantasy-prone individuals' schizophrenia scores, their average schizophrenia scores will be elevated as compared to those of the other groups, thereby providing misleading information.

Moreover, the same problem may afflict Wilson and Barber's questionnaire on fantasy-proneness. Some questions designed to identify fantasy-prone individuals are questions that people with certain mental disorders could, for different reasons, answer truthfully in the same way. For example, both a fantasy-prone individual and a schizophrenic patient might admit to having written a poem while not feeling as if she herself were creating it—the fantasy-prone person because the flow of words seemed to well effortlessly out of her, the schizophrenic because of a paranoid belief that she was being manipulated by radio waves controlled by an enemy.

This would mean that some of the people identified by Wilson and Barber's questionnaire as fantasy-prone may in fact be less fantasy-prone than their scores indicate. Instead, they may be schizophrenic or suffer from some other disorder. For these individuals the scores would provide misleading information, characterizing an individual as fantasy-prone who would better be considered schizophrenic. Individuals such as these may have been among the seemingly fantasy-prone individuals who were hospitalized. And it might be this misleading information in both the fantasy-prone questionnaire and the MMPI measures that led to the modest association between them.

This is not to argue that heavy daydreamers are necessarily models of psychological health. They are probably as much subject to mental disorder as other groups are, and the possibility of slightly poorer average psychological health cannot be ruled out. But the conflicting evidence on their psychological health can be laid at least partly at the door of imperfect methods used to study them. This means that it is too early to draw final conclusions about the psychological health of heavy daydreamers except to say that in most instances it is quite sound.

## GROUP DIFFERENCES IN DAYDREAMING PATTERNS

Our personalities and our concerns reflect in part the groups we belong to: our country, ethnic and racial heritage, professions, education, wealth, and neighborhood. And this, too, shows up in daydreaming. As yet, we do not have extensive information regarding the impact that being in a specific group has on our daydreaming. In fact, where researchers have investigated, the differences between groups usually appear modest. But differences do appear to exist. Most of our information about group differences in daydreaming comes from Leonard Giambra, who has given the Imaginal Processes Inventory to more than a thousand people on two continents. His findings shed light on differences between the rich and poor, the better and less well educated, African- and European-Americans, and Americans and Australians.

### Financial Means, Education, and Our Daydreams

Two major distinctions between groups in the United States are in how financially well-off we are and how much education we have. Being well-off and well-educated have important psychological advantages, and even our daydreams benefit. Those of us who are well-off and well-educated have more options in life and are on the average generally less bored than the others. Presumably, this translates into having more things to look forward to and having a wider average range of interests. These factors are reflected in our daydreams, which for well-off, well-educated people are more satisfying, more often about solving problems and overcoming difficulties, and less often about self-doubts, self-criticisms, and feeling guilty.

### Average Daydream Differences Between African- and European-Americans

In the United States, one of the key components of our personal identities is our ethnic group membership. Of the various ethnic groups, African-Americans are among those for whom ethnicity is a central issue. African-Americans have, of course, a long and tragic history of brutal victimization through slavery and, after that, economic discrimination and deprivation. For them, race is historically connected with, on the average, much greater poverty, poorer education, poorer health, discrimination in employment, and the chronic humiliation of belittlement and hostility from many European-Americans. These factors inevitably influence our personalities and goals. It is therefore not surprising that African-Americans daydream on the average more or less often about certain things than European-Americans.

To pinpoint these daydream differences, Giambra surveyed African- and European-Americans ages seventeen to thirty-four in Maryland. Although the differences were not striking, African-Americans reported on the average somewhat more vivid daydreaming; more frightening, hostile, and guilt-ridden daydreams; and more daydreams about occupational success. These average differences in daydream patterns would seem to match the American realities. On the average, African-Americans have to put up with more unpleasantness and must struggle to succeed against greater odds. A larger proportion of them than of European-Americans live in dangerous neighborhoods, which would be reflected in the frightening and hostile daydreams of being attacked, of self-defense, and, in general, of participating in an often violent society. The frequent insults and humiliations forced on African-Americans must also make for more hostile daydreams, including daydreams of striking back. The fact that many often start with disadvantageous educations and first jobs means that they have farther to go to reach desirable positions at work. This would account for the larger number of daydreams about succeeding. We find, then, that African-American daydream patterns reflect the problems they must cope with.

**National Differences in Daydreaming**

Which country we live in also seems to make a difference, even among cultures as alike as the United States and Australia. According to observers of the Australian scene, writes Giambra, Australians are more easygoing on the average than Americans. They place less emphasis on individual achievement and more on getting along with companions and coworkers. They are more egalitarian and suspicious of authority, and they place a higher value on having a good time.

Their daydream patterns accord with those differences. Australian men and women ages seventeen to twenty-three reported:

- more pleasant daydreams than the Americans
- more sexual daydreams
- fewer daydreams about dealing with problems
- fewer daydreams of criminal daring
- more outlandish daydreams
- more daydreams about the present
- fewer about their personal future
- minds that wandered more, raced more, and went blank more often
- less boredom

Somewhat older Australian women, ages twenty-four to forty-four, were somewhat less accepting of their own daydreams than the Americans, and they daydreamed more about their relationships with other people. Like the younger Australians, they daydreamed more about things in their present lives than the Americans and, in general, they differed from the Americans in the same direction as the younger Australians did, although the differences were weaker and less significant. Overall, then, the reported lifestyle differences between Down Under and the United States extend to average daydreaming patterns.

Taken together, all the findings on class, ethnic group, and nationality seem to make one general point: our daydream patterns reflect the realities of our life situations, including the personality traits, goals, and obstacles they engender.

CHAPTER 5

# How Our Daydreams Reflect Who We Are: Daydreams, Storytelling, and Self-Discovery

Psychologist Bill Henry had a special talent. Taking a made-up story often only a few lines long, he could tell you a surprising number of things about the storyteller: his or her intelligence, thinking style, expectations, emotions, treatment of other people, and ways of dealing with stress. Onlookers might be astonished or skeptical, but much of the time Henry was right.

This was no sleight of hand. Much like a frontier tracker looking at a patch of forest floor, Henry looked at the seemingly commonplace and saw the subtle clues to the human individual behind the story. He knew that every word, every idea, and every choice about when and how to say something reflected the person telling the story.

When you read a novel such as *The Thorn Birds* or a Sherlock Holmes mystery, you are reading a highly refined literary product; but the original raw materials for that product were much the same kind of imaginative flow that goes into daydreaming. If you think back on your own efforts at creative writing—whether as a professional author, a hobbyist, or a student in a composition class—you may be able to remember what you went through to start filling a blank page. You needed to get a creative flow of ideas moving through your head. It may have felt wrenching at times, a little like starting your car in third gear or moving a mountain. But once you got the flow going, it probably had many of the properties of a daydream.

Storytellers have certain things in mind that they want their listeners to pay attention to—a story line, the looks and feelings of the characters, the leads that build suspense—and those are often the things the listener notices. But storytellers unwittingly tell us much about themselves beyond the plot line or lesson of the story itself. They create their stories out of their own mental substance: they decide what to say because it occurred to them, and therefore it reflects them. The person who knows enough to listen for the hidden messages can find them in what storytellers choose to tell about, what their characters are thinking and feeling, what events lead to what actions, and what actions lead to what consequences.

The same is true of daydreams. When we look at a daydream, we normally pay attention to what it is about, or who did what, often overlooking its deeper clues to the character of the daydreamer. Our daydreams have a certain flow and movement, a setting, sound and color, action, and often, like a story, a plot and outcome. All of these are our own creations, and their specific details tell us a lot about ourselves, including some things we might not otherwise have realized.

Thus, even a brief, humdrum daydream contains a considerable amount of information about an individual's personality, and the reason it does so is that daydreams reflect the personal makeup of the daydreamer: feelings, wishes, concerns, beliefs, expectations, thought patterns, strategies, temperament, and relationships.

## DAYDREAMS AS AN INFORMATION SOURCE FOR MANAGING OUR LIVES

With all that daydreams, night dreams, and stories can tell us about ourselves, they obviously constitute a powerful channel of information. Tapping into this channel can benefit us on two different levels. At the first level, it opens up a path to greater self-understanding, with all of the pleasure and self-assurance that it brings; on another level, this self-understanding can make a large difference in how well we manage our lives.

When we make decisions about ourselves—about whom to marry, which career to pursue, or where to go on vacation—we base those decisions partly on the beliefs we have about ourselves. Insofar as those beliefs are incorrect or incomplete, we risk making bad decisions. Using the information inherent in our own fantasies can help correct beliefs about ourselves and therefore lead to better life decisions.

You might think that because our daydreams reflect our concerns and feelings, we must already know everything they can tell us, but this is not the case. Often, we delude ourselves into believing that we want something or do not want it simply because we believe that we *should* feel that way about it. For example, you may be miserable in a relationship that on the surface appears reasonably good. You tell yourself that you are happy with it, because you think you *should* be happy with it.

We are less likely to delude ourselves in this way in our daydreams. They are more apt to reflect our discontent and what we are missing. If you are missing respect, you may daydream about a romance with someone who remains in awe of your fine qualities. You feel deep gratification over this imaginary other person's tender regard. If you are missing raw sexual excitement in your partner, you may daydream about a sexual encounter with someone extremely passionate.

Or let us suppose, as often happens, that a person decides to pursue a certain career for the wrong reason: not because the work will bring pleasure but because being in that career will win someone else's approval. For example, an extroverted, people-oriented individual might decide to become an engineer like his father instead of a stockbroker or social worker. His daydreams will probably contain plenty of clues that this decision is wrong for him. When he imagines his life as an engineer, his daydreams may be devoid of warmth. He may conjure up images of steely, sterile rooms and a meticulously ordered life. In other daydreams, he may imagine himself full of deep feeling as he champions distressed clients or full of ebullience as he negotiates stock trades. The contrast in feeling will be a strong clue that his career decision may be a mistake; and the contrast in the situations he imagines—isolation in the one case, human contact in the other—will be a clue that he would be happier in a career involving interaction with others.

If we pay attention, then, daydreams can give us information about ourselves that we may not be taking into account. Sometimes, that information is crucial for optimal planning of our lives.

**Information from Daydreams**

It is always a good idea for us to know our own minds, to know who we are and where we intend to go with our lives; and staying in touch with our daydreams can keep us plugged in to ourselves. But when the going gets tough—for example, when we come under pressure from people close to us or from our job commitments—it is especially easy to lose sight of what we really feel and want. Then more than ever, as we face making crucial decisions, we benefit from keeping occasional tabs on our daydreams to stay in touch with what they might be expressing about us.

The possibilities for extracting information from daydreams range from the completely informal and intuitive to the highly systematic. For most of the nonscientists among us, informal and intuitive methods are usually enough. We do not and need not analyze every daydream.

In fact, to do so would be quite disruptive. We automatically tend to remember and pay attention to the most emotional of our day and night dreams; but, unless we deliberately focus on them, the rest generally come and go without leaving much of a conscious memory trace. They may very well leave us some benefit in learning from them; but just as we learn to play musical instruments or develop athletic skills through much practice while forgetting the specific occasions on which we practiced, we quickly forget what most of our daydreams were about or even that we had them. Psychologists do not yet know how they escape our memories, but it is clearly a good thing. With daydreams of one kind or another making up a third to a half of our thoughts, it would be hopelessly cumbersome to focus on and record each one.

Nevertheless, it is still a good idea to pay attention to some daydreams now and then. That includes the quiet, everyday variety that we might otherwise overlook, because it is often those very daydreams—the ones most characteristic of us, the relatively automatic ones—that reveal our basic assumptions about ourselves and our world. Daydreams can provide us with clues about our desires—both the surface ones and those deeper down—and our methods for turning wishes into reality.

*Clues to our needs and wishes.* You can gain insights into your needs and wishes by keeping track of what you are trying to do in your daydreams. Daydreams are internal action. In them we take action in our minds, using some of the same brain systems that we would use to perceive and act on the world in reality. Even though our daydream perceptions are freed for the moment from the sensations of the outside world and our daydream actions are freed from real-world consequences, it is ultimately we who are acting in those daydreams. And actions, whether real or imaginary, are organized around our goals. Therefore, the goals in your daydreams are often goals you would actually like to reach. In the daydreams and dreams described later in this chapter, people go to visit parents, retrieve their money, arrange a job, complete a lab report, want to hear from a boyfriend, buy beer for someone, avoid harm from a malfunctioning car, and lambaste an obnoxious character. Each of these daydream actions is aimed at some kind of goal, and those daydream goals are in most instances no doubt closely related to an actual goal.

But often things are more complicated than that. For one thing, the wish for the daydream goal might not be wholehearted. For example, you might wish for a torrid love affair but be more afraid of the risks than you want the affair, and you therefore would not pursue it in reality. Your daydream about such an affair would tell you that you want it, but in this situation that is only part of the story. If you were afraid of the consequences, you would very likely have other daydreams—or perhaps simply some sober thoughts—about disastrous outcomes. Or perhaps the disastrous consequences would be part of the same daydream that features the affair. In either event, daydreams would provide information about both halves of your ambivalence, the desire and the fear.

Sometimes it is not the particular daydream goal itself that you want but something that reaching the goal can provide for you, which is often something that reaching other goals might provide equally well. Goals are valued partly for their own, intrinsic value—how they themselves make you feel once you have attained them—and partly for what else they lead to. For example, people might visit their parents because they enjoy the contact for itself, intrinsically, or they might visit so as to avoid feeling guilty or to keep from being cut out of a parent's will—for extrinsic benefits. Often, a particular goal combines a number of different benefits, some intrinsic and some extrinsic. When you pursue a particular goal in a daydream, you might be after only one of its benefits and not care very much about the others. If you can remember a number of your daydreams, you can ask yourself what benefits the daydream goals have in common. In that way, you may be able to zero in on something fundamentally important to you.

For example, you might have daydreams about giving a great speech to loud applause, rescuing a pedestrian from a mugger, and inducing someone reluctant to have sex into becoming wild with sexual excitement. It might not seem as if these daydream themes have much in common, and yet they do have a common thread: they all depict a major emotional impact on someone, whether adulation for a speech, gratitude for a rescue, or a shift to strong sexual desire. That is, they all satisfy a wish for power over other people's feelings—the power to compel their affirmation and reaction.

A wish of this kind might conceivably, though not inevitably, signify a need for greater power, respect, or acknowledgment, perhaps because of feeling overpowered, belittled, or ignored. You might never wholeheartedly want to give a speech, undertake a rescue, or pressure a reluctant partner for sex. But understanding the yearning to enjoy greater status with other people or greater control over your life circumstances would enable you to confront a wide-ranging problem and, having formulated it, take steps to solve it.

For example, you might decide to become more assertive in your friendships and on your job, thereby making yourself less ignorable. You might make plans to do something that would bring you greater recognition, such as volunteering to work with people who need help or developing some skill or achievement. Or you might examine whether you really are being ignored and slighted relative to others or whether you only feel as if you are, in which case you could work on finding out why that is so.

*Clues to our assumptions and methods for dealing with life.* Beyond needs and wishes, daydreams also reflect the way we go about dealing with life. Your daydreams contain information regarding how you imagine going about getting what you want. Daydreams also contain some of the stock things you do or say to yourself, and these reveal a good deal about your orientation toward solving problems.

Once you have an idea of how you go about solving a particular kind of problem, it is necessary to think about your problem-solving methods critically. You could consider how realistic and effective your methods are—whether this is the best way to go about solving the problem. As you see yourself, in your daydream, choosing a particular approach, you could ask yourself what assumptions you were making about the other people and what other approaches you left out.

For example, suppose that you have been daydreaming about a troubled relationship with your boss. You feel that she has been picking on you, criticizing you unfairly and loading you down with more than your share of work. Your daydreams sometimes have you telling her off in no uncertain terms, loudly and abusively. Sometimes you daydream about sabotaging her efforts by destroying crucial documents, at other times about boobytrapping her chair. In reality, you do what she tells you, express very little, and smolder.

Your daydreams are telling you that you are very angry with your boss, which is not news to you. But they are also telling you that thus far your only daydream alternative to sullen, withdrawn obedience has been abusive language or sabotage. Your daydreams would have left out important alternatives: unaggressively describing your feelings to your boss, asking about her point of view, negotiating with her, finding out about channels for filing grievances, organizing fellow employees, and so on. The methods you have daydreamed about would have indicated an unspoken assumption of yours: people in power over you impose that power unilaterally and cannot be engaged in rational discussion or negotiation. Of course, this assumption is correct for some people, but fortunately not for a great many more. Understanding your original assumption, you are now in a position to imagine alternative assumptions and, based on them, to work out alternative approaches to your problem, approaches that you might not have seriously considered before.

Daydreams are themselves a way of discovering creative solutions to problems. People who daydream imaginatively can sometimes find solutions that would not occur to them were they to work on the problems deliberately. That is because our deliberate attempts tend to use the rational methods we have learned, and when these fail to work, we may be stumped; but daydreams can be more playful and can therefore allow us to explore new approaches, some of which may happen to work.

Unfortunately, people sometimes get into ruts that show up in their daydreams as much as in their outward behavior. Locating those ruts in your daydreams and then intentionally trying out a different approach in further daydreams may help you break out of an unproductive pattern. For example, I had been trying to make up a lecture on the connections among the parts of our personalities. As I daydreamed about various ways of giving such a lecture, it kept coming out dry and repetitive. In my daydream, I visualized my class sitting stony-faced, dutifully taking notes; and I sensed that the point would not get across very effectively. Trying to break out of this rut, I focused on the word *connected*, and as I did so, I began to hum to myself "the toe bone is connected to the foot bone, and the foot bone is connected to the ankle bone, . . ." and then began to daydream about standing before my class singing this song with altered words: "Perception is connected to cognition, and cognition is connected to emotion. . . ." After I finished laughing and giggling, I reflected that this just might get the point across. Never before had I *sung* a point to a class, but the next day I did—and it was probably the best-learned point in the whole course!

*Some guidelines for interpreting your daydreams.* Just as a professional would never draw a firm conclusion based on a single piece of evidence, you should never regard a conclusion about yourself based on a daydream analysis as rock solid. Anything you infer about yourself from your day or night dreams must be taken as a hypothesis—as your current best guess—to be tested against other things you know about yourself. If a conclusion doesn't feel right, there is a good chance it isn't right.

Besides considering what is in a daydream, you can obtain important information by knowing what set it off. If you can identify the event that triggered it, you will have learned something about the connections your mind makes between that event and the concerns underlying your daydream; because without such connections, the event would not have triggered a daydream involving that particular concern. For example, when Blaine heard the words "the powers of a man of learning," he launched into a daydream about becoming rich and famous. That connection tells us that Blaine connects learning with wealth and fame, and that in turn reveals some of Blaine's probable motivation for going to college.

When you look at your daydreams one at a time or a feature at a time, you get only a very partial view of yourself. That is because a daydream may reflect only a particular desire or a particular way of doing things and may leave out other desires or ways of doing things that conflict with the first one. For example, you might like the idea of being a celebrity and daydream about yourself being on a talk show, but you may prize your privacy even more. As a result of your fear, you might daydream of being held up to ridicule by a group of strangers. In real life, despite your liking the idea of being famous, your even greater fear of public exposure might motivate you to avoid the public limelight; but you would never have anticipated this decision had you considered only the first daydream. For this reason, a single daydream—or even a few daydreams—taken out of context is more likely to reflect your inner inclinations, such as wishing you were famous, than to be a reliable predictor of the decisions you would make in reality.

Useful as daydreams are for knowing ourselves, it is hard to be completely objective about ourselves. If you have serious doubts about yourself or are having difficulty dealing with personal problems, remember the value of enlisting the judgment of a professional, such as a qualified clinical psychologist or psychiatrist or some other kind of licensed psychotherapist or counselor.

Finally, remember also that daydreams are more than cold sources of information to be analyzed. First and foremost, they are themselves a way of exploring information that is important to us in that, within our daydreams, we are already scrutinizing our lives and drawing conclusions. And beyond this, as we shall see, daydreams are for many of us a prime source of stimulation and entertainment, a way of having fun with life and a medium for creative expression.

**Vanessa's Daydream**

Here is a fairly typical example of a very plain, everyday daydream that nevertheless reveals a lot about the daydreamer. A young woman named Vanessa reports on a spontaneous reverie she had one spring.

"I was thinking about going home and visit my parents tomorrow. [Then] I was thinking about going into the store tomorrow and trying to find the payment of mine that they lost. The [next] thought segment . . . was concerning a job —whether I should get a part-time job now and keep it through the summer. The last thought that I had going through my head was about what I'm going to be doing this summer, specifically where I'm going to be working this summer."

Apart from some rudimentary facts—Vanessa's parents are alive, the store lost her money, she is thinking about a job—there might not seem to be much material here on which to base an assessment of her personality. In fact, if there is anything significant at stake—as there is, for example, in a clinical diagnosis or a job interview—no one should draw firm conclusions about someone else on the basis of so little evidence. Rather, interpreting daydreams is like detective work. You treat each tentative conclusion as a working hypothesis, and no more, until you have firm evidence that you were right. But looking for hidden messages gradually trains you to be more sensitive, both to others' internal reality and to your own. For example, there is more information in our snatch of Vanessa's daydreaming than meets the eye at first glance. It tells a considerable story about her.

From Vanessa's reverie we learn that she still has a relationship with her parents, but on this occasion her thoughts about them are limited to "going home and visit." This thought seems perfunctory. She does not dwell on the visit. She gives no evidence of looking forward to it, nor does she express apprehension. She does not seem to imagine the details of the visit. Instead, her thought about visiting her parents immediately sets off a thought about money. It is unclear what that means regarding her relationship to her parents—is it encumbered with concerns about finances?—but it suggests that the visit holds limited emotional value for her, or perhaps strong ambivalence, since otherwise she would most likely have stayed with the theme longer and said more about it. She is probably no longer closely tied to her parents.

Not only is Vanessa independent of her parents, her reverie casts her as a take-charge person, an assertive individual who is actively running her own life. For one thing, she is not prepared to let the store get away with losing her money. Furthermore, imagining getting her money back led to thoughts about earning it and imagining how she would do that during the coming summer. We learn thereby that she responds to needing money by taking steps to earn it, and she thinks strategically about what kind of job would be best for her. She plans ahead. Considering all of these thoughts together, there is a take-charge quality to this reverie. Vanessa seems to feel in charge of her life and is prepared to take action when problems arise.

This is a fairly elaborate picture of Vanessa's personality—quite a lot to infer from four brief thoughts. But it turns out to agree remarkably well with other information my research team found out about her.

For example, Vanessa's highest score on the California Psychological Inventory was on dominance—taking charge in relationships with others. Her second-highest score was on self-acceptance, a quality that helps her to accept her feelings and needs and to act on them. She scored lowest on conforming to rules, self-control, tolerance, and trying to make a good impression. That is, she is very much an individualist who acts independently of others. Although she comes from a down-to-earth, working-class background, she told us that she hoped to become active in the arts and to live a life very different from that of her parents, and she described a number of alternative plans for achieving this goal. This information jibes completely with the take-charge quality that emanates from her daydream and with the independence and tendency to plan we found there.

Had we questioned Vanessa more closely about the specific images and feelings in her reverie, we would have found out much more than we did. It is in such details that we often find the keys to individuality. We would want to ask her exactly how she visualizes her parents. (As she imagines visiting them, are they standing side by side or does she imagine them doing different things in different parts of the house? Are they smiling or grumpy, attending to her or to something they are doing, spunky or downhearted?) The answers would tell us the kind of people she imagines her parents to be and the relationship between them. That would in turn tell us something about the images she carries around inside her that help to shape her own behavior and relationships.

Many thoughts also have sounds or other sensations associated with them. What does Vanessa imagine herself or her parents saying? Are they greeting her? Quarreling with each other? Does she smell freshly cut hay, manure, a meal cooking, a house odor? What emotions does she feel as she thinks about the visit? (Elation? Quiet anticipation? Nervousness? Reluctance?)

The answers to these questions would tell us something about the way Vanessa expects to be received by her parents, whether happily and attentively, with irritation and detachment, or in some other way. They would tell us something about the voices she carries around inside her that direct, support, criticize, and nag. And they would tell us something about the feeling tone, both theirs and hers, that she associates with her parents and their household at this time in her life. For example, when she is under stress, she might carp at herself the way her mother did, or she might say gently supportive things to herself the way her mother said them to her, even down to using her mother's intonation and the timbre of her voice. She might imagine her parents' home under a pall of tension and discontent or as a place suffused with warmth and respect, and that may well color her expectations and fears for the home she will create.

When Vanessa visualized going to the store, she might have imagined herself striding in confidently to solve a problem, stomping in angrily to berate a clerk, or slinking in nervously to raise the question. The way she imagined this scene probably corresponds to the way she usually handles confrontations, unless her daydream had a "pretend" quality about it, in which case it might reflect how she wished she could handle it. She might have imagined the clerk or the supervisor as agreeable and concerned or as overbearing and impatient, and that would tell us how she expects or fears others will react. And how she imagines herself reacting to them would tell us much about her orientation to the world around—her level of trust and self-confidence, her expectations of people in stores and more generally in business relationships, and her methods for dealing with difficult business and interpersonal situations.

By the time we had added similar questions about the imaginary summer jobs in her daydreams, we would have the material for a wide-ranging sketch of Vanessa's personality. We didn't ask those questions because we had already asked her so many others. But when you consider your own daydreams, you are under no such constraints. You can plumb your own daydreams to your heart's content, and perhaps you will learn some things about yourself that you have not suspected. When you daydream about yourself with a person in your life, what exactly is your mood like? Sometimes, it will be different from what you think it must be. How are you dressed? How is the other person dressed? What are your relative body sizes? Who has the more assertive voice? Which of you seems the more eager to assuage the other and avoid conflict? Much of the time, your answers will be the expectable ones, but not always. If in your daydream you feel unsure of yourself, that the other person is better dressed, larger, and with a firmer voice, and that you seem to be making all the compromises and apologies—especially if the daydream is contrary to reality or exaggerates it—that *may* tell you that you feel psychologically and socially smaller than the other person, perhaps more dependent on that person and at his or her mercy.

## GUIDED DAYDREAMS: A DETAILED LOOK AT IMAGINATIVE DAYDREAMING

Psychotherapists who use imagery methods often probe their clients' images in great detail. They do this both to understand their clients better and to help their clients experience their own images more fully, which helps to expedite the personal growth that stands at the heart of this kind of therapy.

One method by which psychotherapists harness daydreaming for these purposes is called "guided daydreaming" or "guided imagery." Most kinds of guided imagery begin with the client relaxing and the therapist suggesting a starting point for the daydream—a setting such as a meadow, an object such as a lion, or perhaps the end of an interrupted dream the client had. The client focuses on this starting point, lets the waking dream unfold, and keeps the therapist posted on its progress.

This experience differs from ordinary daydreaming in that the client communicates what is happening in the imagery continuously as it unfolds. This casts the client into the role of not only experiencing the daydream but also systematically observing it and putting it into words. The therapist may even ask questions or make suggestions during the daydream. It might seem as if this procedure must be very disruptive and that the resulting daydream would be at best a weak, watered-down version of a normal one, but in reality the opposite is true. The therapist's questioning actually seems to deepen the imagery by drawing the client's attention to its details. These experiences are often very intense and powerful, so much so that they are sometimes called "waking dreams."

The therapist might choose a starting point that relates quite directly to one of the client's problems, in which case the waking dream might portray elements of the problem quite directly. For example, a therapist working with a client who has a marital problem might suggest starting with a conversation between the client and his wife. But often therapists will choose more open-ended starting points, such as imagining a meadow, a house, or two animals walking down a road together having a conversation. The waking dreams that start in these nonspecific settings sometimes work their way toward dealing quite explicitly with the clients' concerns. For example, a client who is working through her relationship with a parent might begin with imagining a house, going in, and suddenly finding this parent in the bedroom. But often the waking dreams reflect those concerns more subtly. For example, someone depressed about a life with little satisfaction might try to imagine a meadow but end up with an image of a desert.

In my own work with waking dreams I have mostly

followed the method developed by West German psychiatrist Hanscarl Leuner, which tends toward relatively long imagery periods, usually ten to twenty minutes but often even longer, and treats the imagery experience as the central "active ingredient" in the therapy. One feature of this method is that the therapist can ask the client a lot of questions during the daydreaming and thereby get a great amount of rich detail about it as it unfolds. Because the client describes the imagery as it evolves, less detail is forgotten than would be the case afterwards; and the therapist does not have to depend on the often rather laconic accounts that people give of their daydreams when they are asked to write them down after they have had them. Therefore, we can learn much more about the detailed imagery of daydreams this way than from accounts of daydreams given after they are over. In my own practice, I never fail to be amazed at the wealth of detail that is present in daydream images and how well they fit what I know about my client from other sources. Here are two waking dreams drawn from a client in this kind of therapy.

**Lucille's Guided Daydreams**

Lucille is a young woman who was distressed by her relationship with a man. The relationship was in itself a satisfying experience for her, but since this man had no apparent intention of marrying her, it was also a relationship without prospects. She was, in a sense, trapped within the relationship unless she wished to deprive herself of its emotional benefits.

The starting point for Lucille's first guided daydream session was a meadow. As she let an image form in her mind, she saw a cow pasture in late summer, one getting a bit brown, surrounded by woods. The sky was overcast. A wire fence ran around most of the pasture's perimeter, but the pasture sloped downhill to the left, and at the bottom of the slope there was a short stretch that was not fenced in. Suddenly, Lucille sensed a man standing next to her, someone who seemed very familiar, and he took her hand. She could not see him in the image and could not make out his identity.

Briefly, she enjoyed their togetherness amid this scenery. She looked over toward the trees and noticed mushrooms growing there. As she ambled down the hill toward the unfenced area, the man vanished.

Lucille's waking dream continued for a considerable time beyond this scene. She left the enclosure, discovered a lake with a sunken ship in it, went for a swim, came out, and felt good. But I would like to focus on the first part of the experience and consider how its details correspond to the other things we know about Lucille.

*The meanings in Lucille's first guided daydream.* The correspondence between the waking dream and the rest of Lucille's life is quite striking. The overcast sky reflected her downcast mood. Given that she was to imagine a meadow, she imagined a literally nourishing one: a pasture. Pastures nourish cows in a physical sense, and satisfying relationships nourish people emotionally. Her pasture was already past its prime and starting to brown, just as Lucille's relationship was starting to wear thin because of its limitations. In the pasture, she was largely fenced in, just as in her situation she was fenced off from developing more promising relationships. Within the pasture she enjoyed her friend's physical and emotional closeness. As she left the pasture, he vanished, as he would have to largely vanish from her life if she ended their relationship. After she left the pasture, she was able to enjoy other experiences and ended up feeling good. Symbolically, she had tried out leaving the relationship and found the outcome satisfactory.

Or so it would appear. One can never be absolutely sure of getting this kind of interpretation right. But a fit that is as good as this one in so many details generates confidence in the interpretation. At the same time, it illustrates the extent to which nuances of concern, feeling, and expectation shape the details of daydream images. And insofar as they do, it indicates the possibility of working backward from the images to shed light on the daydreamer's life outside the daydream.

*Lucille's later guided daydream and its meanings.* A few weeks later, Lucille's preoccupation with her relationships had broadened. Conscious that she was getting older, she reflected with me on the fact that her current relationship was in one important way like her previous ones—that she had a pattern of bonding with unavailable men. She had gotten along well with several more suitable men, but these relationships somehow never succeeded in becoming sexual. This realization saddened and frustrated her.

The starting point for Lucille's guided daydream on this occasion was a brook in a meadow. She saw herself sitting on a steep embankment over a very narrow, fast-flowing brook. It was too small for swimming. Across the brook and a bit downstream stood a large weeping willow whose branches hung in the water like a curtain. Behind it, the sun was setting. It was getting dark. A little boat made out of folded paper came floating along and was caught in the willow branches. The stream had now become wider near the willow—in fact, wide and deep enough to swim in. She stepped into the stream and swam toward the willow. She longed to reach its branches—the "curtain"—but, just as emphatically, she did not want to swim through the branches, did not want to get behind the curtain. As she swam, she sensed some kind of resistance, as if she were swimming against a current. Try as she might, she could not seem to reach the willow branches. Then, suddenly, the image vanished. She felt, as at the outset, slightly saddened.

There are again many correspondences between this waking dream and Lucille's life situation at the time. The setting sun might well symbolize her fear that her time for establishing a suitable relationship with a man was running out. The weeping willow probably reflects her depressed mood. The brook was at first an inhospitable one, too small for swimming and too far below the embankment for dangling her feet in it. It tantalized her; it made her want to swim or splash her feet in the water but prevented her from doing either one. She felt frustrated, much as she was frustrated by the inhospitable social situation in which she found herself. That, too, surrounded her with something she wanted—potential male partners—without satisfying her needs. When the brook widened and she was finally able to swim, the experience turned into the waking equivalent of a frustration dream. Just as she felt repeatedly frustrated in her search for a suitable relationship, she was unable to make headway toward her objective in the stream.

A feature of a dream or daydream need not represent only one particular thing. Sometimes, a feature represents two or more things simultaneously. Sigmund Freud, the originator of psychoanalysis, called this *overdetermination*, because the same feature is determined by two different factors in the person where one might have been enough. This is illustrated in Lucille's waking dream by the tree. It was a *weeping* willow, probably as a reflection of her depressed mood. But in light of her persistent, ardent efforts to reach its branches, it also probably stood for an important life objective, one she couldn't seem to reach. Her effort and her frustration seem to parallel her frustration at the time in finding a suitable relationship with a man, which suggests that this is what the tree symbolized. In addition, its branches hung in the water *like a curtain*, concealing something that she did not want to face. In her waking dream she explicitly did not want to swim through the branches. Her palpable fear of doing so suggests that the branches concealed something dangerous, or at least something unpleasant. If the tree indeed symbolized for her a relationship with a man, then her resistance to finding out what the branches concealed suggests that there is something threatening to her about a full relationship with an available man, where the relationship is not limited at the outset by the man's unwillingness to make a commitment. Conceivably, she feared the new demands that such a relationship might make on her, demands that she could perhaps not foresee or control.

Lucille's guided daydream illustrates the connections between our daydreams and the moods, concerns, and events of our real-world lives. It also provides the basis for illustrating one way to generate possible interpretations of daydreams, as well as possible questions about ourselves. Lucille's second daydream suggests that some force kept her back from whatever lay behind the curtain of willow roots. If it were your daydream, you might wish to find out the nature of that force—the threat of a stable relationship, as I suggested (as only one possibility!) for Lucille, or something else? To discover what it is could be of pivotal importance in reorienting your life.

## HOW DESIRES SHAPE OUR DREAMS

If daydreams and "waking dreams" are this revealing of a person's individuality, so are night dreams, which Sigmund Freud once called the "royal road to the unconscious." They, too, reveal our deepest concerns and the ways we are inclined to deal with them; and dreams, too, are shaped by the cues inside and around us that touch on our concerns. For example, Barbara, a student of psychology, reported the following dream:

"I dreamt I was sitting at the table in my apartment. I was doing homework—I think I was working on my MCL [motivation, conditioning, learning] lab report results 'cause I remember trying to draw graphs. It must have been late at night because the curtains were open so I could see outside and it was completely dark out. Then suddenly I was waiting for a letter from [her boyfriend]. I was ignoring the papers and stuff that was cluttering the table. I remember listening for the mailman because you can always hear when he comes. I walked to the door once and looked out when I thought I heard him but he wasn't there. I came back in and sat down. Then I woke up."

This is a common form of dream, and it, too, provides a wealth of revealing detail. It encompasses two main activities, drawing graphs for a laboratory course and waiting for a boyfriend's letter, with a sudden transition from one to the other. Part of the explanation as to why Barbara dreamed about these two things is plain enough: both represented unmet goals. She was in reality faced with a deadline for handing in her lab report and she was in reality still building the relationship with her boyfriend. These concerns disposed her to react emotionally to cues related to her lab report and to her boyfriend.

But that explanation doesn't tell us why she dreamed about them at that particular moment; we need something more to explain the timing. We do not know what triggered the dream segment about the lab report—perhaps it was something in a previous dream—but we do know the cue that nudged her dream over to her boyfriend: As Barbara slept, an experimenter had just read to her her boyfriend's address. Still fast asleep, Barbara immediately reacted in her dream by shifting her attention from the lab report to her boyfriend.

The way in which Barbara's dream changed tells us something important about the way cues influence dreams, daydreams, and thoughts: they often unleash a new action sequence. The cue in this case was the address of Barbara's boyfriend, but the address itself never occurred in her dream. Instead, it triggered a change in Barbara's behavior. She watched and listened for the mailman, and then she walked to the door and looked out. In her dream, the cue had sent Barbara into action.

Even though the address as such did not appear in Barbara's dream, it still had a specific effect. After all, Barbara dreamed that she was looking for the mailman rather than making love to her boyfriend on the sofa or talking to him on the telephone. Her boyfriend lived in another city; we associate addresses with letters; and hence she began to dream about awaiting mail. Had we read Barbara her boyfriend's telephone number, she might have dreamed about waiting for a telephone call. Had we simply uttered his name, she might have waited for him to arrive in person.

The fact that she waited for mail, rather than starting to write him a letter, tells us something about Barbara and their relationship. There are a number of possibilities. Perhaps she had already written to her boyfriend but he had not yet replied; or perhaps she was in the habit of waiting for his initiatives in the relationship and felt little sense of control over it. There are also other possibilities. From the information in this one dream, one cannot be sure which one is correct, but the details of the dream suggest the likelihood that Barbara feels cut off and dependent on her boyfriend's wishes. After all, despite her obvious desire for a letter, when the letter did not arrive she did nothing in the dream to contact him.

There is one more noteworthy feature of this dream. Hearing the address did not simply wipe away the dream Barbara had already found herself in. She remained in the same room and, for a while, at the same table; only her attention and actions changed. Sometimes cues do lead to a brand-new dream sequence, but more commonly they change the direction a dream takes, or change a few details in it, while carrying over some of the dream's features from before the cue.

Here is another dream that illustrates the same principle. Howard was a young man with a low-paying job, a girlfriend, and an aging car. Recently he had been concerned about the condition of his car, fearing that it needed repairs he could ill afford. About ten seconds after reading him the word *car* three times, we woke him up and he reported: "My car broke down on me again. Let's see. I was in Lake Brooten. I was just cruising around and stuff. . . . It was Friday night, and I was supposed to pick up my girlfriend. There was another girl I was going to buy some beer for. And anyway I went over to my girlfriend's house. Just as I pulled up to the driveway it felt like my car had a flat tire, but the whole car was just going from one side to the other. Something was really wrong with it. My girlfriend's friend pulled up and I think we got in with her. Then I woke up."

Since Howard was in the middle of a long dream about "cruising," his dream probably already included a car before the experimenter introduced the "car" cue. But before the cue the car served as background to the main action, picking up his girlfriend and buying beer. These themes reflected his ongoing concerns about the relationship with his girlfriend and about his use of alcohol. After the "car" cue, the dream changed and focused on the car, which behaved in accord with his worst expectations. That is, the dream then played out the kind of experience that Howard expected and feared from his unreliable car.

Barbara's and Howard's dreams illustrate how events influence the timing of changes in dreams and daydreams: when something reminds us of a concern not already represented there, our images shift focus to the new concern. Knowing this can help us to make additional sense of daydreams. When a daydream starts or shifts focus, we can try to figure out what happened just before the shift to trigger the change. It might have been something outside the daydreamer, or it might have been something in the daydream just before the shift. If we can identify what that something was, it will give us additional information about the daydreamer's mental associations with the new concern.

## HARNESSING DAYDREAMS THROUGH STORIES ABOUT PICTURES

In the 1930s, Christiana Morgan and psychiatrist Henry A. Murray assembled a set of pictures that people might use as jumping-off points for spinning a yarn. If you went through this procedure, you would be asked to look at each picture and then to make up a creative story about it with a beginning, middle, and end. You would also describe what the people in your stories were thinking and feeling. This procedure became famous as the Thematic Apperception Test (TAT), still a widely used method for assessing personality.

The stories that people make up for the TAT are in some ways similar and in other ways sharply different from naturally occurring daydreams. The differences are perhaps most obvious. Most daydreams occur spontaneously and are brief impressions or fragments of stories, but telling a TAT story is a task, something undertaken quite deliberately, that is supposed to result in a complete story. Furthermore, the storyteller is aware that others are listening to the story or will be reading it, which virtually guarantees a certain amount of impression-management by the storyteller.

Nevertheless, daydreams and TAT stories are in some important ways similar. Both necessarily draw on our beliefs and abilities, and both reflect our current concerns and emotions. Therefore, some of what psychologists have learned from studying TAT stories is also applicable to daydreams.

Here are three examples of such stories. All were written by young men in response to the same picture, which showed a group of men sitting around a table and one man standing and apparently looking out the window. The first storyteller, Gene, writes:

"The end of a poker game. All are happy except for two of the players. One is getting up to leave, the second is standing looking out a window in deep thought. The one who is looking out the window is the biggest loser.

"The man looking out the window has lost very much more than he expected. He must tell the news to his wife. Money will have to be borrowed and something she always wanted will not be bought. He is thinking of the heel he is. The other players are too happy with their winnings to take any note of this. They don't realize his mistake. He will however have to suffer for it a great deal before he is again at ease and has regained self-assurance."

Remember, the picture Gene was looking at was simply a bunch of men around a table, with one standing and looking out the window. However, Gene's story centers around a colossal mistake and wretched feelings of guilt—a personal crisis that jeopardizes his main character's marriage and finances. Evidently, his mental associations to group activity with other men include taking risks to compete, making mistakes, losing, and disgrace. Furthermore, the other men give him no support; they are too busy exulting in their winnings. Most likely, Gene expects little of a positive nature from other men. And there is one more significant feature of this story: the most important part of his loss is having to tell his wife and having to deny her some things she wants.

As far as we can infer from this one story, Gene's emotional life revolves around a woman—perhaps a real woman, or perhaps only one he imagines for himself in the future. Either way, the woman of the story could also stand for his mother, with whom he may have had a very emotionally dependent relationship. He fears being done in while competing with other men, from whom he expects no help. He has a gloomy, pessimistic outlook on life, one that crops up again in other stories he wrote on the same occasion.

The preceding story gives us a remarkably individualized portrait of Gene's inner life. Very much like a daydream, it tells us about his desires (to win and to please his main woman), his fears (of failing at both), and his expectations (that he must go it alone with little help or comfort and will probably fail).

The second storyteller, Jonathan, takes a very different view—much less punishing, remarkably dispassionate, and concerned with conflict. He writes:

"A number of men are arguing the best way to make their company greater. The man pointing is trying to convince his colleagues of his theory but one of them will not listen. The man in the center of the picture is new to the company and the man at the window resents his genius for youth. The man in the center wants his way to be accepted. The other men around the table are all concerned with making the company greater. The man at the window does not want the others to succeed. The man in the center will have his plan adopted. It will work well and he will achieve good standing with the company."

Stories such as Gene's and Jonathan's contain a great amount of information, enough to be confusing to someone trying to form a picture of the storyteller. In order to make these kinds of judgments easier and more reliable, psychologists David C. McClelland and John W. Atkinson and their students devised elaborate techniques for scoring stories such as this. These techniques require looking for fairly specific kinds of features: what the different characters are doing, thinking, and feeling, and how much help or hindrance they are getting from the people and physical environment around them.

For example, a skilled story analyst would note that in Jonathan's story the characters around the table, except for the man in the center, are motivated by a desire for corporate prestige—to "make the company greater." The man in the center is mostly wrapped up in making a personal impact on the others. But making the company greater and making a personal impact on others are both forms of exercising power and gaining prestige. The story would therefore score high in the need for power. Insofar as some of Jonathan's other stories follow suit, the story analyst is likely to conclude that Jonathan himself has strong needs to be powerful—to be able to make an impact on others, to carry high prestige.

There are other revealing features of Jonathan's story. For example, the story presents people in conflict with one another, in that one character resents another's "genius for youth" and wants the group to fail. Evidently, in Jonathan's inner world men are inclined toward resentment and possibly toward subversion, perhaps even treachery. His need for power may in part reflect his desire to protect himself from the hostile peers that he imagines people his world.

By way of contrast, here is Gary's story, again about the same picture: "A classroom has begun a tangent. The teacher has been shaken from the subject, and the class 'brain' is giving his opinion on the tangent. The subject they were talking on was boring anyway so why not learn about something interesting, although, naturally important. The students seem impatient and restless and the sooner they get out of class the better. The teacher is also quite bored, although the students must be exposed to this material. The teacher will finally drag his disorderly class back to the subject and they will proceed."

This story reflects a bad case of the academic blahs. There is little indication in it of a need for achievement, power, human relationships, or for much of anything else other than change—for relief from boredom. The characters are locked into a system that seems to defeat all their desires in that situation. We can probably conclude that Gary is not very happy as a student, feels trapped in classroom situations, and sees little hope for improvement in the system. He is mature enough not to blame the instructor, whom the story casts as another of the system's victims, but perhaps not mature or gifted enough to transcend academic frustrations.

From a single picture, we have three drastically different stories. They are very suggestive, and based on them I have offered a lot of educated guesses about Gene, Jonathan, and Gary to illustrate the way one can take TAT stories—and naturally occurring daydreams—and glean information from them. They are not, of course, firm conclusions that you would be safe basing decisions on, any more than you are ever safe in drawing firm conclusions about someone's overall personality from a few stories, dreams, or daydreams.

Psychologists who assess personality know that the impression obtained from a single source of information about someone can be highly misleading. They therefore generally base their conclusions on a collection of two or more sources, such as a diagnostic interview, a Minnesota Multiphasic Personality Inventory (MMPI), a Rorschach inkblot test, a TAT, and perhaps various measures of intelligence. If you were performing a professional assessment, you would treat each of your inferences about Gene or Jonathan or Gary as a hypothesis about him that you would check against the other sources of information. Only if you could confirm these impressions in the other information could you place much credence in them.

## HOW VALID ARE INTERPRETATIONS OF STORIES?

Because it is much easier to collect TAT stories than naturally occurring daydreams, most of what we know about the validity of daydreamlike interpretations comes from research with stories. That research shows that stories provide useful information, although they have limitations of which we must remain aware. Because both TAT stories and daydreams draw on our imaginations, what we have learned about the validity of stories probably applies in part to daydreams as well.

The validity of TAT stories as clues to personality has been assessed by thousands of scientific investigations. Their results provide a picture of what one can and cannot do with them. They tell us that there is no simple one-to-one correspondence between our TAT stories and our lives, either in relation to our outward actions or our inner experience. But, on the whole, there is a reasonably close relation between TAT stories—and therefore probably daydreams—and needs, feelings, beliefs, abilities, and cultural experiences.

For example, if we walk around angry much of the time, we are more likely than others to people our stories with angry and violent characters; if we feel guilty about our anger, we more often create story characters who feel guilty or who, having transgressed, come to a bad end. When we are hungry, we tend to create characters who are trying to find food. Similarly, if we get excited about achieving excellence, we often make up characters concerned about achievement. And when we are sexually aroused, we are likely to tell about sexual exploits.

And so on. These are all ways in which TAT stories, and most likely daydreams, relate to our inner realities—how we feel and what we want. If we look at them simplistically, stories and daydreams relate less closely to outward behavior. For example, some people who hardly ever attack anyone, even with words, produce unusually violent TAT stories and daydreams. Those people are very likely to describe themselves as aggressive because they feel angry inside much of the time, and yet they might never actually behave aggressively on the outside.

Here, the story or the daydream tells us something very important: that the person is seething inside and keeping the anger all corked up. This information is all the more important for its *not* applying to the person's actions. The discrepancy between inner reality and outward behavior can pose a major psychological problem, one that can shut the person out of truly intimate relationships, undermine good sexual experiences, and take a toll on his or her health.

The reason for this difference between inner and outer realities is that taking action has very different consequences than wanting and feeling do. When we go about translating our wishes and feelings into action, we usually consider the constraints of reality: whether a given action is a practical thing to do and what we will get or lose by doing it in a given situation. And that often puts us in conflict. For example, we might very much like to get into a relationship with someone but know that the person is probably unavailable. Because of this we might worry about being rejected and embarrassed, which might keep us from following our inclination to approach the other person.

But daydreams and stories often provide information on both sides of a conflict such as this, especially if we look at a series of daydreams or stories by the same person. For example, if you were in the conflict situation described above, you might daydream about running into the other person at a company picnic. In your daydream, the two of you get into a conversation that gradually becomes personal and intimate. You make eye contact, and it becomes evident that the other person is interested in you. And there the daydream might end—or it might just keep getting more intimate. This particular daydream would not have revealed your hesitation about making intimate contact with the other person. (It might, because of its happy ending, even have reduced your real-life hesitation!) But the chances are that in other daydreams you would play out the other side of the conflict. For example, you might imagine walking out to the parking lot together, trying to make small talk, but that the other person remains cold and distant. You might then suggest that the two of you go get a drink and talk, upon which the other person gives you the brush-off. You feel chagrined and silly.

Had you tried to interpret only the first daydream, it would have seemed as if you had an unalloyed attraction to the other person. But by getting a larger sample of daydreams and looking for all sides of a possible conflict, you get a more realistic picture of what you (or a storyteller) are likely to do.

So the relationship between your daydreams and your actions can get complicated. Here is another example. Two boys have grown up in the same kind of family, and neither one expresses much outward anger. One is prone to internalize his anger and to tell violent TAT stories. For example, he might tell a story about a boy who seized a rifle and shot it at his school, wounding many of his schoolmates and teachers. The other boy's stories contain little violence.

The boys' families had refused to put up with aggression, but this refusal affected them in different ways. The more the first one—who was quick to anger—cursed and hit people, the more he was punished, and because he was prone to anger easily, he drew quite a bit of punishment during what his parents viewed as a "stage." With all this pain, he ended up expressing little of his anger. The other boy was easier-going. Even though he grew up in the same kind of setting, he was less inclined to become violent, and therefore he ran into little punishment for violent acts. Having experienced less punishment for violence, he could feel freer to act out his anger on the few occasions when he became enraged.

Two such people, growing up in the same setting, end

up attaching different consequences to expressing anger and therefore act differently when they become angry. This leads to the seeming paradox that the first person *acts* less angry than the second person and yet tells more violent TAT stories. But the TAT is doing its job: it is reflecting the emotion and the desire to hit. Besides, the first person's violent stories often end unhappily. For example, the boy who shot his classmates is disowned by his family, sent to reform school, and ends up committing suicide. The TAT thereby reflects not only the violence but also the expectation, based on much sorry experience, that acting out invites trouble. By including both sides of a conflict, instead of just one, TAT stories can provide clues to our likely actions.

The point is that fantasy productions, be they daydreams or stories, generally reflect the different facets of their creators. A majority of our daydreams reflect us quite directly: we do most of the talking in our own daydreams and initiate most of the action. Likewise, in our TAT stories, as psychologist Gardner Lindzey established, we usually imbue the main characters we create—the "heroes" of our stories—with our own personality traits. Even though we don't explicitly identify those main characters with ourselves, we often identify with them, and when we do we project into them our concerns, feelings, temperaments, and beliefs.

Although people commonly put themselves into their daydreams and into the main characters of their stories, they also inject other characters. These may be very different from the daydreamer or from the main character of a story, but they are also creations of the storyteller and therefore are also revealing. On the one hand, they may reflect aspects of daydreamers' or storytellers' personalities that they are afraid to identify with. For example, if you have a great deal of trouble owning up to your own anger, you may daydream about someone else acting angry. Even though both characters appear in your daydream, you may feel less guilt if the anger is expressed by a daydream character other than yourself. But quite often these secondary characters simply reflect our views of what other people are like and our expectations of how they will act. When you daydream about having a conversation with a good friend, you are likely to endow your friend with the same voice mannerisms and facial expressions you have learned to expect from him or her.

**Faking It**

Although our daydreams and stories generally reflect us, there is nothing mechanical or inevitable about this, which makes TAT stories a poor basis for "seeing through" people against their will. If we wanted to fool someone about ourselves, most of us would be perfectly able to write stories that hide who we are. Therefore, as clues to our personalities, daydreams and TAT stories are only as good as our willingness to communicate them honestly.

For example, when people are told that their stories will be read by someone interviewing them for a job, they tell different stories than they would have told spontaneously. Their characters are more like the kind of people the storytellers think their interviewers would hire, and the stories become a tool with which job applicants can manipulate the impression they make. Accordingly, the stories become a poor guide to their creators.

Yet even when people try to mislead us, some aspects of their real selves leak into their stories. In writing stories to make a favorable impression, they are presenting their view of good behavior on the job. And this image of good behavior is a part of them, even though it might not be the way they would act once they felt secure in their new job. In other words, even as we try to mask ourselves, we end up revealing ourselves, at least in part. But someone trying to analyze a daydream or a TAT story written under those conditions would have a virtually hopeless task of making accurate sense of it.

So the *reports* we get of daydreams or stories can be readily faked to mislead us, even where the daydreams themselves accurately reflect the daydreamer. This means that using people's accounts of their daydreams or other products of their imaginations gives us no sure-fire, lie-proof insight into their personalities. By the same token, it indicates that we possess the means for keeping this most private part of ourselves truly private.

## HOW FANTASIES REFLECT OUR IDEAS ABOUT LIFESTYLES

Whenever we choose a lifestyle—a certain kind of partner, an occupation, an avocation, friends, possessions, and a personal style and daily pattern—we simultaneously choose not to pursue other kinds of lifestyles, and yet we may be capable of those others, might even find them equally fulfilling, and may know other people who did choose them. We sometimes place ourselves in these different lifestyles in our daydreams or daydream about someone else who has adopted them; and this process is nowhere clearer than in our creative writing.

Like daydreams, literary works reveal a good deal about their authors; and like other daydreamers, creative writers put themselves into their creations. They typically create some characters who seem very much like themselves; but they also create characters who—at least on the surface—seem very different from themselves.

Alabama psychologist Raymond Fowler once induced novelist John D. MacDonald to take the widely used Minnesota Multiphasic Personality Inventory (MMPI) three times: once for himself, a second time as his character Travis McGee might have responded, and again as his other chief character, Meyer, might have answered. Those two characters have lived and evolved through twenty-one of MacDonald's more than seventy novels. McGee is an adventurer, bent on taking risks and trading violence. His close friend Meyer is a quiet, contemplative economist who prefers to stay put and stay safe. Author MacDonald's profile on the MMPI was almost identical with Meyer's but very different from his character McGee's. McGee corresponds to Mac-

Donald's conception of an opposite lifestyle. However, McGee is a person with whom Meyer—and presumably MacDonald—knows how to interact, whom he can understand, and whom he has, in one way or another, come to know. Even though that life would not be his own first choice, it is an integral part of his mind.

Daydreams, too, feature ourselves and other people, and the others need not be just like ourselves. They are the people we know and love or fear, or they are people we would like to know or dread to encounter. In all cases, they are people whom we have somehow made part of ourselves—internalized, engraved in our brains—even though they might not be what we would choose to be. Every time we really experience another person, we add to our own mind another potentiality, another "possible self," to borrow Michigan psychologist Hazel Markus' term. Those others become part of our own psyches. They become a kind of mental repertory company, ready to pop into our daydreams, night dreams, stories, and novels.

For example, you may have had a neighbor whom you found uncommonly kind and caring. If you spent much time interacting with her, her voice and gestures became familiar to you. Eventually, you could readily conjure them up in your own imagination even when your neighbor was nowhere around. And when you felt in need of loving support, you might have done just that: imagined how she might have reacted. You may even have started talking to yourself in that same voice and manner. She became, in the psychological sense, quite literally a part of you. In the language of psychology, you "internalized" her.

Unfortunately, the same applies to the noxious characters in our lives. When we live under oppression, when we are treated with cruel barbarism, as in gang-ridden neighborhoods and concentration camps, we become familiar with the gestures and manner of our oppressors, and then they, too, join our inner repertory company. Psychoanalysts have coined a term for this: "identification with the aggressor."

We may continue to dislike these people and suppress them in ourselves, but our human potentiality for acting like them—and for recreating them in our daydreams and stories—remains.

People probably come into the world naturally equipped to internalize others in these ways. Even day-old infants imitate the smiles and frowns of the people who hover over them. Throughout childhood, we fix our mental gazes on the people around us, turning what we see and hear into images that we can evoke at will. Eventually, we repeat the demeanor and actions of these people in our daydreams and physically mimic their actions when it suits us to do so. It is little wonder that all of us who have been close to loving adults have learned ways to express love, and that all of us who have grown up in a racist society carry within us the images and therefore the potentialities of racial hatred.

The many potentialities that we choose not to act out are just as surely part of us as those we express in action; and they emerge regularly in our fantasies. For example, the woman who daydreamed about being "married to Harrison Ford or William Hurt. . . . We are filthy rich" emphasized that this daydream was "the opposite of the way I am and the pattern of my life." But she also worried about money and the social climate in which she lived. In her daydream, she could try out an alternative self and life—one that could satisfy some possibly very important unmet needs, even though she has chosen not to act on it in reality.

Quite often, these potential selves emerge as foils for ourselves, as conversation partners, love objects, and adversaries. Thus, John MacDonald created a vibrant Travis McGee quite unlike his own outward self, and he also created Meyer in his own image as a stable point of departure.

MacDonald clearly admired McGee, but often these other characters are ones of which we would disapprove if they became real. For example, Meg, a social worker, was raised never to show anger, and, in fact, she behaves unassertively even when she comes across individuals she "would have loved to flatten." Her potential for raw aggression is clearly in place. Even though she keeps it under strict control, it remains inside her as an alternative self. In her daydream, she reports, "I verbally chew out a parent of one of the kids I work with, back him into a corner without cursing. He is particularly repugnant, rude, and aggressive—thinks he can make mincemeat out of me; instead, I render him helpless and walk out." In her daydream she tries out going beyond her usual reaction, while remaining largely true to her usual outward personality: she gives the parent some of his aggressiveness back, and she lets herself prevail—though still without cursing—while giving his obnoxiousness full play.

From literary fantasies to daydreams, then, our imaginations employ both our real selves and our other possible selves—selves that we have learned to know by experiencing them in others, in media portrayals, in the ideals held out to us by society, and sometimes by our own creative ideas of what might be possible for us. Sometimes, like Meg, we try out those alternative selves in our daydreams; other times, like MacDonald, we imagine relating to someone else who personifies those selves. Whatever kind of self we daydream about, our daydreams address our actual goals and explore possible new ones. They thereby reveal those goals, along with our needs, feelings, values, expectations, and the ways in which we might react to events and accomplish our aims.

CHAPTER 6

# Sex and Daydreams

*As I listen to an album I think of my lover. The way her lips feel on mine. The sounds she and I make, the different scents.*

—Anonymous daydream report

Images of love and sex are among our most pervasive daydreams. We embark on them in an amazing array of places and circumstances—on our jobs, in class, in the laboratory, at play, and at home. In our laboratory, Betty is listening to a taped narration with her hand on a toggle switch; but in her mind, before we interrupted her with a beep, "I was thinking about touching, about having another person touching me, and the warmth of the hand. Then I was thinking of contentment in the act of sex."

Sexual daydreams are undoubtedly as old as humankind, probably older; and the forms they take, stripped of superficialities, are timeless as well. The ancients did not record their daydreams as such; but their literature and art give strong evidence of sexual fantasy. Erotic art goes back many centuries. The ancient Greek myths contain numerous accounts of sexual liaisons, many between gods and humans. By one account, for example, Helen (for a time "of Troy") was the offspring of the god Zeus after he, in the form of a swan, ravished the princess Leda. The mysterious woman in the biblical Song of Songs says, "I am weak from passion. His left hand is under my head, and his right hand caresses me. Promise me . . . that you will not interrupt our love." Her account, recorded over two and a half millennia ago, resembles in all but artistry Betty's twentieth-century daydream. Together with research showing that we nearly all experience sexual daydreams, it is plain that they are a characteristic part of being human.

Sexual daydreams come in every degree of emotional depth. Some are relatively light, exploratory episodes. While at work, for example, Dan reported a "sexual fantasy about sleeping with a particularly attractive supervisor, a girl from Reedburgh. I envisioned rolling with her in copulation over one of the work tables." Other sexual daydreams are imbued with profound yearnings and boundless passion, which, as in Betty's daydream, are more implicit and felt than spelled out in people's reports.

Research shows that unless we are engaged in lovemaking, sexual daydreaming makes up only a small fraction of our thoughts. The college students studied so far imagine themselves engaging in something sexual at most only about 1 percent of the time, and about 5 percent of the time when they identify themselves as daydreaming. These average percentages are small, but with very roughly 4,000 or so thoughts each day, we still come out, on average, with perhaps forty thoughts per day about sex.

We tend to remember most vividly the things that arouse us emotionally. Because sexual daydreams are generally so arousing, we probably remember them more often than other daydreams; and therefore, as we look back, sexual daydreams make up a larger share of the daydreams we remember than of those we actually had. For this reason, some people are surprised that the percentage of sexual daydreaming found by researchers is so low. But people vary tremendously in how much they daydream about sex. For some of us, the 1-percent figure is easily believable.

When they began systematic research on sexual daydreaming during the 1970s, researchers were most interested in testing the proposition, popularized as part of psychoanalytic theory, that sexual daydreaming is a sign of sexual inadequacy. The theory stated that daydreaming in general is infantile and that it features unsatisfied wishes. Therefore, sexual daydreaming must be an immature reaction to an unsatisfying sex life. What they found instead was virtually the opposite: the livelier people's sex lives were, the more they also daydreamed about sex.

Investigators were soon looking at sexual daydreaming from a less theoretical viewpoint, simply trying to establish who does it, what they do, and what it is all related to. So far, the overall findings about sexual daydreaming can be summarized as showing that nearly everyone does it at least occasionally; that people who have many sexual daydreams are as well adjusted psychologically as others and that they average, if anything, greater satisfaction with their sex lives; that sexual daydreaming reflects your sexual tastes and preferences and is also a way of exploring sexual possibilities you might not be able or might not want to explore in reality; that it may influence your later sexual behavior; and that sexual daydreaming during sex may enhance lovemaking and help stabilize relationships.

Daydreams about sex have a number of important benefits. When they are about sex with our regular partners—our lovers and spouses—they help to bridge the times we spend away from them. They can also enhance our lovemaking, and they are an important channel of information about our own sexuality.

When we are away from our lovers, we can call up images of them, comfort ourselves with them, and remind ourselves of what we can hope to look forward to. Although the evidence on this is not in, daydreams such as this may help to preserve the bond between us and our sexual partners and perhaps help us to resist the temptation of other liaisons.

Sexual daydreams enhance our lovemaking in at least two ways. First, while we are engaged in sex, most of us sometimes daydream about sex in ways that increase our sexual excitement. Second, while we are engaged in something else, our daydreams often feature new ways to make love that excite us. Afterwards, we may try them out, thereby increasing sexual pleasure. In this way, sexual daydreaming helps mold our lovemaking.

Sexual daydreams are so interwoven with our sexual activities that they also often provide continuing feedback to us about our sexuality. The sexual activities we daydream about tell us something about what we might want and be missing. Or, if they leave out something we are doing, they might be telling us about what we might *not* want. And their emotional tone, along with the way we imagine the person we are with, tells us about the sexual chemistry between ourselves and our partners.

For example, Meg, who is married, has never experienced simultaneous orgasm and has trouble letting go of her self-control and self-awareness during sex. One of her typical daydreams "has to do with conveying to a lover exactly what to do with my body, having him do it well, and being able to enter into a climax together" with a sense of abandon. This daydream reflects something that Meg very much wants. The fact that she finds this satisfaction with a fantasized lover may suggest that she has given up finding it with her husband. However, this is not always so. People with long-term partners often daydream about sex with others even when their marital sex lives are excellent.

The sections that follow present in greater detail how much people daydream about sex; the types of sex we daydream about; how our sexual daydreams reflect our tastes and lifestyles; how our attitudes toward sex relate to our daydreams; how we relate to our partners in our daydreams; who has rape daydreams and what they may mean; and the way we daydream during sex and how that bears on our psychological health.

## SEXUAL DAYDREAMING

Nearly everyone daydreams about sex some of the time, some of us more than others. But just as sex is in our society still a religious, philosophic, and social issue, so is sexual daydreaming. Many of us therefore wonder whether our sexual daydreaming is "normal"—or whether it is a sign that we are morally depraved or psychologically defective. And many of us also wonder what daydreaming about sex as much or as little as we do means about us. Enough research has been completed on these questions that the answers are beginning to take shape.

### Is It Normal?

In the sense that nearly everyone engages in some sexual daydreaming, daydreaming about sex is normal. And people who daydream about it a great deal seem to be, on the average, just about as well off psychologically as people who daydream about it only occasionally. At least, no one who has investigated the matter scientifically has been able to find evidence to the contrary. In one such study of Missouri college students by psychologists William Arndt, John Foehl, and Elaine Good, the total amount of general sexual daydreaming that participants reported was not significantly related to emotional stability. Other investigations of sexual daydreaming during lovemaking came to the same conclusion as well.

This probably runs counter to what you have heard. For most of the twentieth century, psychoanalysts taught their belief that people who daydream much about sex are probably compensating for unsatisfying sex lives; but mounting evidence is showing that, if anything, the opposite is true. Although problems in sexual relationships—or not having a sexual relationship—may certainly stimulate you to daydream about sex, you are also likely to daydream about sex a good deal when you are sexually most active and satisfied with your partner. In the Missouri study, for example, the women who reported the most sexual daydreaming reported experiencing more orgasms and greater sexual satisfaction. Other investigations, too, have found that those of us who report many daydreams about sex also report more sexual experiences, more orgasms, and generally more satisfying sex lives than others do.

**Why We Daydream About Sex as Much or as Little as We Do**

How often we daydream about sex seems to reflect primarily the intensity and pace of our sex lives. When these are high —when we get actively involved in more sexual relationships, seek more orgasms, and generally make sex a more important part of our lives—we also daydream more about sex. And this holds true for people of every age, from the late teens to old age. One reason it holds true is that every relationship we value, and every plan or design we have for a sexual experience, is a kind of goal for us, which sets us up to daydream about it.

When we are cut off from opportunities for sexual expression with others, we may continue to daydream about sex. If we are accustomed to an active sex life, being deprived of one may stimulate a host of sexual daydreams. But that is probably true only if we intend to resume an active sex life and have credible prospects for doing so. When people genuinely curb their sexual appetites and plans and commit themselves to celibacy, for instance as adherents to a strict religion, their daydreams reflect that decision too: the amount of daydreaming they do about sex falls off as well.

### Sexual Daydreams and Guilt

Sexual daydreaming also reflects your attitude toward sex: whether you view it as a positive human activity or as something negative, about which we should feel shame and guilt. Some of us have been raised to accept and enjoy sex, to treat it responsibly as one of life's great pleasures. But our different upbringings may have instilled different rules about where and when we may enjoy it—anytime we have a chance, with good friends, within a stable love relationship, or strictly within marriage. Others of us grew up learning that sex is dirty, unworthy of us, something to be hushed up in decent society and expressed only for procreation or as a personal failing. Still others grew up with families who conveyed the first message in what they said but, in their own avoidance and discomfort with sex, communicated the second. As a result, many of us, whatever we may believe rationally, carry a load of shame, guilt, and anxiety about our own sexuality.

Both restrictive attitudes and negative feelings about sex affect our sexual daydreams, but they do so in different ways. Restrictive attitudes seem to reduce our sexual daydreaming as such. This becomes plain in a series of studies by North Carolina psychologist Steven Gold and his colleagues and by Utah psychologists Jerri Brown and Darrell Hart. They asked their research participants about how liberal or conservative their attitudes toward sex were, how strong their ties to religion were, and how strict or permissive that religion is. They also asked them to record some of their daydreams. Those who had liberal attitudes toward sex, weak religious ties, or a religion that is relatively permissive engaged in significantly more sexual daydreaming. They reported daydreaming about sex more often, and their sexual daydreams were on the average longer, richer, and more explicit than the daydreams of people with conservative attitudes or strict religions.

If we feel guilty about sex, we may average almost as

many daydreams about sex as others do, but it will be harder for us to tell others about them. When asked to write down their sexual daydreams, as South Carolina psychologists Denise Moreault and Diane Follingstad had participants in a study do, people who feel guilty about sex communicate less about their daydreams than do others. For example, they write shorter reports with less vivid images, and they feel much more embarrassed doing so.

This is consistent with what we know about the way guilt affects people's sexuality. On the one hand, people who feel guilty about sex get physically aroused by sexual stimulation just as others do. On the other hand, they may not feel as subjectively aroused as their bodies really are; and, of course, they end up feeling guilty about what arousal they do feel.

In sex, as in other areas of our lives, how guilty we feel about something and how much we engage in it are two very different things. Many people who feel guilty about sex engage in it anyway. They may be in conflict over their sexual relationships, but they still pursue them and hang on to them when they have them—and feel chronically bad about themselves.

All that, including the guilt, shows up in our daydreams. It shows up in the embarrassment and guilt we may feel about our sexual daydreams, as well as in daydreams of being rejected and punished. For example, Larry is strongly attracted to Dolores, although he does not know her very well. Sometimes he daydreams about making love to her, after which in his daydream she tells him that she has lost all respect for him and wants nothing more to do with him. At other times he imagines Dolores leading an uninhibited sex life with other men. Then he daydreams about making love to her as one of many men in her life, and he proceeds to worry about having contracted AIDS from her. His sexual images express his desires, whereas their unhappy endings express his feelings of guilt and fear.

**Daydreaming About the Kinds of Sex We Enjoy**

There is probably no kind of behavior about which humans have displayed more ingenuity or performed in greater variety than sex. It has taken place with almost any number of partners, old and new, same-sex or opposite-sex, human, animal, or inanimate, with any of our body orifices or other parts of our anatomy, in every conceivable place, public or private, as participants or observers, and with a rich variety of props and rituals. All are potential grist for our daydreams.

The kinds of sex we actually daydream about depend on the kinds of sex we enjoy. As reported in a study conducted by psychologists Sharon Lentz and Antonette Zeiss about women's daydreams during masturbation, women who daydreamed more than average about having intercourse were also achieving orgasm somewhat more often in their actual intercourse experiences.

One likely reason for this is that women who experience orgasms during intercourse are more satisfied with intercourse and are therefore more likely to give it a prominent place in their sex lives. If they take enjoyment from intercourse, they also probably feel free to enjoy their sexual daydreams. And because our daydreams are woven around the kinds of goals we pursue, intercourse would then also crop up more in these women's daydreams.

Our daydreams reflect our sexual preferences, whatever they may be and whether or not they are currently—or will ever be—a part of our actual sexual repertory. British psychologists Chris Gosselin and Glenn Wilson interviewed hundreds of people interested in various kinds of unconventional sex. They found that sadomasochists—who get sexually stimulated from humiliating or hurting their partners, or from being humiliated or hurt by them—daydreamed a lot about hurting or being hurt, about spankings and whippings, and about being tied up or tying up their partners. People with leather or rubber fetishes daydream a lot about leather and rubber. Transvestites have many daydreams about dressing up in the clothing and accoutrements of the opposite sex.

Apart from their particular sexual preferences, the sexual daydreaming of people in the unconventional groups was not very different from that of anyone else. They differed only slightly in their amount of daydreaming about intercourse with a partner they loved, intercourse with a new partner whom the daydreamer knew but had not yet slept with, homosexual daydreams, watching others have sex, performing oral sex, and so on.

**Daydreaming About It Versus Doing It**

Although your sexual daydreams reflect your lifestyle and taste, having a daydream about an experience doesn't mean you will necessarily have it. For example, a good many consistent heterosexuals have some homosexual daydreams and many homosexuals have some heterosexual daydreams, but this does not change the preferences they feel and act on.

People are capable of experiencing at least some sexual pleasure from a wider range of activities than they actually choose to engage in. Our bodies can register pleasure regardless of whether some activity is socially approved, unless our emotional revulsion or anxiety get in the way of our enjoyment. Gentle skin contact, stimulation of our erogenous zones, and orgasm are in and of themselves pleasurable; but some forms of these feel better to some people and other forms feel better to others, and we therefore develop distinct preferences. Furthermore, our sexual arousal and our emotional readiness to engage in sex are heavily dependent on our cultural conditioning—what we have learned to value and the differing emotions we have learned to attach to different kinds of sex—which tends to bring our sexual behavior more in line with social conventions. Nevertheless, we retain the potential for pleasure from a wider range of sexual activities, and, at some level, we are often aware of that fact.

Therefore, you may recognize that some kind of sex might feel good but ordinarily be too put off by a variety of other reactions, such as rational judgment, loyalty, personal integrity, self-esteem, embarrassment, disgust, shame, or guilt, to try it in reality. This means that you could be intrigued by the possibility of sex inconsistent with your orientation, or even attracted by selected aspects of it, without ending up deciding to engage in it. In fact, many consistent heterosexuals have tried out actual homosexual experiences—and many consistent homosexuals have tried out heterosexual ones—and then have chosen their final sexual orientation because it worked better for them or felt right to them.

In the private arena of our daydreams, we are able to experiment with different forms of sex without the risks and emotional dislocation of acting them out in reality. This relative safety lowers our inhibitions and makes mental experimentation more likely. It thereby enables us to enjoy in our daydreams some of the sexual activities we might in reality avoid.

For example, Jonathan likes variety in his sexual partners. He is also very much concerned about AIDS and therefore has limited his sexual partners to people he knows reasonably well. But his daydreams often take him into a different world. He sometimes daydreams about being at a large party in a sprawling suburban house. The lights are subdued, and there are couples dancing and making love all over the house. A strikingly attractive woman comes over to him, puts her arms around him, and gives him a very long, deep kiss. They topple over onto a couch and begin petting and gradually disrobing. Wordlessly, although he has never seen or heard of this woman before, they progress to intercourse. A short time later in his daydream, he spots another stunning individual and ends up in intercourse with her. This continues through a wide variety of partners. After his daydream, Jonathan has a rueful twinge of reservation about it. He knows that had his daydream been reality, he would have put himself at substantial risk of infection with a sexually transmitted disease. But STDs did not exist in his daydream world, nor did guilt, social disapproval, rejection, or any other impediments, and he could therefore enjoy the sex and avoid the consequences.

Daydreams are often a way to try something out without losing privacy or having to pay the costs of doing something in the real world. That is true whether your daydreams are about business dealings, vacations, violence, or sex. Within daydreams, you have the luxury of pretending that some realities do not exist. For example, you might pretend that you can overcome the laws of gravity to fly like a bird, that you have won the lottery, or that AIDS has not yet come into being. Practically everyone learns to pretend in early childhood, and many people apply pretending in some of their daydreams. They typically know they are doing it, and that keeps them from confusing their daydreams with their real prospects. But in their daydreams, they are exploring expanded ways of being, testing assumptions, and trying out new ways of looking at things. In the end, it is often a constructive process for them, adding to their insights about themselves as sexual beings and sometimes helping them decide what they will and won't do about their sex lives.

## VARIETIES OF SEXUAL DAYDREAMS

Our sexual fantasies take every conceivable form. Most of them reflect kinds of sex we would like to experience with actual sex partners, but they often go far beyond what daydreamers would be willing to do in reality. Confirmed heterosexuals indulge in occasional homosexual fantasies, and life-long gentle individuals embark on rape fantasies. Daydreams sometimes go even beyond the bounds of the anatomically possible, as in imagining intercourse positions that no normal pair of human frames could sustain or erections that reach enormous proportions.

Our daydreams often exaggerate the pleasures of sex and deemphasize or banish discomforts and misgivings. In our daydreams we may test the limits of possibility, trying for the circumstances that yield the greatest satisfaction. We often focus on the main features of our daydream actions and ignore the pesky details. We imagine ourselves making love naked in the grass and forget the twigs and stones that might gouge us, the mosquitoes and chiggers that might bite us, and the neighbors who might come upon us.

Nevertheless, like all daydreams, sexual fantasies are not limited to fulfilling our wishes. They also reflect our experiences with reality and its limits; and that often means that even in our sexual daydreams society remains, at least in the background, very much with us. Sometimes, in an automatic flow of their associations with sex, people experience mounting anxiety and guilt that cripples their enjoyment, their imaginary partners condemn or abandon them, or the forces of society discover, interrupt, and punish.

Carola had two male friends, Mel and Rock. During intercourse one day with Mel, she fantasized that she was making love to Rock. But in the middle of her daydream she envisioned Mel's hurt if he knew about her sexual activities with Rock. She imagined him bitter and stony-faced, their relationship crumbling. In her upwelling guilt, the daydream faded, and she returned her full attention to her intercourse with Mel. Even in our daydreams we do not completely escape sexual reality or cultural conditioning.

There are no clear-cut categories for sexual daydreams. They intersect and overlap one another, and no short list can do justice to the many variations. Sexual daydreams may be about:

- being admired
- a previous or future sexual experience
- doing something wicked or forbidden
- variety in positions, actions, places, or partners
- sex with multiple partners
- humiliation, pain, domination, and rape
- being of or dressing like the opposite sex
- sex with a partner who is not of the gender you normally prefer

Their moods may be gently romantic or wildly passionate, self-possessed or frenzied.

## ROMANCE, ADMIRATION, AND PASSION

In the most common daydreams, at least in middle-class America, somebody is paying the daydreamer a lot of sexual attention—with admiration, passion, or love. The daydreams of women more often carry an aura of romance, whereas those of men are more often suffused with raw passion.

For example, here are the percentages of women reporting different kinds of daydreams on a questionnaire given them by University of Missouri psychologists William Arndt, Jr., John Foehl, and Elaine Good.

| | |
|---|---|
| a man kissing her breasts | 92% |
| in a secluded place, a man gently removing her clothes and having sex with her | 90% |
| being a very glamorous woman and having sex with a very handsome man | 71% |
| having sex with a man where they risk being caught | 65% |
| being at a party where famous men admire her charms | 64% |
| wearing skin-tight clothes, with men staring at her | 51% |

The following were the most common sexual daydreams reported by the men in this study.

| | |
|---|---|
| being excited by "a woman's shapely legs" | 96% |
| "kissing a woman's large breasts" | 91% |
| a woman "forcing her intentions" on him | 87% |
| getting "a woman so excited that she screams with pleasure" | 87% |
| a woman telling him that she wants his body | 86% |
| two women exciting him sexually | 84% |
| several women admiring his nude body | 65% |

being "at a party where everybody is having sex with everyone else" 62%
"watching a man and woman having sex" 60%

The figures show that most of us—both women and men—like simply being admired. For women especially, romantic settings and themes play an important part in their sex-related fantasies. When people record sexual daydreams as they happen, as psychologists Kimeron Hardin and Steven Gold had a group of college students do, women mention themes of romance and commitment more than men do, whereas men focus more on explicit sexual activity and its variations, such as group sex.

One of the women, for instance, reported daydreaming "about getting married and the kind of sexy wife I'll be. I daydreamed about the way I would take care of him."

Compare this with a daydream by one of the men: "I daydreamed about my girlfriend, making love to her in Florida over break, the places we would go and things we would do"—a much more matter-of-fact daydream that focuses more on activities and less on the relationship as such.

These differences in women's and men's daydreams are consistent with average differences between women and men in their approach to relationships. Women on the average place more value on the relationship as such—on communing, conversing, and interacting. Men seem to focus more on what the relationship can provide. This is a difference in emphasis rather than an all-or-nothing difference. Relationships are extremely important to both sexes, and, in fact, men on the average hang on somewhat longer and suffer somewhat more when they break up.

*Different or multiple partners.* For those of us in ongoing relationships, one of the most common daydreams is about sex with a partner different from the regular one. Most often these daydreams feature one partner, who may be someone we know of and desire, someone we once knew and enjoyed, or a pure creation of our fantasies. But people of both sexes—though men more often than women—also daydream about having sex with numbers of partners, including anonymous partners they know nothing about.

In the Missouri study, more than three out of five men reported daydreaming being "at a party where everybody is having sex with everyone else." Among the women, two out of five reported daydreaming of having sex with two men at the same time. And one out of three women reported daydreaming of being "at a party where I summon each man I desire to have sex with me."

These daydreams are telling us that, whatever we may choose to do or not do about sexual partners in reality, variety is attractive. There are many indications that for many of us sexual excitement with a steady partner declines over the years. The prospect of a new partner or group of partners is therefore relatively exciting. In most instances, we will be too unwilling to sacrifice the other benefits of our steady relationships to throw them over just for sexually more exciting alternatives, but in our daydreams we can try on the newcomer free of cost. That way our daydreams serve as means both to gain some sexual enjoyment and to explore the possibilities for greater enjoyment in reality.

*Daydreams and gender preference.* Substantial numbers of heterosexuals have daydreams about some kind of homosexual activity. For example, 22 percent of the men in the Missouri study daydreamed that "another man and I are fondling one another," and 8 percent of the women daydreamed that "a woman is holding my hand while I masturbate." In fact, homosexual fantasies are fairly common during masturbation. Among a group of French Canadians and Europeans surveyed by Quebec sexologist Claude Crépault, nearly half the women and nearly a quarter of the men reported occasional homosexual masturbation fantasies. Even during sex with a partner of the opposite sex, homosexual fantasies occurred occasionally to more than a third of the women and nearly a fifth of the men.

These figures are much higher than estimates of active homosexuality in the general population, though not greatly higher than the percentages who have ever had a homosexual experience. They probably do not represent a desire for actual homosexual relationships so much as the potential for sexual excitement and fulfillment with same-sex partners. The fact that so many people choose to have these daydreams during masturbation and intercourse, when they are presumably trying to heighten their excitement, indicates that they are being turned on by the homosexual elements in their daydreams, and daydreaming provides them with a way of exploring and enjoying the prospect.

Just as heterosexuals sometimes daydream about homosexual encounters, homosexuals sometimes daydream about heterosexual ones. Although most of the daydreams of homosexual men and women are homosexual, they also explore sexual modes in daydreams that most of them would reject if they were given the choice in actuality.

### Active, Passive, and Mutual Sexuality in Daydreams

The traditions of our society prescribe that men and women will take on very different roles in lovemaking. Men are expected to take the initiative and to be the active partner, whereas women are traditionally cast as the passive recipient—of contact, of courtship, and of sexual penetration. In recent decades, these traditional expectations have been countered by movements for greater mutuality in relations between men and women, the sexual counterpart of sexual equality. Our cultural expectations seem to be evolving. Accordingly, researchers have sought to find out to what extent the roles we play in our daydreams are keeping pace.

Research has found the same variety of role-playing in our daydreams as in reality. In some sexual daydreams, we take the initiative and become the more active partner in foreplay and intercourse; in others, we let our partner take the initiative and become more of a passive, if blissful, recipient of sex. In still other daydreams we imagine ourselves and our imaginary partners as equally active participants.

Both men and women daydream of all these variations. But, consistent with their real-world behavior, men mostly daydream about themselves as the active partner and women mostly cast themselves as the passive partner in their own daydreams. In the daydreams collected by the Missouri psychologists, the most common daydream for women was having a man kiss their breasts, whereas the second most common daydream for men was of doing the kissing. Additional information comes from New York psychologist Robert Mednick, who in the 1970s asked people to write down the most frequent daydreams they recalled having while they were just daydreaming, while they were masturbating, and while they were having sex with a partner.

Judging from Mednick's daydream reports, people daydream about themselves and their imaginary partners in equal roles less often than they daydream about taking an active or passive role. For his participants, whose average age was thirty, daydreams of mutuality in sex made up only about 20 percent of the total.

Not only were daydreams of mutuality in the minority overall, their number shrank the more involved the daydreamers were in actual sex. Themes of mutuality occurred:

- 27 percent of the time during just daydreaming
- 22 percent of the time during masturbation
- 4 percent of the time while men were having sex
- none of the time while women were having sex

Evidently, the closer people are to sexual activity, the more they move toward either an active or a passive role in their daydreams; and the role they choose will conform five out of six times to the traditional roles, active and passive, of American men and women. For example, Myron daydreamed at work that an attractive female coworker came over, pulled down his pants and performed fellatio on him.

He thoroughly enjoyed this daydream, in which he took what for an American male is the unconventional role of responding to his daydream-woman's vigorous initiative. He also felt a considerable amount of guilt, shame, and anxiety about this daydream, much more so than about daydreams in which he played a more active role. Probably, his negative feelings stemmed from imagining himself in a role different from the one society had prepared him to take. But playing this role in a daydream disturbed him a lot less than doing it in reality would. Therefore, the excitement he felt in his daydream outweighed his negative feelings. We have no daydream samples from Myron while he was having sex, but if his daydreams during sex were like those of Mednick's men, he would have imagined himself taking the lead and controlling the intercourse.

This trend—toward greater mutuality the more removed the daydream is from actual sex—might be telling us that people really yearn for more mutual sex, but that they gravitate toward stereotyped sex roles, even in their daydreams, the closer they are to real sex. Whether this pattern will change with changes in American cultural patterns we do not yet know.

## DOMINATION AND RAPE

Among the striking findings of research on sexual fantasy is the prominence in our inner lives of daydreams about rape. Most of these findings have been incidental: researchers knew that rape daydreams occur and placed them on their lists of daydream themes to investigate. The findings, which are in a number of ways surprising, are about:

- how much both men and women daydream about rape
- how large a portion of the normal population engages in rape fantasies at some time
- how both sexes daydream about both raping and being raped

- how both sexes find most of these daydreams sexually stimulating
- how daydreaming about rape is in itself not a sign of psychological disturbance

Rape daydreams come up while just daydreaming, while masturbating, or while engaged in sex with someone else, and most of them are sexually stimulating. Yet, those who daydream about rape are in many ways a cross-section of the population rather than a particularly disturbed group.

We have long known that forced sex is deeply ingrained in our culture, as it probably is in the majority of the world's cultures. Among Connecticut college men surveyed by psychologists Donald Mosher and Ronald Anderson, three-quarters admitted having deliberately gotten women drunk or high on drugs in order to make them amenable to sex, and a majority admitted having bullied, threatened, or manipulated women into sex. A majority of American high school and college students—even a large, though smaller, number of women—believe that men are under some circumstances justified in forcing women to have sex with them. The concurrence of so many women in condoning some instances of rape indicates the extent to which rape is a cultural malady and not simply an aberration of individuals.

Among many groups, in the United States and worldwide, quintessential maleness carries with it a certain aura of rape. Within those groups, the potentiality of rape colors and even helps define relationships between men and women. This potentiality increases the implicit power of men over women and contributes to fear and caution in women's behavior toward men.

That men daydream a lot about raping women is therefore not particularly surprising. What *is* surprising is that men daydream as much as they do about being raped *by* women.

That American women daydream about rape is not surprising either, given the pervasive threat and high incidence of man-on-woman rape. What is surprising here is that, contrary to women's reactions to real rape, a substantial portion of women's daydreams about rape have an erotic quality. Also surprising is that many are daydreams of the women raping men.

**Daydreams About Being Raped**

One of the most surprising findings to emerge from contemporary research into daydreaming is that, while more women than men daydream of being raped, men actually daydream more often about being raped than about doing the raping. Even more surprisingly, they daydream about it almost as much as women. In fact, daydreams involving forced sex were the second most common variety of sexual daydreams among 120 people studied by researchers Mark Schwartz and William Masters at the Masters and Johnson Institute in St. Louis.

Of course, women do daydream more often about being raped than men. Findings of a number of investigators show clearly that daydreaming about being forced into sex is extremely common among normal women despite different backgrounds, life stages, and activities when daydreaming. These investigators have established the following percentages of women who have various kinds of force daydreams.

| | |
|---|---|
| being "overpowered or forced to surrender" | 49% |
| being "forced or overpowered into a sexual relationship" | 36% |
| being "a slave who must obey a man's every wish" | 30% |
| being "tied up and stimulated sexually by a man" | 48% |
| having to "submit to aggression" | 42% |
| "pretend to fight and resist before yielding to the sexual advances of a man" | 39% |
| being "subdued and compelled to have sexual relations with one or more strangers" | 23% |

| | |
|---|---|
| having "sexual relations against your will with a man whom you know" | 20% |
| being humiliated | 15% |
| being beaten | 14% |

These figures are based on very varied groups engaged in different activities. The first daydream was based on interviews with suburban women about their daydreams during sex, studied by psychologists E. Barbara Hariton and Jerome L. Singer. One out of seven women reported daydreaming about this theme "often" or "very often." The percentages for the second and third daydreams are based on over 300 questionnaires returned by American college women about any of their sexual daydreams, not just those during sex; more than 200 were surveyed by psychologist David Sue and 138 were surveyed by Arndt and colleagues. The other percentages are from 66 women surveyed in Quebec and Europe by Claude Crépault's team about daydreams during sex.

The percentages for men are not greatly different.

| | |
|---|---|
| being "forced or overpowered into a sexual relationship" | 21% |
| being "kidnapped by a woman and must do as she orders" | 46% |
| "a woman ties me up and then has sex with me" | 42% |
| being "raped by a woman" | 46% |
| being "tied up and stimulated sexually by a woman" | 36% |
| "pretend to fight and resist before yielding to the sexual advances of a woman" | 27% |
| having to "submit to aggression" | 17% |
| being humiliated | 12% |
| being beaten | 5% |

Here, the first daydream is from more than 200 college men surveyed by Sue, the second and third from Arndt's 125

Missouri students, and the rest from 94 men surveyed in Quebec and Europe by Crépault's research team about daydreaming during sex.

Again, large numbers of normal men tell us that they daydream about being forced into sex. A smaller group of both sexes have daydreams in which they specifically suffer humiliation and pain, often as part of being raped. Both men and women report these daydreams, but women more often than men. About one in four of Arndt's Missouri women reported daydreaming that they are being "made to suffer before a man will satisfy me sexually" and that "a man is holding me down and tells me there is pleasure in pain."

One woman told British psychiatrist Glenn Wilson the following fantasy, which illustrates typical kinds of humiliation and abuse and also the erotic tone that suffuses them:

"I am kidnapped and taken in a car to some building. . . . I am stripped naked in front of a group of men and they tell me to lie on the bed. I think only one of them ever makes love to me, and this is over a period of some time. If I do not do what I am told the men whip me and beat me. I am also given an extravagant wardrobe of gorgeous clothes to wear, mostly long formal gowns, and I am given expensive jewelry. They make me go to the bathroom standing up (as if I had a penis) while they watch, and do all kinds of different styles of intercourse, sitting on chairs, lying on floors, beds, and so on. At first I am afraid, but then I gradually begin to experience pleasure and happiness and I feel an overall sensation of wonderfulness."

*Why we do it.* Daydreams of being dominated and even raped, unlike really being raped, are for many people sexually exciting and stimulating. The clearest indication of this is that people choose these daydreams to heighten their excitement during masturbation and during sex with partners.

It may seem hard to explain why we would choose to daydream about being raped and like it. However, many people clearly link force with sex, and for them it is a potent, exciting combination in fantasy, regardless of whether they are the rapist or the victim.

Of course, those who daydream about being raped have no intention of becoming rape victims. They would not end up enjoying being raped in actuality; they would most likely be severely traumatized by it.

Psychoanalysts have long held that sex and aggression are intimately entwined—that sex normally has some aggressive components, and that the combination might feel particularly gratifying, even to victims. But others find this concept unlikely and have proposed a number of other ideas. Although only a little basic research has been done on this question so far, what we know allows us to form a fairly good guess as to the explanation for daydreaming about being raped. There are at least three reasons: imagining being forced to have sex can make different people feel more wanted, less guilty, and appropriately punished for misbehaving.

*Feeling more wanted.* First of all, many daydreams about being forced to have sex—at least the ones that are sexually exciting—portray the other person as filled with desire and passion. This is often mixed with some cruelty, but in daydreams the violence is typically limited to something far short of permanent injury or disfigurement. The imaginary perpetrators of force are consumed with passion for the daydreamer and want her body. Feeling intensely wanted is itself exciting, and it is heightened further because the circumstances in the daydream give you the chance to let your own passions go. In your daydream, you can ignore the complications and social inhibitions that go with real human relationships and can at the same time feel free of the physical risks that accompany real rape. Your real passion and the other people's imagined passion meet and end up arousing you sexually so much that both can achieve imaginary gratification, often on a tremendous scale.

For example, Bertha daydreams that she is grabbed by three rough men who beat her into submission and successively rape her. She feels the blows, which are painful enough so that she submits, but they are not crippling. In her daydream she sees their wild-eyed determination to have her, feels their desire, and experiences their entering penises as enormous, hard, and violently thrusting—and feels her own excitement rising. In her daydream, Bertha focuses on the passion and the sex rather than on the violence. The aggression and pain are in a sense the props that make the plot possible.

Although Bertha imagines feeling frightened in her daydream, her real fright is kept within tight bounds. The men in her daydream, after all, are figments of her imagination. To that extent, they are ultimately controllable and safe.

That is a very different scenario from actual rape. There, the perpetrators are motivated much more by anger or a lust for domination than by sexual passion. And the victims, completely turned off sexually, suffer through a painful, humiliating assault.

*Feeling less guilty*. Another reason for daydreaming about being raped is that people who harbor guilt feelings about their own sexuality don't have to take responsibility for enjoying it. Guilt puts a powerful damper on sexual pleasure, and imaginary rape absolves you of guilt. You can't help being raped.

Women who feel a lot of guilt about their sexuality report more sexual daydreams of being forced, such as "I imagine I am being overpowered or forced to surrender" and "I enjoy imagining that I am being dominated sexually and that I am helpless," as South Carolina psychologists Denise Moreault and Diane Follingstad have shown.

Conversely, the Missouri women whose daydreams featured domination or suffering as part of sex reported suffering more in general from negative feelings in their lives, such as anxiety and guilt. In contrast, other women who daydreamed heavily about sex, but without much focus on rape, had no special problems with feeling bad.

This suggests that those who daydreamed about domination and suffering may have felt less secure and more guilty about sex than others. This could have induced them to daydream more about sex being forced on them in order to assuage their guilt. In fantasies about rape, they can absolve themselves of blame, which increases their pleasure in sex.

This, too, is different from actual rape. Many rape victims groundlessly blame themselves afterwards and carry a long-term burden of guilt and shame.

*Feeling appropriately punished.* A third likely reason for daydreaming about being raped, as well as for enjoying fantasies of being beaten or humiliated, is that it comes with built-in punishment. If you harbor feelings that sex is dirty and sinful, you are also likely to fear that engaging in sex will bring some kind of punishment down on your head. If during it you fantasize that you are already being punished—by having a rapist brutalize you or having someone beat or humiliate you—the punishment, in fantasy, is already in place. You have arranged your own punishment, at least in imagery, and have therefore lessened the fear of punishment from outside. For example, Beth could get excited during sex only by daydreaming at the same time that she was being whipped all over her naked body.

*Terrifying rape fantasies.* Fantasies of being raped are by no means always pleasant. For some, they are a terrifying anticipation of a hazard all too prevalent in modern society. As such, they may turn into frightening episodes of violence.

Take for example Janice's daydream: "Again, I dreamed about getting raped. This time it was a terrifying experience. There was one *big* guy. He was very rough on me. He hurt me very much. He made me perform oral sex. He said he would be back."

Daydreams such as this reflect the daydreamer's concern about her vulnerability much more than her sexual interest as such. Presumably, her power to pretend collapsed in the face of her real fears of rape.

Daydreams draw on our normal stock of expectations, feelings, and behaviors; and all women regard real rape as a terrifying prospect. We can sometimes hold these fears at bay by "pretending," but they can readily sweep back into our daydreams and overwhelm us.

Terrifying rape daydreams may be the residues of actual sexual abuse in our past. Whenever we are traumatized—whether by battle, floods, earthquakes, or rape—we are at risk for a delayed reaction called "posttraumatic stress syndrome." This syndrome includes both flashbacks to the events that traumatized us and related upsetting images in our daydreams, such as terrifying daydreams of being raped.

They may also arise out of our fears of the dangers around us. Our daydreams explore the negative possibilities in our lives as well as the positive ones. Even if we have never been raped, most of us have heard or read enough accounts, or seen rape presented graphically enough in films and television programs, to have the raw materials for creating our own rape images. Stimulated by our fears, real or imaginary, we then recreate the rape images in our daydreams.

Often these rape images are accompanied by images of self-defense or escape. We may even create several different endings for such a daydream, each one trying out a different method for coping with the threat. In this way, our daydreams help prepare us for the events we fear.

### Daydreams About Doing the Raping

Another surprising discovery about sexual daydreams involving force and rape is that, while more men (up to half) than women daydream of raping someone, a substantial number of women (up to a quarter) also daydream about doing the raping.

A further remarkable finding is that for the men, as for the women, daydreams of being raped are more common than daydreams of raping someone else. In two different surveys, 46 percent of the men daydreamed about being raped, compared with 39 percent and 33 percent who imagined raping.

Research shows the following percentage of men who report some form of raping daydream.

| | |
|---|---|
| "forcing others to have sexual relations with me" | 24% |
| "forcing a woman to have sex with me" | 39% |
| "woman you are seducing pretends to resist" | 45% |
| "tie up a woman and stimulate her sexually" | 39% |
| "raping a woman" | 33% |
| "attacking someone" | 27% |
| "humiliate a woman" | 15% |
| "beat a woman" | 11% |

Here, the first two daydreams are based on Sue's and Arndt's American college students and the rest are daydreams during sex in Crépault's survey.

Between a third and half of these normal men daydream about using force on women. Two of the daydreams, which involve tying the woman up or her "pretending" to resist, could be interpreted as being instances in which the woman cooperates with the man; but "raping a woman" is unambiguous. Fewer women than men daydream they are doing the raping, but the percentages are still intriguingly high.

| | |
|---|---|
| "forcing others to have sexual relations" | 16% |
| "I capture a man and force him to have sex with me" | 25% |
| "several boys are tied in a row. I bring each of them to erection" | 10% |
| "attacking someone" | 27% |

The first three daydreams are from Sue's and Arndt's American college women, the fourth, during sex, from Crépault's Quebec and European women.

Up to a quarter of these normal groups of women daydreamed about raping men. But these figures are still considerably lower than the proportion of women who daydream—especially during sex—that they are being raped.

*Why we do it.* Science still has only very preliminary explanations for why we daydream of committing rape. There is no hard evidence. But what we know about the motives for real rape suggest some likely reasons: to feel powerful by dominating someone, to vent anger at some person or people in particular, and to gain sexual gratification through the violence itself. This information comes from Connecticut prison psychologist Nicholas Groth, who has interviewed at least 250 convicted rapists.

*Power.* Power means control: your ability to get from other people the response you want. To a degree, how powerful we feel contributes to our sense of self-esteem, our sense of being worthwhile. Many of us feel a sense of powerlessness, a sense that other people are in control of our lives, and then we feel correspondingly diminished.

When we feel this way about our relationships with our sex partners, actual or prospective, we may be motivated to assert power by whatever means we have at our disposal, including force. In the realm of sex, asserting power means getting our partners to respond in ways we wish. Most men want their sexual partners to be responsive, to experience a passionate desire for them. When men can imagine women swept away with their own passion and at the end gratified by the man's sexual power even during rape, they experience a sense of great power, sexual and otherwise. Under these circumstances the prospects of rape are very arousing to them.

This scenario of men able to provoke women's passion through force seems to be a key factor in many rape fantasies.

They frequently take the form of women initially resisting but finally becoming sexually excited and orgasmic. This excitement of the victim seems to be important to the fantasizer's sexual satisfaction. For example, reading stories of rape in which victims become sexually aroused, as Winnipeg psychologists Neil Malamuth and James Check had people do, leads to much more sexual arousal than reading rape stories in which the victims remain disgusted throughout.

Exciting though the turn-on-through-force scenario may be, it is completely unrealistic. Anyone who has been raped or has worked with rape victims knows that such victims are thoroughly turned off by the experience. They feel full disgust and loathing at the time or anesthetize themselves psychologically by experiencing themselves off to the side or up above, watching themselves going through the ordeal, only to have the full horror come home to them afterwards. A residual depression over the rape persists for months.

Yet, the scenario of the aroused victim plays a substantial role in the fantasy lives of real rapists. For example, Warren, one of Groth's prison interviewees, was motivated like most rapists by his desire to dominate. He was in a stable sexual relationship, but he explained that he experienced much more gratification when he could imagine breaking down a woman's resistance through force than he could experience with a willing partner. He, like other domination rapists, regularly daydreamed that his victims ended up becoming excited and gratified. He would then try to live out this fantasy by finding a real victim to rape. Inevitably, the victim would fail to become aroused. This frustrated him and made him feel even more inadequate, and this heightened inadequacy made his fantasy rapes yet more exciting, and so he would try once more to turn his mistaken fantasy into reality.

Most people who engage in rape fantasies will never actually commit a rape; they would in fact be repelled by it. And yet it is likely that the same desire to assert our power even against the odds, to do exactly what we want and be done with it, plays a role in normal rape fantasies. There we are able to reorder reality and imagine the satisfaction without the distressing costs of the real thing.

*Anger.* Some men are motivated toward force by their anger at women. Often the anger is at someone they know, perhaps a current or past lover or spouse. At other times men feel great anger at women as a group. Both kinds of anger can spawn rape images.

Anger and sexual arousal are to some extent interwoven. After men are provoked to anger, as psychologists Andrew Barclay and Ralph Haber once did, the stories they make up are both more aggressive and more sexual, and blood tests show them to be sexually more aroused. This suggests that being angry can stimulate more sexual daydreams, but these are bound to be colored by the anger. Anger combined with sex is likely to equal force.

When things go amiss in our sex lives, images of forcing sex and inflicting pain are likely to increase. In research by British psychiatrist Glenn Wilson, participants who reported those images were both sexually more active than average and less satisfied than average with their sex lives. One likely reason that they would be given to images of force and pain is that sexual frustration breeds anger, which disposes them toward sexual aggression.

*Sexual gratification in violence.* A few men gain their sexual satisfaction through violence. Apart from clinical observations, little is known with confidence about them, and their daydreams have not been studied systematically. What is known is that the act of violence itself excites these few sexually. To that extent, their violent sexual daydreams would also heighten their sexual gratification.

*The difference between daydreaming about rape and doing it.* Of the many people who daydream about rape, only a small portion are likely to commit rape in the future. We probably all have at least flashes of fantasy in which we do violence to others, and many of us imagine in loving detail the injury we would do to those who incur our wrath. However, fewer of us would be capable of translating those daydreams into action. That is because any one daydream may reflect only a facet of ourselves, whereas a real decision to act draws on all the relevant factors within us.

Most men, including actual rapists, have very mixed feelings about rape, such as sexual arousal, self-disgust, and anger toward the victim. But the mix of feelings depends partly on the man's personality and partly on the woman's reaction. Asked by Mosher and Anderson to imagine being the rapist in a realistic rape scene, the average research participant experienced a number of negative feelings. They especially felt disgusted, angry, frightened, distressed, and contemptuous —along with experiencing some sexual arousal.

The more macho men felt fewer of the negative feelings and just as much sexual arousal. They also admitted to a more extensive history of coercing women into sex. In other words, there is a part of the male population that gets excited by forced sex and has fewer emotions that might get in the way of enjoying it. That both motivates and frees them to enjoy a daydream about raping someone.

Daydreams reflect the many sides of who we are. Even the majority who would not commit a rape often have some of the personality components that contribute to rape, such as the capacity to become sexually aroused by it and a reservoir of impatience, frustration, and anger toward their rape victim's sex, and that is presumably what our rape daydreams reflect. Given the makeup of the daydreamer, the daydreams follow as a matter of course.

There is as yet no evidence as to whether daydreaming about raping changes the likelihood that you will actually ever commit rape. Insofar as daydreaming helps you to explore possibilities, to rehearse actions, and to plan your future, it seems possible that under certain conditions daydreaming about raping people could make an actual rape somewhat more likely. But the conditions would be that you find the daydream more enjoyable than distressing, and that you formulate what you consider to be a safe enough, workable plan. If your daydream ends up reminding you of your victim's agony, if the circumstances are such that in reality you would probably be caught, or if the whole daydream takes place in a spirit of unreality, it may very well make a real rape less likely than before.

In any event, it is clear that a few rape fantasies do not make a rapist out of you. Far more people engage in rape fantasies than commit rape.

*Inflicting humiliation and pain.* In daydreams involving humiliation and pain, as in other kinds of force, more men than women daydream that they are in the dominating role—again consistent with average sex roles in Western society. For example, one out of five men in the Missouri study but only one out of twenty-five women reported daydreaming about spanking someone of the opposite sex, whose bottom is typically bare. One out of seven men reported daydreaming that he "requires a woman to say, 'I've been bad, please punish me.' " Fewer women have this daydream.

The reasons for daydreams about inflicting humiliation and pain are most likely similar to some of those for daydreaming about rape: they assert power and vent anger. The Missouri study led by William Arndt found that people who daydream a lot about humiliation and suffering are also likely to daydream more than average about rape. In Wilson's British group, those who daydreamed about such things as whipping or otherwise hurting someone, like those who daydreamed of forcing someone into sex, were above average in sex drive and relatively dissatisfied with their sex lives.

Those of us given to these kinds of daydreams seem to have personalities that are not very different from others. Women who daydream a lot about humiliation and suffering seem to score on the average as emotionally less stable than others, judging from the Missouri study led by William Arndt, but did not differ in other respects. Men who daydream more than average about these topics and about using force have personality scores not significantly different from those of other men.

## FANTASY DURING SEXUAL ACTIVITY

There are few things as sexually stimulating as your own sexual daydreams. Highly imaginative people can actually daydream themselves to orgasm. Even during sexual intercourse, sexual daydreams increase many people's overall arousal level and sexual pleasure. Anthony Campagna once compared the arousal power of sexual daydreams with that of reading highly arousing erotic stories. He asked one group of men to develop their own sex fantasies and the other group to spend the same length of time reading erotic stories. When all of the participants rated how aroused they felt, the group who had spent the time daydreaming reported significantly more arousal than the other group.

Most of us have made use of our sexual daydreams to increase our excitement during sexual activity. In fact, we probably daydream most about sex while engaged in it. That is especially true during masturbation, but it also occurs quite often during sex with partners.

People often daydream to compensate for their declining ardor with their steady partner. Sexual daydreaming within sex seems to take hold as relationships ripen and age. Sexual relationships generally become less passionate with time and repetition. A little experience with a partner makes for better sex on the average than no experience, and with a great amount of satisfying experience sex becomes more relaxed and comfortable. But sex with a new partner has a special excitement about it, and sex within new love is particularly piquant. Sexual daydreaming during sex can restore some of that edge to sexual excitement.

### Masturbation Fantasies

Most of us make fantasy part of our masturbation. The reason is that masturbation fantasies are overwhelmingly made up of sexually exciting images that increase enjoyment and help the process along toward orgasm. In a survey of 129 Yale freshmen, Connecticut psychologist Anthony Campagna found that a third fantasize every time they masturbate and three-quarters do so more than occasionally. Masturbation fantasies are about the same kinds of themes that occur in other sexual daydreams and in roughly similar proportions.

**Fantasies During Sex with Another**

Most of us occasionally entertain sexual fantasies while actively making love to a real partner. About a third to half of us spin them fairly often during sex or even every time. The rest do so occasionally. Relatively few sexually experienced people have never had a daydream while engaged in sex with a partner.

The longer relationships go on, the more people begin to daydream during sex. Women end up engaging in fantasies during sex about as often as men, but with any given partner men seem on the average to start daydreaming sooner in the relationship. Among Sue's college students, a third of the men who ever daydreamed during intercourse reported doing so from the very beginning of the relationship. Only half that many women began right away, but a third of them reported doing so within about a month.

By the end of the first year, about three-quarters of the men and two-thirds of the women who ever daydreamed during intercourse were doing so. Only about 5 percent of the men waited as long as two years before daydreaming during intercourse, as did only about 20 percent of the women.

*Why we do it.* There are several reasons for daydreaming during sex with a partner, according to David Sue's participants, but they all probably boil down to increasing sexual excitement and pleasure. The percentages were as follows.

| | |
|---|---|
| "facilitate sexual arousal" | 42% |
| make their partner seem more attractive | 26% |
| imagine doing things that they and their partners "do not engage in" | 16% |
| "relieve boredom" | 4% |

Sexual daydreaming has for many people become another sexual technique, a resource, and an integral part of their sexual practices. Daydreaming makes sex more exciting and pleasurable. Just as physical attraction and love, foreplay, and good timing contribute toward better sex, so does daydreaming.

*Spontaneous daydreams.* Some daydreams during sex are spontaneous. These images are just part of the natural flow of your thoughts, which do not stop for sex. While engaged in sex you may be reminded of a previous time or you may spontaneously imagine being elsewhere with your partner, or doing something else, or being with a different partner.

*Intentional daydreams.* Other daydreams during sex are quite intentional. Many people use them to heighten sexual excitement and pleasure by imagining something even more arousing than what is occurring.

Occasionally, people use daydreams to cool things down, as when they feel themselves moving too quickly toward orgasm. Then they might daydream about something nonsexual or less arousing to cut the rise in excitement.

*What we daydream about.* The daydreams people have during sex are very similar to sexual daydreams in general. The most common daydream for Hariton and Singer's New York suburbanites was to think of "an imaginary romantic lover" while making love to a spouse. Other common daydreams were to "relive a previous sexual experience," pretending "doing something wicked or forbidden," imagining "being overpowered or forced to surrender," or imagining being "in a different place, like a car, motel, beach, woods, etc." Each one of these themes cropped up in the fantasies of about half the women at least occasionally during intercourse. About a quarter of these women occasionally imagined themselves as striptease dancers, harem girls, or prostitutes. Sue's participants reported very similar experiences, except that the most common daydream during coitus, entertained by more than half of both men and women, was of oral-genital sex.

The apparent function of these fantasies is to increase excitement by adding to our sexual activity one more exciting component. Clearly, the activity we daydream about in these situations is one we find enjoyable, even though it might bring too many problems with it to carry out in reality. For example, imagining oral-genital sex might simply add excitement to the level of excitation already produced during our actual intercourse. But for some it may be especially arousing by virtue of it not being available in actuality, perhaps because of a reluctant partner or our own inhibitions or beliefs.

*When does it start?* Daydreaming may occur at virtually any time during lovemaking. More men than women start early in their lovemaking and continue to the end. About four out of five men who daydream during sex begin during the period when they are just getting sexually excited, whereas half the women start that soon, according to the reports of Crépault's participants. This suggests that men may feel the need or want the additional excitement of fantasy more than women to get them fully aroused and going.

The other half of the women and the rest of the men begin daydreaming as they approach orgasm. Possibly they need more help from daydreaming to sustain excitation at this critical point. All of the women and most of the men stop daydreaming at the point of orgasm, though one out of six of the men report continuing on into orgasm.

*Is it psychologically healthy?* No one has yet found evidence that sexual daydreaming during sex reflects anything wrong with the daydreamer. Crépault and his colleagues asked their participants a number of questions about their backgrounds and sexual practices, including the following: How did they get along with their parents? What were their religious practices? When did they begin to masturbate? How often did they have sex? The amount people reported daydreaming during sex had very little relationship to the way they answered most of these questions.

Because people use daydreaming to heighten their sexual excitement, it might seem as if they are compensating for poorer-than-average sex lives. However, that does not seem to be the case. The women in Hariton and Singer's study who engaged heavily in erotic daydreaming during sex were on the average neither more nor less satisfied with their sex lives than those who did little or no erotic daydreaming during sex. Therefore, many people seem to daydream about sex within an already satisfactory sexual relationship for the purpose of making their experiences even better.

*Who does it?* Women in the above-mentioned studies daydreamed during sex slightly more if they were well educated, if they daydreamed more in general, and if, in general, they were highly sexed—had begun sex play and masturbation before adolescence, reached orgasm relatively quickly, experienced their orgasms as both in the vulval and vaginal areas, and masturbated once or more per week.

Men who have a more open, exploratory approach to sex and have come up with definite preferences are more likely to daydream about sex during sex. The participants in the studies noted daydreamed during sex slightly more if they had better orgasms with partners than with masturbation, preferred less conventional positions such as rear-entry and side-by-side for intercourse, generally made love in the evening rather than during the day, had at some time had a homosexual experience, had experienced psychotherapy, and had pronounced preferences regarding the circumstances around making love, such as time of day, degree of nudity, and who initiates the act.

People who have discovered that sexual daydreaming helps them toward better lovemaking are on the average more highly sexed, sexually experienced, and more prone to daydream in general; and are likely to engage in highly erotic, pleasurable fantasies and feel pleased with the experience.

*The benefits of daydreaming during sex.* Daydreams help us to explore the territory, to try things out, to become familiar with certain ways of acting, and to refine actions in light of imaginary experiences. And as we gain experience and insight, we become more confident and readier to act. Daydreaming during sex can help to:

- raise sexual excitement thereby enhancing the experience
- blot out an inadequate or ugly sexual reality
- identify problems in a relationship
- stabilize a relationship

We have already seen the many ways in which daydreaming enhances many people's arousal during sex. However, some people may daydream during sex to blot out the reality of a partner they do not like. For them, daydreaming may be the only way to achieve an acceptable sexual experience with the current partner; it may help them overlook things their partner is doing that they dislike or not doing that they wish he or she would. It can help them become sexually aroused when they are unable to do so with the real partner alone.

At the same time, those daydreams already represent the daydreamer exploring and rehearsing new possibilities for love relationships—the search, perhaps not fully conscious, for a way out. That way out may lie in discovering things they could induce their partner to do so as to make sex more exciting, or it could mean locating a different partner more to their liking.

Yet again, others may daydream during sex, but their

daydreams may be fearful or angry ones. Their relationship may be in deep trouble, they may have been traumatized by a previous relationship, or they might generally be plagued by feelings of guilt, anxiety, or resentment. They will have difficulty attaining a fulfilling sexual experience, at least on those occasions when their daydreams intrude on sex to remind them of the things that are wrong with their lives.

What we daydream about tells us something about what we are missing. Sometimes, the missing ingredient is something no longer possible with our steady partner. There is no way to make an old relationship new again, for example, although certain changes can sometimes help—changes of posture, sequence, manner, context, timing, and locale.

Daydreaming during sex may help to stabilize an ongoing relationship with a spouse or steady partner. A fair number of Hariton's and Singer's suburban women reported that their "fantasies are a substitute for having an affair with another man."

But not infrequently the daydreams reveal things the daydreamer would like the partner to do or be, and these sometimes could be realized within that relationship if only the desires were communicated and possible sources of the partner's resistance to them were allayed.

When people start using daydreams to cover up their dislike or distaste for their partners, the relationship is in serious trouble. And yet sometimes those daydreamers are still trying to make the best of a bad bargain, may still be masking their dissatisfaction even as they mask the reality of their partners during sex. Looking their daydreams in the face may nudge these daydreamers to come to grips with their problem and to do something about it before it dims too much more of their remaining lifetime.

Daydreaming can also be a way of warding off psychological involvement in sex. People who use daydreaming for this purpose have typically been reared in a way that has made sex frightening or disgusting to them. Faced with an eager sex partner and a relationship they value, many such women still go through the motions of sex in accordance with the Victorian ideal, treating it as the duty of a devoted wife. But they feel little pleasure, and their minds may well be elsewhere, such as on compiling grocery lists or solving problems at the office. Some men of this kind may find themselves impotent with their spouses. In today's sexually frank world, they are likely to realize that something is wrong. They may not realize that one of the things wrong is what they are doing with their minds during sex. Imagining car repairs does not promote sexual arousal or fulfillment.

Sex therapists today recognize the importance of the stream of daydreams that accompany sex. They can coach their clients to set aside thoughts that interfere with sex and to focus on the sexual here and now; and they can also teach clients to use their daydreams to explore their desires, to arouse themselves sexually, and to help themselves to maximum pleasure by drawing on the rich resources of their fantasies about sex.

For example, daydreaming about intercourse as you masturbate to orgasm may help link intercourse with orgasm in your mind. That would make you more aroused during actual intercourse and therefore make you more likely to come to orgasm there as well. Sex therapist Antonette Zeiss and her colleagues worked with women who had problems reaching orgasm during intercourse. The therapists put these women through a training program in which they fantasized about intercourse as they masturbated themselves to orgasm in the presence of their male partner. By these means, the women eventually experienced more orgasms during intercourse. So deliberately daydreaming about intercourse during masturbation may also strengthen a person's enjoyment of intercourse itself.

CHAPTER 7

# What Our Daydreams Are Made Of: The Stuff of Mental Imagery

*I dream thee with mine eyes, and at my heart I feel thee!*

—from "A Day-Dream" by Samuel Taylor Coleridge

For many years daydreams were thought to be completely insubstantial, something that wafts through your mind without leaving a trace, something that expresses you and perhaps pleases you but does not change you in any important way. If that were true—if daydreams were really a one-way street—daydreams could not serve as the medium for personal growth and self-management that they in fact seem to be.

But daydreams have a thoroughly substantial base. They hold their power for learning and personal growth because in an important sense they are an integral part of you: whenever you daydream about seeing or doing, you are mobilizing some of the same brain systems that you would use if you were actually seeing or doing. So when you see your lover in your daydreams, you are using much of your brain's equipment that you use in actual seeing. When you feel your lover stroke you in your daydreams, you are activating some of your brain's systems that you use to feel real stroking. When you daydream about stroking your lover, you invoke a large part of your brain's channels for actually stroking someone. And as you daydream these things, you feel much of the emotion you would be feeling if your daydream experience were real.

In other words, the brain systems you use for daydreaming are part of those you would use for doing the things you daydream about. To put it yet another way, the brain centers and pathways you use for daydreaming *overlap* the brain centers and pathways you use in real life, in that you use some of the same ones for both daydreaming about doing something and actually doing the same thing.

This overlap in brain systems between daydreaming something and doing it is crucial for two reasons. First, it explains what daydreams are made of—the material out of which they are constituted; and second, it means that when you daydream about doing something—when you rehearse some action in your daydreams—you are giving some of the same brain mechanisms a workout that you will use later to perform that action. Therefore, what you learn in that daydream can later transfer into your real life, as a benefit of your daydream for your personal growth.

## DAYDREAMING AND REALITY

It may be hard to accept that our daydreams have so much in common with the perceiving and acting parts of us. One reason for this is our habit of contrasting daydreams with reality, as if daydreams were all in our head and reality were all out there in the real world. But what we experience as *out there* is in our heads nearly as much as daydreams, thanks to the wonders of the phenomenon we call consciousness.

Consciousness is so much a part of us that we hardly notice it. You look out a window at the sun lighting up the trees and roofs beyond, and you believe, quite automatically, that the picture you see is out there, real and palpable, but that is illusion. The objects may well be out there, but your brain has created that picture from millions of bits of energy striking the back of your eyeball. The energy is converted to nerve pulses, a form of information that is transferred to your brain. What you experience as "seeing" is actually your brain's partial and somewhat distorted recreation of the scene, beautiful, sophisticated, and—marvel of marvels—inspectable, knowable, and reportable.

What the brain creates out of all that energy coming in from the outside world—or at least the part of which we are conscious—is called sensory imagery. Sensory imagery constitutes the brain's model of the outside world based on the sensory information available to it.

### Mental Imagery—The Raw Material of Daydreams

The brain can also create images without sensory information from the outside. Just as it can follow the guidelines of sensory energy to create a model of the outside world, so it can create a new model based on our memories of the models it created in the past. In fact, a large part of consciousness is made up of *mental* imagery—the sights, sounds, smells, tastes, and bodily sensations that we experience in the absence of the things they represent. You can imagine the smell of an orange or the sound of your best friend's voice without either the orange or the friend having to be anywhere near you. That is mental imagery. Mental imagery is a large part of daydreaming, which is always *about* something, and the something is represented in your consciousness as you daydream.

So far as we can tell, all of us with an intact brain are capable of mental imagery; and one or another kind of mental imagery seems to be part of almost every thought. As you try to convert a Fahrenheit temperature to centigrade, you briefly "see" the fraction 5/9 and perhaps a whole series of arithmetic steps. You think about a colleague's abilities for a certain job and "see" her face, perhaps also hear the lilt in her voice. You wonder what to cook tonight and imagine the different dishes you could prepare—how they look and perhaps how they smell and feel. At different points, you might "see" your grocery list, your cookbook, and your refrigerator.

Most often we experience our daydreams visually, as if we could see what we are daydreaming about. Our daydreams very commonly also include voices and other sounds, as well as bodily sensations, smells, tastes, and movement. So to find out what daydreams are made of, we need to consider what mental images are made of.

*What mental images are made of.* Mental images are the conscious face of psychological processes that go much deeper; they are the conscious tips of psychological icebergs. Only a small part of our psychological machinery becomes conscious, just as only a small part of what your electronic hand calculator does shows up on its display. When you start a letter by writing down the date, you are conscious of knowing the date and going through the motions of writing. However, your brain went through many steps of determining the date, laying out a plan for writing it, and coordinating your writing movements, although few of those steps became conscious. In fact, most of them were probably incapable of becoming conscious, any more than the calculator can display its own circuits. But part of your mental activity does become conscious, and you experience it as mental imagery.

Exercising your mental imagery is what we call imagining. When we imagine seeing or doing something, we create the images of scenes and actions. But we cannot move the tips of icebergs around without moving the icebergs themselves, and in an analogous sense we seemingly cannot imagine without mobilizing the deeper psychological and mental processes of which the images are only the conscious face.

*Imagining and really doing—how they differ and how they are alike.* Clearly, imagining is not exactly the same as actually seeing or doing. For one thing, imagining goes on largely cut off from the outside world. We may be doing something in imagination while our muscles are doing nothing at all. During intense mental imagery, our eyes may be looking at the outside world without consciously seeing it, because our consciousness is at that moment shielded from the impact of that world on our sense organs. So there is a definite difference between imagining and really perceiving or doing.

Nevertheless, even though pure mental imagery is cut off from the outside world, it still uses some of the same brain machinery that you would have used were you really perceiving and acting. When you daydream that you are hitting a home run, your mental imagery ignores the furniture in the room around you, and you remain physically still. But at least part of the brain that would be involved in hitting a ball, and watching it disappear over the left-field fence in fair territory as you round first base to the cheers of the crowd, is active.

## WHAT DAYDREAMING HAS IN COMMON WITH REALLY SEEING AND HEARING

This view of the mental images in daydreams—as something that shares underlying processes with actual perceiving and doing—rests on many kinds of scientific findings. To begin with seeing and hearing, psychologists have been able to show that:

- we can be fooled into confusing mental images with reality
- visualizing something makes it harder to see something real, unless it happens to be the same thing you are imagining
- brain areas active in seeing are also active in mental visualizing
- brain damage that knocks out your ability to see certain things also knocks out your ability to imagine them

## Believing That What You See Is What You Imagined

One piece of evidence that our mental images have much in common with actual seeing is that we can mistake the one for the other.

It is still unclear how we know when we are seeing and hearing rather than just imagining. Some investigators have suggested that we can identify the sensory images of actual seeing and hearing by the fact that they are more intense, detailed, and stable than our purely mental pictures. Others have suggested that we expend more effort to imagine something than to actually see or hear it, so that the amount of effort we exert provides us with a clue as to which one we are doing.

If these theories are true, then if for some reason our actual sensations became less intense, detailed, and stable than they usually are, we might be fooled into thinking that what we are seeing is something we are imagining. And that is just what psychologists have found: under certain conditions even perfectly healthy, sophisticated people can confuse what they see with what they imagine—not only in retrospect, but even at the time that it is happening.

The first scientific indication of this came in 1910, when psychologist Cheves Perky asked people she knew to stare at a white mark on a window and to imagine some "colored object." Some of these people were children; others were graduate students with extensive practice in observing their own conscious experience. Unbeknownst to all of them, the "window" that the white mark was on was a ground glass screen; and behind the screen was a secret dark room, in which two experimenters were scurrying about with colored glass, cardboard cutouts, and a "projection lantern" to create visual images on the screen. They could, for example, put cardboard with a round hole in it over a sheet of red glass, hold them both in front of the lantern, and project onto the back of the ground glass a filled red circle; from the front, it would look something like a tomato. As each participant looked at the screen, the experimenters in the dark room gradually turned a light up until it was distinctly visible, though still very faint. They muffled the outlines of the figures with gauze to keep the outlines from being too sharp, and an experimenter gently moved the cardboard so that it would not appear too fixed—all in an elaborate ruse to make a sense impression act like the kind of mental image that goes into daydreams.

The unsuspecting participants were instructed to look at the screen and *imagine* a colored object. Nevertheless each participant reported "imagining" the images that happened to be projected on the screen—without realizing that what they firmly believed they were imagining was actually something they were seeing. If the image on the screen was a banana, the participant would report imagining a banana: "The banana is up on end; I must have been thinking of it growing." Sometimes, people added imaginary features to what they were seeing: "I can see the veining of the leaf." But they were nevertheless convinced that it was all in their minds, even when the experimenter asked them whether they were "quite sure that (they) had imagined all these things." Some even felt insulted that there could be any doubt.

Evidently, most of us, children and adults, can be made to mistake what we saw for what we imagined. This confusability tells us that sensory images and mental images share much in common—that seeing something "out there" and seeing it purely in our mind's eye are most likely two different ways to use a single underlying brain process. And because mental imagery is the main ingredient in daydreams, Perky's finding anchors our daydreams in the basic machinery of the mind—that same machinery that lets us see, hear, feel, taste, and smell.

**Mental Images Can Interfere with Seeing**

Over the next eighty years, research moved from Perky's "projection lanterns" to far less pronounceable "event-related cortical potentials" (brain-wave reactions to controlled stimuli) and "single photon emission computer tomography" (scans that measure blood flow to different parts of the brain). In the process, psychologists have firmed up the evidence that our mental images share brain mechanisms with our real-world activity.

The next interesting finding was about what happens when we have a mental image at the same time that we are attending to our surroundings. If imagining and seeing use the same brain systems at the same time, you would think that they would compete with each other for access to these systems and thereby weaken each other, unless we happen to be imagining the same thing we are perceiving. And that is just the way it turned out. Our mental images actively weaken any simultaneous real-world perceptions when they are about something different and strengthen them when they are about the same thing.

For example, suppose that sixty years after Perky's experiment you are a research participant for New York psychologist Sydney Joelson Segal. You sit across from a screen wearing earphones. You have been trained to stay alert for faint pictures of a blue arrow on the screen and for a harmonica chord played softly through the earphones. Whenever the experimenter asks, "What was it?", you are to answer with "sound," "picture," or "nothing." Some of the time you are also asked to imagine things, either visual mental images such as a volcano or auditory mental images such as the sound of a typewriter.

While you are imagining something visual, such as a volcano, if you are like Segal's other participants, you miss seeing more arrows than usual, but you detect harmonica chords almost as well as when you are not imagining anything. While you are imagining something auditory, such as typewriter sounds, it is the other way around: you miss significantly more harmonica chords than blue arrows. It is as if imagining seeing an image ties up part of the brain system for seeing but not the system for hearing; and imagining hearing a sound ties up part of the brain system for hearing but not the system for seeing.

The mistakes you made could not have been chalked up simply to the distraction of trying to have a mental image. Distraction would have affected both seeing and hearing to about the same degree, regardless of what you were imagining or whether you were being presented with arrows or chords. The fact that the mistakes were so specific shows that the mental imagery of seeing uses some of the same brain channels as actual seeing and the mental imagery of hearing shares brain channels with actual hearing. It is as if mental images preempt their brain systems and make them unavailable for perception.

All this anchors daydreaming all the more securely in these basic perceptual parts of the brain. It means that when you are imagining a scene, you are exercising your brain's perceptual systems.

**Imagining Often Acts Like Seeing**

Taking earlier research a step further, Harvard psychologist Stephen Kosslyn showed that "seeing" in one's imagination acts in many ways like seeing in reality. When we search for a mental image, we act very much as we do when searching with our eyes. In designing some of their experiments, Kosslyn and his students made use of a commonly recognized fact: if someone asks you whether the sidewalk in front of you is dry, you will look down and quickly answer yes or no; but if someone asks you whether the sidewalk down the street is dry, which is farther away and harder to make out, it will take you longer before answering. Kosslyn wondered whether it would also take longer to make out the details of imaginary things when you imagine them to be far away than when you imagine them to be up close.

In one experiment, Kosslyn asked people to imagine a small animal such as a rabbit standing next to an elephant (which people usually imagine as fairly far away) or standing next to a fly (which they usually imagine up close). Then he asked them questions about the animal: Does it have a nose? Does it have a back? Just as in actual looking, it took people longer to answer these questions when the thing they were imagining was far away than when it was up close.

In another experiment, people were asked to memorize a map. They were then asked to imagine moving their eyes from one point on the map to another. It took longer to do that when the points on the map were farther apart than when they were closer together. This demonstrates again how much our images have in common with our perceptions.

**Brain Linkages Between What We Imagine and What We See**

Some skeptics still worried that participants in experiments such as Kosslyn's were so eager to please the experimenters that they put on an act and reported what they thought the experimenters wanted to find. If that had been true, which it probably wasn't, all those results would tell us nothing about mental imagery as such or about the daydreaming of which it is such a large part.

But now we have even harder evidence about the biological link between mental imagery and behavior: the brain areas most involved in mental imagery turn out to be the same ones most involved in actual seeing. This means that mental images resemble vision not only in behavior but also in brain anatomy.

You have probably had an experience like the one I had recently. I was looking for a book on my shelves, which have a great many books on them. I had a distinct memory of how the book looked and I knew its author and title. I let my eyes sweep through the likely parts of my shelves but didn't find it. I looked again, trying to read titles and authors quickly as I went, but still didn't find it. Feeling frustrated, I tried once more, this time reading every author and title *very carefully*, and found the book—right there, where I had twice passed over it. I suddenly realized that the book was a different color and shape than what I had recalled and imagined. Despite my eyes sweeping over titles and authors, the discrepancy in appearance led me to go right by it. Had I been imagining the right color and size, I would have spotted it in an instant. It is as if mental images add to actual vision when they are similar; but when they are out of kilter, it is harder to make sense of what you see.

This is the principle that Carnegie-Mellon psychologist Martha Farah seized on and applied to the brain. Farah reasoned that if mental images and vision were similar enough, it should be possible to add up their effects. When you look for something that is hard to make out, you should be able to spot it faster if you happen to be imagining the very thing you are looking at. Likewise, the parts of your brain, such as the occipital lobe, that get active when you are looking should be even more active when you are looking *and* imagining the same thing. Farah's findings strongly confirmed this theory.

Farah's participants monitored a screen that periodically flashed a letter *H* or *T* for one-fiftieth of a second, immediately followed by a pattern that would make it hard to know whether there had been a letter or not. Each time, her participants were asked to signal just one thing: Was there a letter, or wasn't there? Some of the time, they were also asked to *imagine* either an *H* or a *T*, and the flashes came while they were holding the image. When the letter being flashed matched what they were imagining, they could detect it much more accurately than when the letter on the screen was different from the one they were imagining.

But what about the brain's activity in all this? The heads of these participants were plastered with electrodes, little metal cups connected by wires to a machine that recorded changes in electrical voltage. When letters flashed on the screen while participants were imagining the same letter, some of their brain areas registered stronger changes in voltage than when the letter came on without that image. It is as though the brain had added up the two sources of activity:

that from the image and that from actually seeing the letter, just as if both were using the same brain circuits. If the two were different, their activity was not added up.

In addition, the mental images had their largest effect in the same brain areas that are most active in vision itself: the back of the brain, including the occipital lobe and certain surrounding areas. The farther forward the electrodes sat, the less the voltage fluctuations were enhanced by the mental images.

Farah's findings indicate that the visual-imagery aspect of daydreams does indeed exercise the same part of the brain as that used in actual seeing. And they are supported by other findings using different methods. For example, imagining increases the amount of blood flowing in that same rear brain area—the occipital lobe—that showed the most effect in Farah's experiment and is essential for vision. Also, when victims of brain damage lose certain very narrow abilities, such as being able to recognize colors or to recognize living things, they also lose the capacity to *imagine* seeing those things.

The systems involved in your mental images go beyond your cranium all the way out to your eyes. When you see an actual color, the eye's retina sends certain signals to the brain that correspond to the color. Massachusetts psychologist Robert Kunzendorf has shown that when you only imagine that color, the eye sends signals to the brain that are in some ways very similar. Even more striking, when you imagine seeing red while actually looking at green (or the other way around), your eye sends signals that correspond to what you were imagining rather than to what you were seeing!

The retina in the eyeball is a tissue that evolved from the brain. In a sense, therefore, it is an outlying part of the brain. But the fact that it is activated during mental imagery underlines how extensively our mental images use the same brain systems that we use for seeing. And that means that our daydreams—or at least their shapes, colors, sounds, tastes, smells, and bodily sensations—are squarely rooted in the brain systems that underlie our usual five senses.

All this means that your daydreams are not something completely apart from your real-world activities but are an interior version of them. When you daydream, you exercise parts of your brain that are responsible for the activities you are daydreaming about. When you exercise these brain systems in such a way as to teach them something new, that learning alters them and sets them up to apply their learning to the next real-world occasion for which they are relevant. And that is what makes the mental images of daydreaming a medium for personal change and growth.

For example, we have already encountered Max, who one day daydreamed about fixing wiring and holding electric cords in his mouth. As his daydream flowed on, he "saw" his little daughter imitating him and electrocuting herself in the process. Because this was a very distressing daydream for him—a taste of the distress he would feel in real life—he resolved to be a better model for his child by no longer using his mouth to hold cords.

Max learned through daydreaming: in his daydream he noticed something that he had not noticed before—his little daughter nearby, ready to imitate him. This sensitized him to the real-life situation he faced on his return home, so that he would now be much more likely than before to notice what he did with the electric cords and the whereabouts of his daughter.

Max's daydream did not necessarily improve his perceptual skills as such. But when we practice seeing, hearing, and so on in daydreaming, we exercise our brain systems for seeing and hearing and can therefore theoretically change the very skill with which we see or hear. The opportunities for improving these perceptual skills in daydreaming may be limited, but the opportunities for improving other kinds of skills, such as motor skills or social skills, are much more numerous. As we shall see, these also share brain systems with our corresponding real-life activities and can benefit from daydreaming.

## IMAGINING MOVING AND REALLY MOVING

When we think of mental images, we tend to think of "pictures in the mind." But actually, when we daydream, we often imagine ourselves doing something—talking to someone, going somewhere, pitching a ball, making love. These are images of action, and they are images just as much as mental visions of scenery or of other people's faces.

If we are to improve our motor and social skills directly through daydreaming, mental images of moving our muscles, as in playing a sport or talking, would have to work the same way as our mental images of seeing or hearing: they would have to rely on the brain systems we use in really moving. We now have good reasons to believe that this is so.

Just as visualizing or using other senses in daydreams shares brain systems with actual behavior, imagining moving your muscles likewise uses parts of the brain that serve actual movement. When you daydream about returning a tennis ball that zings right past your opponent, you are using the part of the brain system that you play tennis with. When you imagine a conversation, you are using brain areas involved in speaking.

Thus there is a certain degree of correspondence between daydreaming that you are doing something and actually doing it. When you practice doing something in imagination, that practice carries over to real life. The reasons for believing that this is true are as follows:

- Imagining moving a muscle produces low-level electrical activity in that same muscle.
- Imagining movement activates brain areas used in actually moving.
- When you practice some skill in your mind, such as playing the piano or shooting baskets, your mental practice by itself improves your physical performance when you next try it.

• Imagining yourself acting socially more effectively, such as asserting yourself better, carries over into real life.

We do not normally think of daydreams about walking or playing a sport as having a direct connection to our muscles. Most of us know that our mental states can affect our bodies: when we worry, we get tense, and we may develop headaches, indigestion, and other physical symptoms. Research now shows that there is a direct connection between our action images and our muscles; they use some of the same brain pathways.

**Electrical Activity**

The first researcher to provide solid evidence that imagining movement affects the muscles was University of Chicago physiologist Edmund Jacobson, one of the pioneers of muscle relaxation. Since mental states can change people's tension levels, Jacobson was interested in how mental activity affects muscles.

To provide an objective measure of relaxation, Jacobson developed a highly sensitive method for measuring electrical activity in muscles, the technique of electromyography, or EMG. His form of EMG was so sensitive that he could measure low-level tension changes in muscles that to an outside observer seemed completely at rest throughout.

In the late 1920s, Jacobson brought in a series of volunteers, strapped electrodes over their right biceps—the muscle in the upper arm that we flex to show off our "muscles"—and asked them to imagine various activities. For example, he asked them to imagine bending an arm, picking up a ten-pound weight, pulling on a gear shift, or sweeping the floor. At other times, Jacobson asked his volunteers to imagine that their arm was paralyzed, to relax an arm, or actually to move some limb. The question he sought to answer was what happened to electrical activity in their right biceps while they imagined moving.

The results were clear-cut. When these people imagined bending their right arms, electrical activity in the right biceps almost always went up, usually sharply, which meant that the muscle suddenly tensed up. When they imagined an activity that involved the right arm, such as lifting a weight, much the same thing happened. When they stopped imagining the movement, the electrical activity in the muscles quickly went down again. If a volunteer imagined bending the left arm, or actually did bend it, this left the right biceps unchanged.

These findings established that imagining doing something with the right arm tenses the same muscles that would be involved in actually performing the movement. The major difference was in amount. During movement imagery, the electrical activity was much weaker than in actual movement—too weak to actually move the arm. This suggests that when you daydream about lifting a baby or rowing or tackling the opposing ball carrier, the muscles involved are activated, though at a level too low to notice without sensitive equipment.

Another set of muscles that humans use regularly are the ones involved in speaking. To see whether these respond to imagery in the way that arm muscles do, Jacobson attached electrodes to his volunteers' tongues and lips. While the volunteers imagined doing things such as talking, doing mental arithmetic, or recalling a poem, the EMG records showed tongue and lip muscles tensing up. There was no such muscle activity when the participants were doing something that did not entail language. Just as imagining arm activity activated the right biceps, imagining speaking activated the muscles people use in speaking.

Since Jacobson's work, many other investigators have confirmed and refined his findings, ranging from the great Soviet psychologist A. N. Sokolov to Virginia psychologist Frank McGuigan. They have shown that almost any language-related mental imagery activates speech-related muscles. Even just listening to language seems to produce some low-level activation there. In many literate people, language-related imagery even seems to activate the muscles in the forearm that the person uses for writing.

Finally, the idea that movement imagery activates the brain areas involved in real movement has been confirmed by direct measurements of brain activity. As shown by a Danish research team led by neurophysiologist P. E. Roland, when you imagine moving your fingers, you increase the amount of blood flowing to part of the brain region involved in actual finger movements.

What all this indicates is that when you imagine engaging in an action, as you often do in daydreams, you are using parts of the brain that you would use if your action were real. In fact, those brain systems become so active that their activity spills over into the corresponding muscles and can be picked up there by the EMG. For the brain, the difference between moving and imagining moving seems to be mostly a matter of letting the movement commands reach the muscles full force, in which case you move, or blocking them before they can create actual movement, in which case you only imagine moving, as in daydreams.

The brain activities that produce mental images of movement and those that produce actual movement overlap to such a degree that the first have to be held in check to keep them from producing actual movement. Even so, sometimes the restraints on our movement commands break down, and then we move unintentionally. For example, sometimes we get so caught up in an imaginary conversation that we find ourselves speaking the words aloud. Sometimes a dream will spill over into movement, and we sleep-talk or sleepwalk.

## YOUR DAYDREAMS AS MEDIUM FOR CHANGE

Based on the foregoing, anything you learn about managing your muscles during movement imagery ought to carry over into "real life." It makes mental imagery—including the mental images that make up daydreaming—a safe arena within which you can try things out and learn, knowing that you can put the lessons you learn to use in real life.

In point of fact, that does seem to be one of the ways that people spontaneously use daydreaming. When Alexandra, an educator, is scheduled to give a talk, she spontaneously rehearses that talk in her daydreams repeatedly before giving it. As she hears herself make a point, she also sees how her imaginary audience reacts. Often, the imaginary reaction leads her to reformulate that part of her talk. She has found her daydreams to be most helpful when she is familiar with the room in which she will talk. In fact, like many speakers, she finds that focusing part of her mental imagery on the physical arrangements—the size of the room, the location of the podium, projector and screen, the seating for the audience—will help her function in the setting. When possible, she tries to get an advance peek at the room so that her daydreams can integrate it and prepare her for it. In ways such as this, mental imagery—and therefore daydreaming—can be an internal medium for self-improvement and personal change.

If our mental images are the tips of psychological icebergs—the conscious faces of underlying psychological and brain processes—that must mean that when they change, so do the processes they represent and therefore so do we. Research has demonstrated that mental images can indeed change, and that when they do, so do our physical and social skills and our ability to cope. Specifically:

- mental images can be shaped through learning
- mentally practicing physical skills such as shooting baskets can improve the level of the physical skill
- working through mental images can help people to change their emotions
- working through mental images can help to improve social skills and other aspects of personal growth

Daydreams, therefore, can be harnessed for self-improvement. They are in part flexible tryouts for real life, internal proxies for the real-world school of hard knocks; but some of their benefits come naturally and effortlessly just as a result of normal daydreaming.

**Mental Images Change with Learning**

It may seem strange to think that our mental images can be changed in the same way as other behavior. Yet, our mental images are shaped by our experiences with reality, and that shaping takes place through some of the same basic, sometimes primitive processes of conditioning and learning that change outward behavior.

You are probably acquainted with the work of the Russian physiologist Ivan Pavlov with dogs. Like humans, hungry dogs begin to salivate when they sense food. After ringing a bell each time he was about to feed his dogs, Pavlov got them to the point where they started slobbering whenever they heard the bell, even in the absence of food. Remarkably, we can also change—through conditioning—the mental images that go into our daydreams.

Any doubts I may have had about that vanished through an unforgettable personal experience that is probably very similar to one you have had. One year I moved from my old office to a smaller one. I had grown attached to a portable blackboard in the old office, for which the new office was too small. But since the blackboard was mounted on wheels, I took it along and put it in front of some file cabinets across from my desk. Whenever I looked up from my desk, there it was staring me in the face, and whenever I needed to get into the file cabinets, I had to wheel it aside. Eventually, the blackboard became enough of a nuisance that I gave it away. What followed was completely unexpected.

For nearly two weeks, whenever I looked up from my desk, I had a brief image of the missing blackboard. Of course, I realized each time that my image was completely mental and that the blackboard was gone. Even so, for the first few times its absence hit me as a surprise. As the days went by, the image became fainter and the surprise disappeared. This left no question in my mind that mental images could be conditioned and learned.

There is laboratory evidence that backs up these experiences. In one experiment, the American psychologist Douglas Ellson apparently succeeded in conditioning his volunteers to hear an imaginary tone when they saw a real light. He asked volunteers to listen for tones and to press a button whenever they heard one being played. Each tone came on and off very gradually, slowly becoming louder and then slowly becoming softer again, in order to make it harder to detect. For some volunteers, Ellson turned on a light just before each tone. The idea here was that, in the volunteers' minds, hearing the tones might become so linked to seeing the light that when they saw the light they might actually "hear" the tone—even when there was none. To test this, Ellson later occasionally turned on the light without playing a tone. On those runs, about 80 percent of these volunteers pressed the button as though they had, in fact, heard a tone.

Apparently our mental images, just like our other behavior, be it salivation or love or fear, are molded by our experiences—experiences with what to expect, what things are associated with each other, and what works. Consider, for instance, the following experience.

Tony had invited Katherine to go sailing with him. Katherine knew Tony only slightly—they had talked at a party and on the phone—and she felt attracted to him. He seemed confident and forceful, competent and bright. But she also felt vaguely uneasy about the date, and she didn't know why. In a daydream about it, she imagined flashes of sailing in the bay and afterwards going to a restaurant with Tony—and then, in her daydream, he took over. He decided where they were going next, and he acted completely convinced that his suggestions and decisions were the right ones. Katherine had no sense of choice as he rolled right over her feelings and preferences. Fearful of a relationship with him, she broke the date.

Katherine's daydream draws on sailing images that she had developed as a result of her sailing experiences. Less obviously, her daydream unfolded as it did because of what she had learned to expect from men like Tony. In some ways his manner reminded her of her father, with whom she didn't get along, and her daydream completed her picture of Tony by depicting him as having her father's other, more objectionable, traits.

Her daydream also reflects her experiences with what works and doesn't work for her. At her stage of development, she lacked the feeling of strength she would need to stand up to Tony if he were as she had daydreamed. As a result, in her daydream she found herself unable to resist his initiatives and capitulated to them, despite her strong feelings to the contrary.

At a later stage in her development, when she had a clearer idea of how to handle people like Tony, her daydream might have portrayed her standing up to him. The first such daydream might have emboldened her to go through with the date. But as it was, she was unwilling to risk it.

As your daydreams unfold, they often go in unexpected directions. You discover things, feel things, and realize things you may never have encountered before. And as you do, you change—a little or a lot—both in your daydreams and in reality.

This is what happened to Katherine. At first, after all, she had accepted Tony's invitation, and she could have expected that her daydreams about the upcoming sailing date would be pleasant ones. But her daydream took an unexpected turn that changed her evaluation of him.

It is hard to know whether breaking the date was the best thing for her. Perhaps she misjudged Tony, but it may also be that her images of Tony correctly foretold how he would have treated her. In any event, her daydream picked up on her forebodings and concretized them. It laid out for her a scenario she felt afraid to let herself in for, and as a result she changed her mind and her behavior toward Tony.

**Imaginary Experiences Can Change Emotions**

Just as we experience emotions in connection with our real-world life, we experience them in connection with the images in our daydreams. In fact, one of the surest ways to stir up an emotion is to ask someone to dwell on images of a past situation that had aroused that emotion. When we conjure memories of a warm, happy event, we begin to feel warm and happy. If we recall someone dear to us who died, we experience renewed pangs of grief. If we focus on something that made us angry, we feel angry all over again.

As we play through our mental images in our daydreams, we sometimes change the emotions that accompany them. You have probably had the experience of something marvelous happening to you and later savoring the experience in your mind. Perhaps it was a compliment from someone important to you or an enjoyable vacation trip. As you played it over in your mind, you most likely felt a return of the original joy and pleasure. But if you tried to make yourself feel good by thinking about it repeatedly, you probably discovered that the joy started to wear out. The memory was still pleasant, but the emotion became fainter; it was time to move on.

The same thing is true of unpleasant emotions. It is part of the folk culture that the way to lose your fear of something is to expose yourself to the thing you fear. If you just fell off a horse, goes the folk adage, get right back on to keep yourself from building up a fear of riding. You may be afraid of driving on busy freeways, but if you make yourself do it repeatedly, you will lose some of your fear. Much the same thing can happen in imagination if you force yourself to imagine doing something that scares you, but without imagining a disastrous ending. This is a principle—called desensitization—that has been harnessed by behavior therapists, who were among the first to make systematic use of mental imagery in psychological therapy.

The most efficient way to treat fears behaviorally is to have patients face up to the things they fear in the real world. For example, the British psychiatrist Isaac Marks reported treating a woman who had a paralyzing fear of riding the Underground, the London subway system. He induced her to ride it anyway all day, until her fear subsided and she was able to take the Underground on a normal daily basis.

But not everyone can tolerate the amount of fear generated at first in such situations. In the 1950s, even before Marks' experiments, the American psychiatrist Joseph Wolpe had worked out a gentler application of this principle by using mental imagery. In a specially designed program called "systematic desensitization," he had patients relax and imagine situations they feared, whether they be standing in high places, going out into crowds, riding on elevators, giving speeches, handling snakes, or whatever else they might have been afraid of. Daydreaming about these things is less threatening than actually doing them; and many investigations have confirmed that when patients follow Wolpe's program, most of them gradually get over their phobias.

Research has also shown that it is unnecessary to follow Wolpe's specific method to achieve the same effect. As long as the person confronts the fear in imagination and does not avoid it—and does not imagine awful things coming of it—the fear will gradually subside.

The success of this procedure shows that emotions can change through imaginary experience much as through actual situations. Furthermore, it suggests that daydreams play a role in maintaining or changing the way we feel about things. When we daydream that something we fear, such as flying in an airliner, leads to disaster, that is likely to maintain the fear. But when we are bolder in our daydreams than in real life and try out new things—and when we let these daydreams end happily—they may eventually help us find the courage to try the things we fear in actuality.

**Practicing Skills in Daydreams Can Improve Them**

As many controlled investigations have shown, daydreaming can also change physical movement and social skills, such as those we use in swimming or tennis or at cocktail parties, just by fantasizing doing them. One of my students, Leslie Meek, recently demonstrated once again that mental practice works. She picked a skill that hardly anyone would be likely to acquire outside the laboratory: mirror drawing. In mirror drawing, people take a drawing of a six-pointed star and trace over its outline. This may sound easy enough, but a screen below their chins prevents these people from seeing the paper or their hands directly. They can only see them reflected in a mirror placed upright in front of them.

Mirror drawing poses obvious difficulties. For example, when the mirror shows your hand moving above the line you are tracing, you automatically try to correct the error by moving your hand towards you; but that makes the error worse, because the mirror shows the reverse of what is on the paper. All of your previous experience with hand–eye coordination now works against you; you have to relearn this skill almost from the beginning. The remarkable thing is that you can improve this skill through mostly mental practice, which indicates that practicing something in your daydreams can improve your future performance.

After a first, error-filled try at mirror-tracing the star, each participant in Meek's experiment received either an eight-minute practice session or no practice. Some spent the eight minutes actually tracing the star over and over, whereas others spent their time just mentally imagining themselves tracing it. To make sure that their mental practice was as vivid and detailed as possible, they were given instructions to "visualize the apparatus and see yourself actually doing the tracing. Try to feel your hand, try to imagine guiding your hand, how the surface would feel, the amount of pressure that you would be applying to the stylus." A third group divided the eight minutes between practicing mentally and practicing physically with the real star and stylus. Before going home, everyone traced the star once more as a test of their improvement over the first time. A week later they came back and, with no further practice, mirror-traced the star one last time.

All of the eight-minute practice groups, even if their eight minutes had been devoted completely to mental practice, improved significantly more than the group that had only the three runs at tracing the star. That was true both for the test right after the practice and for the one a week later. The fact that the participants who practiced mentally stayed improved for a week means that their improvement was not just a mental "warm-up" effect; these people really learned a new skill, even if their practice had been purely mental.

These results are fairly typical. Other investigators have used many different kinds of skills, ranging from various laboratory tasks to such activities as typing, dart-throwing, soccer, and volleyball. Increasingly, athletic coaches have begun using mental practice, sometimes under the name "visualization," in competitive sports. One company, SyberVision, makes a business out of supplying videotapes of expert players for people to watch and imitate mentally. What we have here, then, are disciplined uses of mental imagery that are demonstrably effective in improving physical skills.

The reason for their effectiveness is straightforward when you consider that the brain systems for imagining moving your body overlap the brain systems for actually moving. To use a very crude analogy, after you tune a motor and hear it purr while the car is in neutral, you are not amazed that its performance is still improved after you shift into gear. If the brain machinery for moving in our daydreams, such as that for performing a slalom, is part of the machinery for actual movement, it should not surprise us that after we have improved the movements in our daydreams we move more skillfully in reality.

A number of investigations have shown that this kind of improvement extends to social functioning as well. Rehearsing various kinds of social skills in daydreams makes people smoother operators in social settings. Playing out scenarios ahead of time for asserting your rights to someone, for being sensitive to other people's needs, and so on helps you to perform well when you get to the actual situation. Learning in mental imagery *is* learning, and it transfers right into the real world.

### Daydreaming as a Self-Improvement Medium

A large part of what goes on in daydreaming is reviewing your past experiences and rehearsing for the future. You play through your mind the personal interactions you have had or expect to have—the conversations, lovemaking, victimizations, self-defense, violence—and you assess the consequences. Often, in the process, you change your mind about what will work or will not work. You learn.

The reason this is possible is that your imaginary self is a large part of your real self. In imagining, you are mobilizing some of the same brain systems that would be involved in reality. When you imagine seeing someone, part of your visual system gets involved. When you imagine hugging someone, you activate part of the hugging system. When you imagine confronting an exaggerated fear, you activate real fear and, having called its bluff, weaken it.

In our daydreams, then, we recreate ourselves and our world—not arbitrarily, but by playing out in our sheltered mental arenas the scenarios we have learned for perceiving and coping with reality. The constraints are different in daydreams than they are in reality, which allows us the luxury of trying out things we would not dare try in the real world. But we are the same actors in our mental imagery as in our reality. If we imagine lying on a beach, our brains are reclining, recreating the feel of sand and sunshine. If we imagine kissing someone, our brains are kissing and recreating the feeling of being kissed, recreating the look and feel and smell of the other. And that is why, in a very real sense, we are one with our daydreams.

CHAPTER 8

# Myths and Misconceptions: The Truth About Daydreaming

A surprising number of people worry about their daydreaming—surprising because, as we have seen, daydreaming in one form or another is so integral a part of human life. It is interwoven with our other thoughts, keeping our personal agendas before our eyes, spontaneously grappling with our problems, combing through our past, rehearsing for the future, and generating creative ideas. And yet thinkers from Plato to Freud have regarded daydreaming with attitudes that range from condescension to condemnation. "Men live in their fancy," wrote philosopher Ralph Waldo Emerson, "like drunkards whose hands are too soft and tremulous for successful labor." As a result, even today people are concerned about daydreaming too much, and how they can tell when they reach that point. They worry about whether their daydreaming means that they are particularly immature or maladjusted and about whether they are daydreaming their way into serious mental disorder or weakening their grip on reality as a result of daydreaming. People are also concerned about the kinds of daydreaming that amount to excessive worry and about having their decisions and values distorted by their daydreams.

Modern research has shown that many of the problems people fear in connection with daydreaming simply don't exist. We experience them as problems not because of the real dangers of daydreaming but because of what we have been misled to believe about those dangers—that daydreaming can become an insidious habit, for instance, or that it can lead to mental illness. Not only do these beliefs appear to be false, but recent research even suggests that fanciful daydreaming may strengthen our ability to distinguish fantasy from reality.

The few real problems that do exist are considerably less frightening than you might think. You would, obviously, be ill-advised to do much daydreaming while handling dangerous equipment or cutting across freeway lanes at rush hour. Also, if you are unreasonably afraid of something, such as flying or public speaking, daydreams in which those activities end catastrophically might deepen your fear. Finally, dwelling on something you want but shouldn't have may make it harder for you to resist pursuing it.

Although it is possible to daydream too much by someone's standards, "too much" consists of interfering with other, more important activities, not of any particular amount of time. Because we daydream continually during the spaces left over by our other activities, daydreaming and achievement are usually compatible with each other rather than mutually exclusive. If we daydream a lot and undertake too little in the real world, the fault lies most likely not in our daydreaming as such but in our life situations, which may have frustrated and discouraged us, and in our personal qualities —such as our temperament and coping skills—that shape those daydreams. If we find our daydreams distressing, the cause is most likely in our personal problems, including depression and anxiety, and in our own overreactions to our daydreams.

## FEAR AND CONDEMNATION OF DAYDREAMS

Am I somehow damaging myself by daydreaming? Can my daydreaming undermine my sanity? Can it harm my capacity to function as a normal human being? These are the questions, and behind them the nervous worry, that still haunt many of us as we contemplate our daydreams.

This concern is understandable, backed up as it is by generations of negative judgments from people we thought should know about the subject. The founder of psychoanalysis, Sigmund Freud, had after all written in 1908 that "happy people never make phantasies" and that "if phantasies become over-luxuriant and over-powerful, the necessary conditions for an outbreak of neurosis or psychosis are constituted; phantasies are also the first preliminary stage in the mind of the symptoms of illness." As one result, Anna Freud, his daughter and herself a noted psychoanalytic theorist, struggled through much of her life to suppress her own elaborate and irrepressible daydreams, daydreams that we would today recognize as signs of her creative spirit.

Freud's view fit nicely into our puritanical American work ethic, which emphasizes productive action and equates daydreaming with idleness. In fact, until recent years, American educational psychologists warned against the dangers of indulging in too much daydreaming. They commonly listed it among "defense mechanisms," mental quirks that distort reality in order to help us escape from the anxieties and pressures of real life. Generations of teachers prepared themselves for their profession with textbooks that erroneously warned of the dangers of daydreaming and even likened it to addictive substances. "Fantasy is habit-forming because it is peculiarly satisfying," the distinguished educational psychologist Lee Cronbach wrote in 1963, "one can always make the story come out right . . . fantasy, while it lasts, is completely absorbing and rewarding. So it is that some people come to rely more and more on fantasy. They spend less and less time facing their real problems—and these consequently grow more serious. This vicious circle creates severe mental disorders. Psychotic patients . . . substitute their own wishes for reality."

## CAN DAYDREAMING MAKE YOU CRAZY?

No. But given the misinformation bandied about for so long, it is easy to see why some of us still worry about it. For example, a 1959 textbook by educational psychologists Pressey, Robinson, and Horrocks warned, "Everyone daydreams a bit. . . . The trouble comes when a child settles into habitual daydreaming instead of trying to make good in his work or play. . . . If such 'escapes' are indulged in long enough, the individual may finally even become mentally ill, develop schizophrenia."

Yesterday's experts told us that daydreams are surviving remnants of infantile thinking, of unrealistic wish fulfillment. They saw in daydreams the beginnings of mental disorder, and they spoke of the most seriously deranged as having retreated into their fantasies and lost their sanity. This is a frightening prospect indeed, psychological dynamite—and mostly untrue.

The scientific evidence now available shows that people who enjoy daydreaming are on the average about as well adjusted as other people, whereas people with the mental disorder of schizophrenia are not particularly prone to daydream. Neither your capacity for vivid mental imagery nor your enjoyment of daydreaming are linked with mental disorder. Even people who spin elaborate daydreams in which they get thoroughly absorbed seem to be psychologically about as healthy as those whose daydreams are plain and simple.

This more benign view of daydreaming has now been established in numerous investigations. For example, New

York psychologist Richard Rowe found that people who engage in a lot of daydreaming as measured by a questionnaire suffer from no more anxiety than others; and that holds true whether anxiety is assessed by how they say they feel, using another standard questionnaire, or through polygraph measures of their heart rate and how well the skin of their palms conducts electricity. There are also innumerable life stories of well-known people who were given to elaborate daydreaming and yet made major contributions to the arts and sciences—and also found personal fulfillment.

Some kinds of daydreamers do suffer from more psychological distress than others. People who have frequent daydreams in which they feel frightened or guilty about something experience above-average amounts of anxiety and other neurotic symptoms. Furthermore, as psychologists Thomas Traynor and Leonard Giambra have shown, depressed college students and depressed prison inmates both reported daydreaming more than nondepressed students and inmates, and they enjoyed their daydreams less. They found them more boring, less enjoyable, and less acceptable than others found theirs. Far from being day-brighteners, their daydreams were often gloomy ones marked by failure and guilt.

The fact that unhappy people have unhappy daydreams tells us something important about daydreaming. If fantasy were an escape, you would expect that the people with the most need to escape would have daydreams that make them feel happier, but the opposite seems to be true. The people who most need that escape, those afflicted with anxiety and depression, do daydream somewhat more but, far from providing an escape, their daydreams largely provide yet another domain for feeling unhappy. The daydreams of the neurotic are frightened and guilty; those of the depressed are boring and depressing.

Supporting this curious fact is research by a Western Carolina team headed by psychologist Steven Gold, who asked participants to rate how they felt during and right after each of their daydreams. The people who felt worse right after their daydreams averaged more anxiety, depression, helplessness, and distress in their lives generally. Those who felt better averaged a higher sense of general well-being, reported more positive emotions, had stronger emotional ties to others, and scored overall as mentally healthier.

In other words, people who enjoy and participate in life enjoy daydreaming and get the most out of it; whereas those who have the greatest problems with reality have daydreams that make them, if anything, even more miserable. Our daydreams are extensions of ourselves, whether happy or glum. In our daydreams we survey our possibilities, rosy or bleak, and work over our problems, whether promising or daunting.

**Will Daydreaming Make You Schizophrenic?**

Again, no. Earlier experts saw parallels between elaborate fantasizing and the major mental disorder of schizophrenia —for example, between the irreality of normal fanciful daydreaming and schizophrenic hallucinations and delusions. But the scientific evidence does not bear them out. Among college men and women whom my students and I have evaluated with standard questionnaires, people who enjoy positive, vivid daydreaming score as being no more schizophrenic than others do. Those whose daydreams are often filled with negative feelings such as fear and guilt do score as more schizophrenic. In other words, it is not daydreaming as such that is related to schizophrenia, but unpleasant daydreams, which reflect the negative feelings and experiences that go with higher schizophrenia scores.

Similarly, among psychiatric patients studied by Steven Starker, chief psychologist at the Portland, Oregon, Veterans Administration Medical Center, schizophrenics daydreamed at about the same average rates as other people. It is therefore simply not true that schizophrenics are caught up in extensive daydreams.

*Daydreams and hallucinations.* The longstanding belief linking daydreaming to mental disorder had its reasons. One common symptom of schizophrenia, for instance, is hallucination: the patient hears voices or, more rarely, sees, smells, or feels things that are not there. The patient might hear someone's voice condemning him or might feel half of his head rotting away. These hallucinations are a form of mental imagery and therefore seem to have something in common with daydreaming. However, hallucinations and daydreams are very different things.

If hallucinators were just very vivid daydreamers, we would expect them to have mental images that are more vivid—more lifelike—than other people's. When they imagined a voice or the sound of a piano, it would resemble a real voice or piano sound more than is true for other people. But that is not the case. When Starker's schizophrenic patients were not actively hallucinating—which was most of the time—their mental images of voices and sounds were on the average no more vivid than they are for others; if anything, they were a bit less vivid. Moreover, not all hallucinations are themselves very vivid. Sometimes hallucinators hear their voices only faintly. Therefore experiencing hallucinations is something apart from the hallucinator's usual daydreaming style. There is nothing here to link schizophrenics' hallucinations to their daydreams.

Within the group of schizophrenic patients, there is a way in which normal daydreaming resembles schizophrenic symptoms: those patients whose daydreams include the most sounds are more likely than other schizophrenics to hallucinate hearing nonexistent voices. But the fact that they are hallucinating voices does not make them particularly more disturbed than the other schizophrenics; it only shows that in their disorders, people retain many of the qualities that distinguish them as individuals.

*Daydreams and schizophrenic delusions.* Another common symptom of schizophrenia is delusional thinking: the patient believes others are conspiring to get her, for example, or believes that she is Joan of Arc reborn. To outsiders, beliefs such as this seem to be fantasies and therefore also seem to have something in common with daydreaming. But the fact that a person is deluded does not mean that the person necessarily daydreams very much; and, as we have seen, schizophrenics report no more daydreaming than other people do. Again, we have nothing here to link daydreaming as such with mental illness. We will take a closer look at delusions in a later section.

*Daydreams and schizophrenic distractibility.* A further common symptom of schizophrenia is extreme distractibility. Many schizophrenics have trouble not attending to noises that the rest of us overlook, or they are unable to maintain their own thoughts in a conversation because they feel bombarded by the talking around them. They often disrupt their own thoughts by starting new thoughts in the middle of them. The new thoughts crop up spontaneously, just like normal daydreams.

This begins to sound much like the distractibility I have described as normal, but it is actually a greatly exaggerated version of normal distractibility; and schizophrenics have much more difficulty than others in controlling it. Those of us who are not actively schizophrenic can generally pull ourselves together and concentrate when we need to; during psychotic episodes, schizophrenics cannot, or can do so only with much more effort. Even the schizophrenic's actions may become disorganized by distraction—sometimes even rudimentary actions such as walking or rising from a chair.

The difference between the schizophrenic's distractibility and other people's comes down to a matter of control and balance. Virtually everyone can be distracted. We have seen that this is a virtue, at times a life-saver. But during schizophrenic episodes, the distraction keeps disrupting what you are doing and you have extreme difficulty in bringing your attention back. In normal daydreaming, the disruption is usually minor and you can redirect your attention when you really need to.

In a painstaking look at the inner lives of schizophrenics, Nevada psychologist Russell Hurlburt asked four such patients to carry beepers and to write down a detailed description of the thoughts they recalled having just before each signal beep. Afterwards, he interviewed these patients, carefully going over each thought report to assess in even greater detail just what the participant meant by it and what else might have taken place in the experience. He reported his findings in his recent book, *Sampling Normal and Schizophrenic Inner Experience.*

The thoughts these patients reported varied widely. Many of their thought samples were just like those taken from apparently healthy individuals; a good many others were not. Some contained more fragmented or distorted images—"goofed-up images," in one participant's words—than one would find with most nonschizophrenics. Other thought samples contained broken-off thoughts or a crowding together of multiple thoughts and images. At some points, Hurlburt's patients became too disorganized to report coherently at all. However, none of their thought samples had the quality of being lost in daydreams too pleasant to leave behind; and none of the daydreams were elaborate stories of the kind that would constitute a complete fantasy world in competition with the real one.

Of Hurlburt's participants, Sally comes closest to the popular picture of schizophrenics lost in a fantasy world. A young mother, she often hallucinated voices—of about twenty different characters—that interfered with her daily functioning. Because of their apparent power over her, she referred to these characters as "gods." For example, at one beep, Sally was "talking with her mother about Sally's taxes . . . but . . . she was not paying full attention to her mother. Instead, she was attending to the voice of one of the more important gods who was commanding her to look away from her mother . . . but she could not report them because the gods had commanded her not to do so. . . . the sentence the gods spoke was . . . broken off in the middle . . . , told her to look away (which Sally did in fact do), and started off as a low bass voice and rose to the soprano range by the end of the sentence, there was much intonation and inflection . . . , the words were spoken slower than normal. . . . At the same time as this god's voice was being heard, the rest of the gods' voices were heard humming in the background, a sort of buzzing noise with no particular melody. . . . At the same time as both the 'look-away' and the humming . . . Sally was speaking silently to herself (in Dutch), 'I should take a look at Menno (her son)' to make sure that he was asleep."

This experience is daydreamlike in that the voices were spontaneous—Sally did not intend them to begin at that point—and, of course, they are at odds with the real world around her. But in other respects it is very different from normal daydreaming. The voices felt as though they were real and belonged to others. They were peremptory, they were directed at Sally herself, and she experienced no sense of control over them. In fact, she feared their punishment should she disobey them.

These voices are much like the instructions we often give ourselves, instructions we have often copied from our parents, other authorities, and friends. As it happens, hallucinatory voices are probably just that: one's own voice saying things in one's mental imagery, even when it sounds like someone else's. What makes hallucinated voices seem different from one's own is the insistent belief that they originate outside oneself and are beyond one's own control. At this time, no one knows how this erroneous belief originates, but there is no reason to associate it with daydreaming.

In summary, schizophrenics do not daydream more than other people, and their more bizarre thoughts and images are not much like the pleasant daydreams that some earlier theorists thought schizophrenics escaped into. Schizophrenia, like other forms of major mental illness, is something very different from daydreaming. You cannot daydream yourself into mental illness, and if you were mentally ill you would not be daydreaming much more than you would otherwise.

## DO DAYDREAMS WEAKEN OUR GRIP ON REALITY?

One of the important concerns some people have about daydreaming is that if they indulge in it too much, they might lose their ability to distinguish it from reality. But recent research indicates that there is no reason to believe this can happen.

Normal daydreaming has little in common with the hallucinations of schizophrenia, and even heavy daydreaming will not cause you to start hallucinating. However, daydreaming may play a role in memory distortions, and it is often blamed—incorrectly—for the bizarre theories and beliefs called "delusions."

The fear of losing our grip on reality probably arises from the confusion in many people's minds between excessive daydreaming and many schizophrenics' loss of grip on reality. Actually, there are probably only two ways in which a person can confuse fantasy with reality. One is to have a mental image of something and believe that the image is what you are actually seeing or hearing. The classical examples of this kind of confusion are hallucinations: you "hear" voices, "see" visions, "smell" odors, usually bad ones, or experience tastes or bodily sensations that have no basis in reality. The second way is to recall as real something that only happened in your imagination. In this way, which is a distortion of your memory, it may have been clear enough to you at the time of the fantasy that it was not real, but later you remember it as if it were.

Both kinds of mix-up occur to most of us at one time or another. Everyone's memory for events becomes distorted with time. Most of us have at some time wondered whether we really locked the car or only thought about doing it, and a majority of us have at some time thought we heard a voice that was not there. But in some mental disorders these problems become greatly magnified.

A third way to lose your grip on reality is to have a delusion, but this involves persisting in beliefs that, to others, seem clearly erroneous, rather than mistaking fantasy for reality.

**How Daydreams Differ from Delusions**

When we daydream about being Joan of Arc, we know we are pretending. Not only do we not believe we are Joan, but our sense of pretending underscores that we are not. We probably engage in some mental imagery in which we see ourselves as Joan, feel as if we are acting like Joan, hear the sounds of battle, and so on. The delusional individual, on the other hand, has no sense of pretending and believes that he or she is in fact Joan of Arc. There need not even be much mental imagery associated with this belief.

In fact, schizophrenics do not consider their delusions to be daydreams, and rightly so. Delusions are beliefs that certain things are true. In this regard, delusions are no different from other kinds of beliefs that people have about their world, including your belief that the earth is round or that the U.S. Congress is elected. Beliefs such as these are conclusions that we form about reality, and they then serve as background assumptions for the decisions we make and the way we conduct ourselves. They are not daydreams, any more than your beliefs that the world is round and the U.S. Congress is elected are daydreams. Daydreams are neither conclusions nor background assumptions. They may *reflect* our beliefs about ourselves and the world, but they are not the same things as those beliefs. In fact, we can daydream about something opposite to our beliefs. For example, you might have a daydream of what life would be like on a truly flat world, all the while secure in your belief that the world is round.

What makes something a delusion does not ultimately

reside in the daydreams about it; it resides in the *beliefs* that gave rise to the daydreams—or, more precisely, in our judgments about those beliefs. The astronomer who believes in the Big Bang as the start of the universe daydreams about the day when we will all wind up in a black hole. The theologian who believes in an afterlife daydreams about what heaven or hell might be like and about the activities that might get us there. In another place or time, both of their theories might have been regarded as crazy and their daydreams as warped. Yet today in the industrialized West we regard them as perfectly normal daydreams that reflect a legitimate scientific theory and a legitimate theology.

True delusions are psychotic not because they are theories or because they are daydreamlike but for two other reasons. First, delusions are based on beliefs that seem wildly implausible to the rest of us—so implausible that they alert us to look for other signs of disturbance in the individuals who have them. Second, the deluded individual holds to the delusion unshakably even in the face of what seems to the rest of us to be conclusively contrary evidence.

But despite their implausibility, as Harvard psychologist Brendan Maher argues, delusions are probably a person's best attempt to make sense of bizarre experiences. Many schizophrenic patients experience disturbances in their attention, their senses, and even their movements. Without jumping to the conclusion that they are losing their minds, which none of us would like to conclude about ourselves, how should they explain these peculiarities? They search for an explanation, and when they finally find one they are very reluctant to let go of it—and their daydreams are bound to reflect it.

To see how psychologically healthy people would cope with this kind of situation, Danish psychologist Torsten Nielsen rigged up an experiment. Participants were asked to put on a glove, stick their hand into a box, and look through an eyepiece to see into the box. Their task was to trace straight lines on a sheet of paper on the floor of the box. They all found, to their dismay, that their hands tended to curve away from the straight line. They were unable to make their hands do what they wished. Asked for an explanation, participants said such things as "It seems that my hand was moved by magnetism or electricity." "It was done by magic," "I was hypnotized," and "I don't know, but I began to wonder if it was happening because I am homosexual." Two out of twenty-eight participants theorized that the fumbling hand they saw was not their own but an artificial hand controlled by the experimenters. As it happened, they were right. Had this explanation been incorrect, it would have seemed just as paranoid as the others. The point is that even psychologically healthy people come up with bizarre theories when trying to explain the seemingly unexplainable.

But holding erroneous beliefs is something quite different from daydreaming a lot. It is possible to have completely confused beliefs and not daydream much, and it is also possible with those confused beliefs to daydream a great deal. Likewise, people whose hold on reality is completely firm might daydream little or a lot. Whatever a person's beliefs, daydreams are likely to reflect them.

It appears, then, that delusional beliefs produce delusional daydreams, rather than the other way around. Most heavy daydreamers never become delusional. Most delusional people are not heavy daydreamers.

Even though daydreaming does not appear to give rise to delusional ideas, it is possible that daydreaming about a delusion that already exists could strengthen it. This is a possibility because people can and often do confuse their purely mental images with actual experiences; and insofar as they daydream about their delusional beliefs as if they were true, their daydreams are likely to elaborate those beliefs, to put flesh on their bones, and to add to their appearance of reality.

**How Do We Confuse Our Mental Images with Reality?**

We probably follow a simple set of rules to help us tell fantasy from reality. Because the rules are fallible, we can be fooled. Princeton psychologist Marcia Johnson has compiled a number of ways in which real experiences differ from images, and these differences help us to know which is which. For example, things that really happen to us strike us as more detailed than things we simply imagined. Also, when we imagine something, we have a sense of having generated it and of being able to control it, and that gives it a different feel from the way we experience real events. But when images take on some of the properties of real happenings, or when our memories of the real happenings begin to fade, the memories of real events become more like the memories of images. And at that point, there is a chance of confusing the memory of a daydream with reality.

For example, I once wanted to write an important letter but couldn't get to it right away. Quite spontaneously, with no intent to memorize the result, I began to write the letter out in my head in full detail while walking home from my office. Then a number of other important events intervened, including the writing of a good many other letters. A few days after composing the letter in my head, the impression had grown on me that I had actually written it. Only when I was unable to find a file copy of it and tried to reconstruct what had happened did I realize that the letter never actually got written. This was a case of a memory of an image that was nearly as detailed as a memory of writing an actual letter. After a few days, when the memory of actually writing a letter would have begun to fade, I could no longer tell that the memory was only of a daydream.

**Daydreaming May Distort Memories**

We often confuse our mental images with reality in everyday life. This is probably one of the reasons we get into arguments with our spouses about who did what and with our co-workers about how something was bungled. What we imagined doing or what we daydreamed about it later gets mixed up with our memories of the real event.

A striking example of this is what happens to the memories of witnesses at crime scenes. If witnesses are given false suggestions as to what they saw, they often come to believe their erroneous images even when these contradict the original evidence before their own eyes. For example, some students of University of Washington psychologist Elizabeth Loftus once staged thefts to see whether they could influence what eyewitnesses "recall." Two women would enter a public place, one would leave her bag briefly near some other people, and, while the two women were gone, a male student would pretend to take something out of the bag, hide it under his coat, and quickly walk away. When the women returned, the owner of the bag would express great distress about someone having taken her "tape recorder." They would take the telephone number of the witnesses and, a week later, another student posing as an insurance agent would call these witnesses for information about the "theft."

In Loftus' words, "Although there was in fact no tape recorder, over half of the eyewitnesses 'remembered' seeing it, and nearly all of these could describe it in reasonably good detail. Their descriptions were quite different from one another: some said it was gray and others said black; some said it was in a case, others said it was not; some said it had an antenna, others claimed it did not. Their descriptions indicated a rather vivid 'memory' for a tape recorder that was never seen."

The most plausible way of explaining the witnesses' varied memories of a nonexistent tape recorder is that when they heard the words *tape recorder* right after the staged theft, they formed their own image of what such a tape recorder might look like, and that image is what they reported the following week as reality. Very probably, in the course of spontaneous daydreaming, they went over the theft scene in their minds many times, each time rehearsing their seeing the tape recorder; and with each rehearsal they would become more confident that they had really seen it.

As Marcia Johnson has shown, when we keep replaying a mental image, our memories of the image come to seem more like a memory of a real event. Insofar as a repeated daydream misrepresents something real, there is a chance that it will help distort the daydreamer's view of reality.

Suppose, for example, that you believe someone to be your enemy. Suppose further that you have repeated daydreams about what this person could do to you, about what the person might want to do to you, and about what you might do regarding the person. It may eventually become hard to disentangle what you really know or have actually observed about the person from all the negative encounters you have had with the other person in your daydreams. If you now add to this all of the worst things you have heard others say about this person and ignore all the good things, you will end up with a totally distorted view of the other individual. You may end up feeling not only justified but even self-righteous about doing the individual in. Your distorted beliefs will constitute something of a delusion about the person, and your daydreaming would have played a role in solidifying it.

**Can Daydreams Help Strengthen Your Grip on Reality?**

Surprisingly, that is a possibility. Daydreams—even repeated ones—need not have a distorting effect. When you go about a daydream in the spirit of pretending—of "as if"—you will not only keep your daydream distinct from reality, but you may actually improve your appreciation of the difference between them. Pretending, as London psychologist Alan Leslie has documented, is something that nearly everyone learns between about one and two years of age. When a small child picks up a banana and treats it as a telephone receiver, she generally knows full well that it is really a banana and that she is only pretending to speak on the telephone. There is a clear delineation between fantasy and reality, and the act of pretending provides practice in making the distinction.

As a matter of fact, children who engage in relatively fanciful play are better, not worse, than other children at being able to distinguish between fantasy and reality. A team led by Michigan psychologist Eli Saltz has even shown that children from culturally disadvantaged homes can be trained through play to improve their ability to make that distinction, along with improving their intellectual functioning in general.

Saltz's team tried out storytelling and different kinds of play with preschoolers and then compared their intellectual growth with that of preschoolers who went through standard preschool activities, such as cutting and pasting, fingerpainting, and identifying animals in a picture book. To test the children's ability to distinguish fantasy from reality, the investigators showed them pictures of various scenes and asked them whether each scene was possible or impossible. The group who did best on this test were those who had spent much of the year enacting fairy tales.

This is one more indication that, far from nudging children into psychosis, experience with fanciful play and storytelling builds their imaginations as it firms up their grip on reality. There is every reason to believe that normal fanciful daydreaming yields the same benefit.

## HOW MUCH DAYDREAMING IS TOO MUCH?

Perhaps the most common questions people have about daydreaming concern whether you can daydream too much and how you can tell when you reach that point. The evidence from the research we have seen suggests an answer: daydreaming as such can probably not damage you psychologically; the question is one of balance. At the point where the very positive benefits of daydreaming are outweighed by missed opportunities in real life—at the point where fantasy unduly displaces reality—you have reached the point of excessive daydreaming.

One can do too much of anything. It *is* possible to spend too much time daydreaming, and it is clearly possible to daydream at the wrong times. When you are swiveling a construction crane, taking a timed examination, or controlling air traffic, you are ill-advised to do much daydreaming.

If your daydreaming hinders you from reaching important life goals, rather than supplementing and enriching your life, then you are daydreaming too much. In judging whether you are, the key question to ask yourself is what you would do if you were not daydreaming. Would it release time and energy that you could realistically devote to goals that are more satisfying than the daydreaming they replace?

Where that point lies is very much an individual matter. Whenever we face a question of "too much," the answer depends on answers to two further kinds of questions: Too much for what purposes, or for whose purposes? And how much more important are those purposes—and to whom—than the alternatives? If you are a teacher giving a lesson you hold to be important, then for purposes of getting your lesson across a daydreaming pupil is daydreaming too much. If you are the pupil, bored with the lesson and more concerned about making a good impression at tonight's pajama party, the daydreaming is appropriate. As a teacher, you may be aware of life goals whose importance a pupil may not recognize until much later; or you may be thinking in terms of societal values, such as valuing wisdom, developing character, or outcompeting a foreign economy. Therefore, you do what you can to make your lesson seem more urgent; you enliven, coax, plead, or offer rewards or threats. However, there is still a legitimate clash of opinions about importance. The fact that you have not persuaded your pupil does not impugn the pupil's mental health.

Most people who daydream a great deal usually do so without crippling their real relationships or their productivity. From their own reports, they enjoy daydreaming and reap its benefits. It fills the spaces not occupied by work and social relating, enlivens time spent waiting, and serves as a resource for mental recuperation and private entertainment.

For many, it replaces in whole or part the fabricated fantasies of television, of theaters and opera, and of sports and print media, in which most Americans spend large parts of each waking day. These spectator activities bring their benefits—which include stimulating our real daydreams—as well as their costs, but whether we prefer them to our own internally generated daydreams is a matter of taste.

**Excessive Daydreaming**

People who daydream to the point of excess—rather than simply a great deal—do so because in one way or another their real lives have stalled, not because daydreaming is irresistibly attractive to them. Despite the popular notion of daydreaming as escape, people do not escape into daydreams so much as they daydream by default. Those of us who are most in need of an escape end up with the most unpleasant daydreams, daydreams we dislike and would not choose to escape into. Those of us most intensely and successfully engaged with life have the most pleasant daydreams, but we are clearly not escaping into them. Daydreams multiply when we have time on our hands and when what we are doing is relatively undemanding.

Therefore, the most likely reason for excessive daydreaming is being stymied in important areas of our lives, or having lost confidence in being able to help ourselves. Excessive daydreamers may be deeply depressed. When their real lives are stuck, there is less that they can do about their lives with much hope of succeeding. Therefore, they do less, and that leaves large mental spaces for daydreaming. They may be daydreaming a lot, but their daydreams are likely to be marked by depression, anger, fear, and guilt—a more or less faithful reflection of how they view their prospects, and not the kind of haven people choose to escape into.

Much the same goes for lonely people. If unhappy people escaped into daydreams, you would expect lonely people to launch into vivid daydreams of warm relationships with others. But that is not the way it is. A team of communication researchers in Louisiana, Renee Edwards, James Honeycutt, and Kenneth Zagacki, found that the lonelier students reported fewer daydreams of interacting with others, not more. Presumably, lonely people have fewer others to relate to in reality, and they therefore have fewer people to daydream about interacting with. Those daydreams about interactions that they do have are less detailed, less likely to relieve their tension, and overall neither more nor less pleasant than the interpersonal daydreams of students who are not lonely. Obviously, lonely people do not create many escapist daydreams for themselves, and the ones that occur to them spontaneously are nothing to escape into.

*The real problem with excessive daydreaming.* When people are said to daydream excessively, we usually mean that they engage in too little observable activity of the kind we judge to be good for them. When that happens, it is not the daydreaming that is the problem; the problem resides in the factors that keep these people from moving toward their goals. They may be depressed over a loss, stymied in their pursuit of goals crucial to them, faced by their own or another's serious illness, or forced by circumstances to live a life not of their choosing. On the other hand, their problems may be largely psychological. They may range from ignorance of options and coping strategies to a paralyzing level of inner conflict. Their own fears, inhibitions, pessimism, or low self-regard may be preventing such people from going after what they really want. If excessive daydreamers knew how to get their lives moving again, they would do it, and the amount of time they seem to devote to daydreaming would decrease as they became reengaged in more active living.

For example, Isidora is in many ways a talented and successful young woman, but she is given to bouts of depression and resentment. When something goes wrong, or when something simply fails to go right, she goes into a funk and broods about her difficulties. She visualizes herself as a kind of Calamity Jane for whom everything important that she touches turns to muck. In her daydreams she imagines the disasters awaiting her in her career, her relationships, and her health. She feels ugly and unlovable, and she imagines how others must feel in dealing with her—tolerant, perhaps, and even supportive out of pity for her, but, behind their facades, indifferent, contemptuous, and rejecting. The net effect of all these daydreams is to worsen her depression, to magnify her reverses out of all proportion and thereby to prolong the depression far more than it would have lasted with more positive daydreams.

Furthermore, with this gloomy assessment of others, supported and deepened by her daydreams, Isidora herself becomes irritable and oversensitive. Minor lapses on the part of others, or perhaps well-intended words that Isidora has misinterpreted, offend her deeply. They confirm her gloomy daydreams and sharpen her resentments. People can sense all this and begin to withdraw from her. Her daydreams, unrealistic though they were, have become self-fulfilling prophecies.

There are ways out of situations such as this. The most important thing Isidora could have done would be to focus on her daydreams and examine them, rather than just experience them. She might have recognized what her daydreams were telling her: that she was afraid of failure, distrustful of her own abilities and of others' good will toward her, and in need of reassurance and support. Then she might have taken her assumptions about her future and about others' feelings toward her and checked them against all of her life experiences, not only against the discouraging ones she featured in her gloomy daydreams. She would have realized that she had succeeded at many important things and that there is only slender evidence of the automatic rejection she expects from others. She could then have made realistic plans for finding reassurance and support and for ensuring a rosier future. If she felt incapable of doing that in her everyday personal and work relationships, she might have sought out a psychotherapist to work with her on developing her personal resources for coping.

*When you needn't worry*. Many people worry about their daydreaming quite needlessly. There are no hidden problems behind their daydreams and, in all the ways we have seen in this book, the daydreams themselves are often a positive resource.

For example, Magda worried that her wild, flamboyant fantasies put her on the edge of losing her mind. She did, in fact, spend a fair portion of her time engrossed in elaborate daydreams. Especially when she had to wait for someone, while she rode the bus, as she did dishes, and sometimes while she made love, Magda created an imaginary life for herself, one that she peopled with characters out of her real life or with ones she invented. She enjoyed these fantasies. They not only kept her from being bored, they positively stimulated her. She had a sense of creation from them and a sense of having been entertained. Sometimes she would become so absorbed that she would forget to do something on time or would fail to notice someone she knew who had arrived a few minutes earlier; but except for occasional minor embarrassments, these incidents never compromised her overall functioning. She was still a valued professional and she still had the affection of her friends. But she had heard about people daydreaming their way into schizophrenia, and she was worried about what she might be doing to herself.

Partly because of her concern, Magda volunteered to participate in a research project on fantasy. There she learned that there were no indications that she was in danger of becoming psychotic. She received assurances that even heavy, highly imaginative daydreaming does not cause schizophrenia, and that, as long as she was leading a satisfying life outside her daydreams, she could keep right on enjoying them.

## DO DAYDREAMS SAP MOTIVATION OR WEAKEN RESISTANCE TO TEMPTATION?

For many years, mental-health workers thought that daydreaming about something you want was so satisfying that it could serve as a partial substitute for the real thing. They accepted the assumption of psychoanalysts that by satisfying yourself in fantasy, you would be less motivated to strive for it in reality. But this idea, too, appears in light of research to be mistaken. In fact, daydreaming about something probably makes you more eager for the real thing than you were before.

Whether daydreaming helps or hurts you in this regard depends on how and when you do it. It can help you to strengthen your resolve to do something, or it can nudge you into actions you might otherwise have forgone. You can keep yourself motivated toward a goal by thinking about the good things that reaching it will bring, which arouses your emotions and desire. At the same time, your daydreams are rehearsals for ways to reach your goal, which can increase your confidence and make you more willing to pursue it. On the other hand, if you daydream about something that you would be better off forgoing, these very same consequences of daydreaming about it will make it harder for you to resist temptation.

For example, California psychologist Walter Mischel and his students told children that they could have a choice of two things, such as a marshmallow or a pretzel, but first they had to wait while the experimenter did something in another room. If they waited for the experimenter to come back, they could have their favorite item, such as the marshmallow. If they couldn't wait any longer, they could ring a bell to bring back the experimenter; but then they would have to take the less desirable item, such as the pretzel. Some children were instructed to spend the time while they waited thinking about the food; others were told to think about something else. The group that kept their minds on the food rang the bell on the average much earlier than the second group did. Thinking about the food weakened their ability to wait, even though ringing the bell meant that they would get a less attractive reward.

This does not mean that being a heavy daydreamer makes

you impulsive. People who daydream a lot seem to be just about as self-controlled as anyone else, and there is some evidence that imaginative people have greater control over their emotions. But dwelling on something you want may make it a bit harder for you to put off pursuing it, even when waiting would be prudent.

CHAPTER 9

# Preoccupation, Worry, and Obsessive Daydreams: What They Tell Us and Ways to Deal with Them

We become preoccupied in many different ways. They include:

- healthy preoccupation
- normal worrying
- rumination
- counterproductive worrying
- obsessional thoughts

In healthy preoccupation, we spend a lot of time working over in our daydreams and other thoughts some major project or interest of ours, whether it is an upcoming marriage, an archaeological expedition, a major business deal, or a religious conversion.

In normal worrying, our daydreams are still spontaneously performing their usual positive functions of scanning our past and future for dangers, opportunities, and lessons to learn, and differ from healthy preoccupation mostly by the negative emotions—the apprehension, sorrow, anger, shame, and guilt—that color them.

In rumination, we spend a lot of time daydreaming and otherwise thinking about the same issue well past the point of accomplishing anything.

In counterproductive worrying, distress-ridden daydreams keep cycling through the same topics long past the point of benefiting us.

In obsessional thoughts, we repeatedly experience involuntary daydreams, usually very brief, of something upsetting that we wish did not keep occurring to us.

On balance, most of these forms of daydreaming perform positive functions, and none is by itself very harmful. They do all exact a certain cost, in that they tend to interrupt or crowd out other thoughts you might have had instead. Also, all reflect some kind of challenge, stress, or conflict you are under, and constant worrying might intensify the effect of the stress on your body by prolonging and heightening the negative emotions associated with it.

The main reason we consider the various forms of worrying and obsession to be problems is because of their emotional consequences. Constant worried daydreaming keeps those negative emotions aroused in us and makes us unhappy; and those of us with obsessional daydreams often find them frightening and worrisome. Fortunately, there are ways to deal with them and turn them to our benefit.

## HEALTHY PREOCCUPATION

Most people become preoccupied with matters that are important to them when they are faced with new opportunities, threats to the things they value, or the loss of someone or something dear to them.

Each of these sets up a current concern that, as described in Chapter 2, disposes us to react emotionally when something happens to remind us of it. When we react, we are very likely to have a daydream or other thought about the concern of which it reminded us. We become preoccupied if one of our concerns is about something unusually important and emotionally laden, because then many kinds of cues, including many provided by our own thoughts, will trigger the emotional reactions that start daydreams—and will do so strongly enough to override other things we might have thought about at that point. This is the most plausible explanation for healthy preoccupation, and, as we shall see, it helps explain worrying and obsessional daydreams as well.

As an example of healthy preoccupation, Melanie kept daydreaming about the new major fact in her life: she was pregnant. The test had shown it, and now she knew that her life would never again be quite the same. She wanted the child, as did Jeff; with any luck, they would be parents. In the weeks that followed, Melanie sorted through her life from this new point of view. Nearly everything she did, nearly everything she encountered, reminded her of something she would be doing differently, something she would not be able to do for a while, something she would be able to do now for the first time, something that she needed to plan or prepare for, or someone with whom she would have parenting in common or from whom she might now grow apart.

She continued to sell insurance with as much success as before. Perhaps her excitement about her pregnancy infected her customers, raising their spirits and their willingness to buy. But sometimes it was a struggle to pull herself back from long reveries—about what was happening to her body, about whether the baby would be a boy or a girl, about childbirth, about the child's future room, or about the effect on her and Jeff's relationships with their parents—and refocus on the world of whole life and actuarial tables. This was all the harder because the things she was working on themselves kept sending her into new daydreams. What would her child's life expectancy be? What kind of insurance should she get to protect the child's future? What kind of future would it be, anyway? Melanie was thoroughly preoccupied by her pregnancy in a perfectly healthy way. She needed to think those things through, to test out her future in her thoughts.

## WORRIED DAYDREAMS

Just as healthy preoccupation prepares us for meeting new challenges and threats, so does the kind of more apprehensive daydreaming we call worrying. For example, suppose you find out that you must have surgery. If you live out your fears ahead of time, gathering information and trying it out in daydreams, you will gain a more realistic view of what is in store for you and, most likely, you will react with less upset and stress as you go through the surgery and convalescence. Psychologist Dennis Turk showed that even young children do better in the hospital when they are willing to play out and fantasize their concerns beforehand.

### How Worry Comes About

Worry comes about in the same way as healthy preoccupation: we are driven from daydream to daydream by our emotional reactions. When something is very important to us, many kinds of things are likely to remind us of it. When something reminds us of it, we react emotionally, which means that internally we also start to act; and internal action means daydreaming or other thinking. In the case of worrying, the emotions are mostly negative and the daydreams often anguished.

Worrying tends to feed on itself, because the reminders that trigger these worried daydreams are largely part of our own thought stream. If you have just had a fight with your lover, you may be replaying the argument in a daydream, and as you recreate what your lover said, you get angrier. One reason for your anger might be that you feel especially vulnerable now, perhaps because you have given up other friendships and need this lover more than the lover needs you. As your daydream previews your future moments of loneliness and isolation, you feel afraid, and this surge of fear brings back images of how you suffered with loneliness in the past and how you coped with it or failed to cope with it. Now you experience some self-doubt, perhaps some self-disappointment, and wonder whether anything in your love life will ever work right for you. You suffer a pang of grief at that thought and begin to daydream about your previous relationship and the awful way it ended, which brings you back to the fight you just had. You imagine some of your current lover's least desirable qualities and wonder why you ever put up with them. But as you picture your lover in your imagination you now also see some of the things that attracted you, that you love, and begin to daydream scenarios of reconciliation. And so on.

One thought leads to another by arousing a new burst of emotion that carries with it a new line of mental action. If the issue is important enough to you, the emotions associated with your worry will be strong enough to outcompete the other reactions you might have had. In this way, you stay locked into the same basic theme. If something does finally interrupt you, such as your supervisor bringing you a new assignment, something else will soon again remind you of the fight and your worrying will continue.

**Breaking the Worry Cycle**

A certain amount of worrying is healthy and productive, but occasionally we feel burdened and troubled by it. Perhaps you keep daydreaming about something in the past from which you have extracted all the lessons to be drawn and about which nothing more can usefully be done. Perhaps your daydreams and other thoughts keep going in circles, repeating and tiresomely belaboring the same old themes. And perhaps they interfere with things such as work, studies, or sleep. At that point, worrying has become counterproductive and you will probably want to stop it. Fortunately, there are at least three ways to break out of the worry cycle:

- structuring the problems you are concerned about, perhaps committing them to paper, and marshaling your resources for dealing with them
- clarifying the real problems behind the worried daydreams and dealing with them
- setting aside time periods for daydreaming about your inescapable worries

*Structuring problems and marshaling resources.* Your worried daydreams about the fight with your lover could have gone differently. Suppose that, instead of reacting with self-doubt and self-disappointment, you recalled that you know how to make friends and get along with people. This realization opens up new possibilities to you, so that instead of tumbling into fears of loneliness, you start daydreaming about a more positive new life without this lover. You daydream about calling old friends, taking a vacation likely to yield new friendships, or enrolling in an evening class. In effect, you draw up a set of plans for going forward from here, and you resolve, in case your fight turns into a breakup, to carry them out. As you visualize an alternative future in your daydreaming you feel more in control of your life—better able to control the damage a breakup might do. Therefore, the urgency passes: you feel personally less threatened by the fight, and some of the emotional intensity goes out of the incident. As you calm down, you are better able to turn your mind to other things.

Now we have a possible positive ending for your worried daydreaming alongside the earlier gloomy one. The two endings might have been for two different people, one full of self-doubt and the other self-assured; but they could also be two alternatives entertained by the same person, and as such they point a way toward dealing with situations such as this:

focusing on a situation that "has you going" constructively and imaginatively, laying out your options, and making contingency plans. If the situation is complex enough, it helps to do this in writing to keep track of the complexities.

When you feel you have done as much as you can do about a problem at a given point in time, you will have settled yourself down somewhat. The problem that preoccupied you—whether it is a shaky relationship, trouble at your job, or a sick child—will still be there but will seem under better control. You will feel less vulnerable, and you will be able to get on with your life—your relationships, work, or recreation—without interrupting yourself as much with the worried daydreams that had preoccupied you.

*Thoughts going in all directions because you are overwhelmed.* Sometimes you are preoccupied not with only one issue but with so many that you feel overwhelmed. Your mind is peppered with spontaneous thoughts—a form of daydream—about pressing matters other than the pressing one you are working on at the moment. Your mind feels disorganized and you are getting less productive exactly when you need all the efficiency you can muster.

As you try to prepare a presentation for the day after tomorrow, a brief daydream of your sick child runs through your mind, along with images of your leaving work early to attend to him. That reminds you that the plumber is due in the morning, and you imagine being delayed by that and daydream about trying awkwardly to get away to your presentation. You turn back to preparing it, but your mind cuts away to a brief daydream of getting to the airport right after your presentation for a business trip, which reminds you that you mustn't forget the various things you need for the trip, whereupon you start spontaneously visualizing your home and gathering them all up. In your daydream you go to your desk, which reminds you that you really need to write those seven letters and pay some bills before you take off, and there are the telephone calls to make and the flight to reconfirm.

And so it goes. You go into a worried daydream of your sitter canceling at the last minute, a flash of yourself picking up the suit from the cleaners, and—still spontaneously and unbidden—visualize what you will do for dinner tonight. Consequently, you make little progress on your presentation.

As you worry about forgetting some important part of all that, your anxiety level rises and everything you start to do seems to remind you of some other thing you need to do, which you then imagine doing.

These frantic, starkly realistic little daydreams are carrying out one of the important functions of daydreaming: to remind you of your agenda, to keep you alert to the important things going on in your life. When your agenda gets overcrowded, so does your daydreaming.

In my own experience, the same solution works here as in the previous example: structure the situation, organize the options, and marshal resources. In this situation, I make lists. By putting all the demands on me down on paper, perhaps with an indication of when I need to take care of them, I have relieved my mind of having to keep track of them all. In a sense, the whole list has become programmed, my anxiety level has dropped, and I am better able to tackle the items one by one without constantly interrupting myself with worried daydreams.

Something similar seems to work for athletes. West German psychologist Jürgen Beckmann—who is, among other things, a sports psychologist—describes a procedure used by some coaches before a big game. To keep players from being too distracted by the things on their mind, they are advised to make a list of all their concerns and place them in a box until after the game. Coaches and players report that doing this keeps their minds freer to focus on the action.

*Identifying the real problem.* When our worried daydreams impair our ability to pursue important goals, it is time, if possible, to come to grips with the things we worry about.

However, sometimes we have an erroneous idea of what they really are. Then the first task is to identify them.

Fred is an example of someone who needed to find out the real causes of his distraction. He came to me for help with his studies. He described putting in many hours in front of his assigned readings, but much of that time his mind was elsewhere. If his friends were planning to go to the bar, he daydreamed about them sitting in the bar and having a good time. He saw himself cut off from them by staying home, and then he imagined himself with his friends, an image he liked much better. Or, during his reading, he daydreamed being with a woman he liked or about going home to his parents over the weekend and how the visit would go. Fred pulled himself back out of his daydreams periodically, pictured himself failing his next test, and worried about his future. In between, he read snatches of his textbook. But, since what he read was separated by daydreams into little fragments, he read much of it without understanding its context, without seeing connections, and, not surprisingly, he had trouble understanding it. It was like trying to plough hard, rocky ground.

Fred knew that he had a problem, which he formulated to himself as being unable to concentrate and as finding the readings too hard. Until we sat down to talk about it, he had failed to see that his daydreams were about the things in his life that were of paramount importance to him. He needed warm human contact more than he needed to read any particular assignment. He needed his friends and his family, both for the good times they offered and as reassurance that he was loved, that he would not be abandoned.

Fred had never before made these connections in his mind. He only knew that he kept going into daydream reveries that happened to be about his friends and his family. He could not formulate his actual problem: the conflict between the rigors of being a good student and his hunger for human contact. At a rational level, Fred said that he wanted to do well in college but kept falling prey to his mindwandering. At the level of his emotions, he had another, more pressing agenda of continual human contact. This other agenda was "unconscious" in the sense that he could not have reported it to anyone in so many words, but his daydreams provided unmistakable raw material for recognizing it.

Behind the conflict between studying and being sociable were, of course, further problems: the extent to which Fred needed constant social contact, the immaturity of his social relationships, and his insecurity about what would happen to his relationships if he stayed behind to study. Working directly on these problems would eventually free his mind for concentrated work on his studies.

*Scheduling time for worried daydreaming.* When circumstances keep us worrying, it may be helpful to arrange set times for daydreaming about these worries.

For Eva, coming to grips with her real problems was not enough; they were too numerous and too rooted in reality. Eva daydreamed a lot, but she did not enjoy her daydreams, because so many of them were filled with visions of crises in her life, fearful images of problems she might encounter, yearning for her boyfriend and the things they might do together, and a great variety of other things, some of them entertaining and hopeful, many of them normal and humdrum. She knew that she had trouble concentrating on her studies, and she blamed that on her constant mindwandering. One day she visited her college counseling office to find out what she could do about it.

Eva's emotions were much more tied up with things outside her studies than in them, and there were a great many of them. She felt a constant need for reassurance that only a close relationship could give, but her boyfriend had stayed behind in their hometown when she went to college. Although they often saw each other on weekends, she was apprehensive about losing him. Because her first grades had been marginal, she worried about losing her financial aid.

Her father had recently suffered a coronary, and she was very worried about the chance that he might die. She had many differences with her roommate—about the friends her roommate brought in at all hours, about her friend's loud music, and about tidiness. She would have liked to move out but felt she could not afford to.

Eva was taking courses required by her program, but the courses had little appeal for her. As she sat down to study for them, her mind would drift to her other concerns. Her reading itself often triggered thoughts about her boyfriend, her father, and her roommate. And then, as she caught herself once again having read a page without absorbing anything, she imagined losing her scholarship and feeling disgraced, and she felt despair.

To help her gain perspective on her situation, Eva listed all of the real-life concerns that preyed on her mind and decided what she could do about them, what actions she would have to put off, and what things were beyond her doing anything about. She focused on making as many plans, including contingency plans, as it seemed sensible to make. Just organizing her life in this way had a calming effect. She felt, if not in command of fate, at least in control of what she could do. She felt fewer fears of her life racing out of control and less concern about forgetting things important to her or missing opportunities to reach her goals.

But Eva also used a second technique, because she could not dispel her uncertainties completely. She still worried about her father's health, about losing her boyfriend and her financial aid, and about the conflicts with her roommate. To help keep these worries from intruding on her studies, she used a method pioneered by Pennsylvania psychologist Thomas Borkovec that recognized her psychological need to worry and allowed for the benefits of daydreaming. She set aside a special half-hour time period each day during which to think about her concerns—a scheduled worry session—and tried to postpone her worrying to those daily sessions. In this way, she was able to reduce greatly the amount of time spent worrying during other activities. As a result, she was better able to concentrate on her studies, her apprehension about failing lifted, and her confidence began to return.

## SELF-PERPETUATING DAYDREAMS

Anger, sexual arousal, and fear may intensify and protract your preoccupation with daydreams about them. This is because the daydream images they evoke in turn heighten the emotions that gave rise to them, and the heightened emotional arousal triggers further daydreams in the same vein. It is a circular process, one that can turn vicious.

### Anger

When we are angry, we think angry thoughts and entertain angry daydreams. We often replay the injuries done to us and the unfair advantages obtained by our antagonists. For example, college student Rip had built an elaborate welcome sign for his campus's homecoming; two days later, he found it lying broken on the ground. That afternoon, our beeper caught him still brooding about it. As he said to himself, "I wish I could pulverize the people that knocked down my sign," he was daydreaming a vivid, exaggerated image of doing just that. This kind of daydreaming increases our anger and leads to yet more angry brooding. In the end, we may be ready to exact more retribution than we were to start with, and revenge will seem sweet.

Numerous experiments have borne this out. When researchers enable angry people to brood about the injustices done them, they stay angry or get angrier. Given opportunities to hurt innocent bystanders, they are readier than usual to do so, but doing it does not get back at the person who angered them and therefore does not reduce their anger or their willingness to attack their original adversary.

What does work to reduce anger is distraction. That is why vigorous exercise such as tennis can calm you down—

not, as once thought, because it helps to displace the anger onto the tennis ball or your opponent, but because it distracts you from the reminders of what made you angry and lets your anger dwindle with time. Anything that effectively distracts you is likely to have an equally beneficial effect.

The trick is to substitute new, nonangry emotions for the anger. This can be done in at least three ways:

- by turning your attention to emotions behind the anger
- by reframing the situation to that of a problem to solve
- by distracting yourself with something irrelevant to your anger

Often the anger is a last-ditch reaction to avert some other, more painful emotional reaction to the same incident, such as hurt, depression, or embarrassment. Unpleasant though these emotions are, it may often be more constructive to identify them and deal with them as the real consequences of the damage done by your antagonist than to stay preoccupied with angry daydreams and plans for revenge. If you are unable to identify these other emotions, a competent therapist can help you to do that.

People who have trouble controlling their anger may benefit by breaking off the angry daydream images that sustain their anger and substituting in their daydreams constructive ways of dealing with the situation that provoked them. Sometimes that means learning new techniques for handling those situations. For instance, if an argument provoked the anger, it might be necessary to learn new ways to react to the other person—methods that get you some of what you want without unnecessarily damaging your relationship. In other instances, it might be necessary only to remind yourself of possible solutions you already know about and to use them before you get carried away.

Having an angry daydream about someone can be a signal that you have a problem to deal with. Instead of getting stuck in the rut of angry daydreaming, you can acknowledge the problem with the other person, acknowledge your anger, and then try out some constructive solutions in your daydreams.

The last option is to sap your anger by getting deeply involved in some other activity, whether it be work that you enjoy, sports, or some other absorbing pastime. As long as you are aware of your discontent and take the most constructive steps you can to solve the problem that evoked it, there is no advantage in staying angry.

**Sex**

Sexual arousal probably works in parallel ways. Once you get sexually aroused, you are likely to engage in daydreams about enjoying sex or locating someone to have sex with. These daydreams are likely to keep you aroused or arouse you further, which in turn stimulates new daydreams of sexual activity or actions to translate them into reality—the very picture of being "horny." In the absence of real sexual gratification, this continues unless or until you get absorbed in some other kind of activity or some other emotion breaks into the cycle, such as anger over sexual frustration, guilt about having sexual thoughts, or fear of embarrassment. Or you might simply cut off the daydreams because they conflict with whatever else you are already doing.

**Fear**

When we are afraid, we play out our fears in our daydreams. Sometimes, of course, this leads us to think of ways to protect ourselves, which both lowers our fear and prepares us to cope; but if we still feel exposed and vulnerable after doing all that we can think of doing, the fearful daydreams will maintain or increase our fear. Being afraid, we are more likely to spot reminders of the threat or even to read threats into things that are not threatening, and these will then trigger more fearful daydreams, which further heighten fear and cause us to sense still more threat from the outside world.

This has been demonstrated experimentally, but the everyday world offers its own illustrations. Anyone who has sat around a campfire listening to ghost stories knows how much more threatening the surrounding woods seem than they were before. Coming home from a horror film, you may feel afraid to walk down into your basement. You imagine robbers and burglars or creatures from the netherworld, and you play it safe. Fear begets fear, and it shows up in our daydream images.

Often, people who are afraid of something rehearse their fears over and over in their daydreams. Consider, for instance, someone afraid of flying. Most of us have a probably instinctive fear of being up high without clear-cut support. Most of us are also aware that in an airplane there is nothing between us and the ground except air. Some of us become unsettled enough by realizing this that we become fearful when we think of flying. Such people might repeatedly visualize taking off in a plane and having something go wrong. They sense their own fear in their imaginary predicament and may visualize the horror of those around them; conjure up images of people praying, screaming, or frozen with fear; and imagine the aircraft disintegrating, fire breaking out, and the plane eventually crashing in a fiery finale.

Who would want to fly after that? And, of course, it could really happen to any of us who fly. On the other hand, the probability of it happening is extremely small, much smaller than the proportion of daydreams that end that way for the frightened traveler.

There are solutions to this fear besides staying out of airplanes. One simple-seeming solution, which combines methods called *desensitization* (extinguishing fear by exposing you to what you fear) and *covert rehearsal* (imagining doing something), is to take charge of the daydream and imagine a favorable experience. To be convincing, it helps to look at the statistics on the risks of crashing as compared to other risks in life. Given some rational belief in air safety, you can then relax and repeatedly daydream good experiences in aircraft involving the sheer aesthetics of flight, the surge of power on takeoff, the smooth lift to high altitude, the dramatic vistas, good service, a certain camaraderie, the drama of descent, the seeming miracle of a runway appearing beneath the craft as it approaches the ground, a punctual arrival at the gate, and the benefits that await you at your destination.

This relatively simple approach will not work for everyone. Some will need the reassurance and guidance of a competent therapist; others will need more extensive work with guided daydreams or other therapeutic approaches. But for many, repeating positive daydreams is likely to reduce gradually the level of apprehension and fear. Eventually, actually boarding airplanes and confirming in reality the pleasant scenarios of the daydreams will be likely to bring fear down to a normal level.

## WORRIED DAYDREAMS THAT PERSIST: GRIEF AND DEPRESSION

The worried daydreams that accompany grief or depression do not lend themselves to such neat solutions. In fact, they may be an essential part of working through those emotions and laying them to rest.

We grieve about losses. Perhaps someone close to us has died, our marriage has broken up, we have lost a valued job or bodily function, or our house has burned down. Or perhaps we have only moved away from our good friends. Depending on how important the loss is to us, it is only human to grieve.

There are many dimensions to grief, but one of them is preoccupation. If the loss is of a person, we will find plenty of reminders of that person, and each one will trigger a burst of emotion—often a pang of grief—as well as daydreams and other thoughts. Often, the reveries that arise generate their own reminders and keep the preoccupation going.

Suppose it is Wednesday and, as you think about what you will do tonight, you remember that you will not be doing it with Jean, whom you often saw Wednesday evenings. You experience a sinking feeling, a pang, and visualize one of those evenings. It reminds you of plans you had made for a summer vacation, and you longingly imagine how such a vacation might have been, but you quickly remind yourself that now it cannot take place and experience another pang. You review what you can do instead and conclude that none of the alternatives excites you very much. You feel rather bitter and empty, and you wonder whether you will ever get over the loss. And so on.

This process is part of what is sometimes called "grief-work," and it is probably a necessary part of taking leave from someone or something you value. A team of investigators from Georgia, psychologists Millar, Tesser, and Millar, studied what happened to women as they moved away from home to college. The more the move interfered with a close relationship, the more preoccupied these women were at first with the person they had left behind.

This process of severing ties is not completely automatic, and the longer it takes, the longer people are likely to stay depressed. Psychologist Rosalind Cartwright studied the dreams of women who had recently been divorced. The women whose dreams dwelt on the issues raised by the divorce got over their depression faster than the women who failed to confront those issues in their dreams. Cartwright's findings do not tell us whether dreaming about the divorce itself shortened their grieving, but clinical psychologists such as James K. Morrison and Anees Sheikh have found it useful to guide patients through images associated with their loss as a way of expediting and completing the grieving process. All in all, it seems likely that a certain amount of preoccupation with a loss may be essential to liberating oneself from its grip.

Those of us who are grieving a loss usually know that we are distracted and can tell why, but not always. Many people have not made the connection between their losses on the one hand and their depressions, along with their worried daydreams, on the other. They know that things sometimes go wrong for them, that they are sometimes depressed, and that they sometimes have trouble concentrating; and yet they may not realize that they become depressed *because of* the reverses they have experienced or that their distracted mental state is tied to their depression.

Although some individuals are biologically more susceptible than others to becoming depressed, normal everyday depression is likely to be a reaction to a loss or failure. When depressed individuals recognize what it is that depressed them, they have a better chance to deal with it and to put it in perspective.

Looking carefully at their daydreams may provide clues to their loss. If they can turn the loss into a problem to solve, their daydreaming will become calmer and more constructive and will likely intrude less on their minds when they are trying to concentrate on something else.

## OBSESSIONAL DAYDREAMS

Robert Morphy, a former Gestalt therapy patient, related the following experience. "I used to walk down the street thinking of choking women I saw or grabbing at men's dicks. I don't know how often I'd have these thoughts, probably hundreds of times a day. These thoughts sometimes terrified me. I was afraid I'd do it. Yet I knew I didn't want to. I had no control over the thoughts, had no idea of where they came from or why I couldn't get rid of them."

Like Robert Morphy, a few of us experience a barrage of ideas or images that seem out of our control and that frighten us. We may wish we didn't have these thoughts, but the thoughts pop up nevertheless. These are what psychologists and psychiatrists label "obsessions."

Obsessions may not seem much like daydreams, because they are usually so short—just flashes of imagery and impulse—and feel so uncontrollable, but they are probably an aberration of normal daydreams. Certainly they are fanciful; in them, you imagine yourself doing something that you would ordinarily rule out. And like many daydreams, they begin spontaneously; you did not set out to have them. Apart from the fact that they are likely to keep repeating, the most dramatic difference between obsessional thoughts and normal daydreams is in the person's reaction to them, rather than in their content or the way they start. Unlike our reactions to most daydreams, the obsessional person reacts with revulsion and anxiety and, if these thoughts continue, is likely to seek psychological treatment.

Because they seem so uncontrollable and clash so much with the person's intentions and values, obsessional daydreams often seem crazy to those who have them. They therefore give rise to the fear of "losing your mind," of psychotic illness. Actually, obsessive thoughts do not usually lead to anything more severe. Apart from your emotional reaction to them, they need not of themselves interfere appreciably with normal functioning on the job or in personal relationships. Reactions to them, however, can be quite severe. For example, you might develop elaborate rituals to avoid obsessive thoughts or suffer serious anxiety or depression at the realization of having them. Also, as we shall see, they often indicate being out of touch with your feelings; and because your feelings provide essential information about yourself, being out of touch with them interferes with knowing yourself and with making sound decisions. The bad decisions can in turn cut you off from realizing your potential, can sour your relationships with others, and can ultimately undermine your health.

Obessional daydreams such as Morphy's are only one form of something called obsessive-compulsive disorder. There are a number of other forms. For example, sometimes the thoughts are about things the person fears strongly, such as contamination by germs or his heart stopping, and then they are likely to be accompanied by compulsive behavior, such as overly frequent hand-washing or elaborate precautions to stay away from possible contamination, such as avoiding shaking hands or touching doorknobs. These kinds of conditions present different problems from the kind of obsessional daydreams Morphy describes and may involve different kinds of treatment. What I have to say here does not refer to these other kinds of obsessions and compulsions.

Obsessive thoughts themselves can be about any of many different things but, as with Morphy, they are often violent or sexual in nature. One person might have an image of dropping a baby whenever holding one; another might suddenly imagine killing a loved relative; a heterosexual man might, like Morphy, imagine grabbing other men's penises; a pious individual might imagine uttering blasphemous language, or a peaceful one might visualize herself cutting off her own hand. In most instances, these are very short, daydreamlike episodes. They are likely to keep occurring for a time, perhaps dozens or hundreds of times, usually as variations on a particular theme.

Frightening as they often are to those of us who have them, obsessional daydreams such as Morphy's do not occur randomly. Even though they seem to pop up involuntarily, they most likely do so on certain occasions in reaction to particular feelings or impulses. In the context of those situations, they express something of our underlying conflicts and impulses, and they may indicate some strong blocked feelings.

The meanings of these images may be quite different from what they seem. Moreover, whatever possible meanings such images might have for some of us, they certainly would not mean the same thing for everyone. You cannot automatically assume that a particular interpretation would be valid for you. But the general strategy of finding often easily understandable feelings, impulses, and wishes behind obsessive images does have wide application.

For instance, you may imagine dropping babies without

any intent to drop them. Instead, the image may express either or both of two things: insecurity about dealing with the baby, and frustration at *having* to deal with it. The insecurity may stem from a feeling of incompetence around babies, so that you *fear* dropping them. The frustration, which might be related to the insecurity, may stem from having to hold the baby and not wanting to do so, and this emotion fits with the physical action of simply dumping the infant. The obsessive thought captures both the fear and the desire in one powerful image.

A person who keeps imagining killing another may have this daydream only when talking to or thinking about the other person. Most likely this is in reaction to frustration with the other person. In our everyday language, we commonly express sentiments of wanting to wring someone's neck or bop someone over the head, which are both potentially lethal actions. The obsessional daydreamer may not use the words but represents the same sentiment in mental images. The difference is that the obsessional daydreamer is cut off from identifying accurately the emotion that underlies these images and then is aghast at their violence.

Other kinds of obsessional daydreams can often be explained in the same way. For example, self-mutilating images probably symbolize moments of frustration or anger with yourself, or perhaps disappointment or fear over the consequences of your own actions. Many of us respond to frustration with quietly violent gestures, such as shaking a fist or pounding it on the table, slapping our foreheads, or kicking the ground. When we blame ourselves for our misfortunes, we direct that anger at ourselves. Self-mutilating images probably express those same sentiments.

The meanings of these obsessive images are not particularly unusual. They probably follow the common route of daydreams: an emotional reaction to something in a situation, and internal, imaginary actions that are consistent with the emotions. What might make them feel unusual is that you cannot stand having them.

One reason for the revulsion toward obsessional thoughts is that people take them too literally. Especially in this post-Freudian age, people are likely to interpret any image as representing a wish and a wish as an intention. These images represent a wish in only a rather tenuous, one-sided form that rarely turns into serious intent to act out the image. In our rather violent society, we think nothing of someone saying, not too seriously, "I'll kill you if you don't stop making that racket!" Yet we become alarmed when we express exactly the same sentiment in a snatch of daydream.

Another reason for the revulsion is failure to recognize how the obsessive image is connected to what is going on in the situation. You may not consciously be feeling the emotions the image is expressing and may be unaware of the regularity with which it pops up only under certain conditions, which makes it feel unpredictable and out of control.

**Why We Have Obsessional Daydreams**

Very probably, obsessional daydreams come about when we keep ourselves from experiencing our feelings about something. Therapists have repeatedly reported that people who complain of frightening obsessional daydreams and other thoughts appear to be relatively unemotional and have trouble describing their feelings. It is as if they routinely suppress their emotions, which then find expression in the unwanted obsessional images.

Suppressing something seems to produce a rebound effect. Texas psychologist Daniel Wegner has asked research participants to suppress some thought, such as thoughts of white bears. People trying not to think of white bears quite naturally keep thinking about them, because the act of suppressing requires that you keep in mind what you are suppressing. More unexpectedly, after people are told that they can stop suppressing the thought, they find themselves thinking that thought much more often than they would have otherwise—a rebound. Wegner suggests that obsessive thoughts might represent that kind of a rebound from our prolonged attempt to suppress certain feelings and the ideas that underlie them.

Robert Morphy continued his account of his obsessions: "Obsessional thinking and unblocked feeling are two sides of the coin. As I experience my emotions more directly, I do less obsessional thinking. Glimpses of the blocked feeling and insight into the meaning of obsessional phrases usually precede the return of feeling as part of a process which is typically gradual. One exception [to the gradualness] stands out vividly. I was walking with my friend Norman, talking eagerly, while at the same time, with unceasing repetitiveness, I was thinking of grabbing his genitals. Suddenly, obsessional thoughts disappeared and I felt heartwarming caring for him. The effect was so simple and dramatic that it could serve as a textbook example of how obsessional thoughts block out emotions."

**Dealing with Obsessional Daydreams**

There are a number of ways for dealing with obsessional daydreams. Simply trying to stop the unwanted daydreams whenever they occur doesn't generally work, but some more indirect methods are reported to work reasonably well. These include:

- satiation, paying close attention to each occurrence
- paradoxical intention, deliberately creating the images
- connecting images with feelings
- drug therapy

All three of the psychological methods have one thing in common: they ask you to focus on the obsessional ideas, expand them, and get used to them. The third also tries explicitly to translate them into feelings. In Daniel Wegner's happy term, "We should go ahead and think our unwanted thoughts . . . prescribing the disease as a cure for itself."

Satiation involves paying close attention to each instance when the obsessive thought arises. For instance, British psychologist Brian Glaister had a patient who was troubled by inner voices. These said things such as "take an overdose," "cut your wrist with a razor," or "eat some glass." Glaister instructed his patient to spend half-hour periods "recording the time of the voice speaking, the words spoken and a 6-point rating of demandingness." At the start of treatment, the patient had these thoughts at a rate of about twenty-three per hour. After eighteen sessions, they had dropped to near zero.

Paradoxical intention, devised by Viennese psychiatrist Viktor Frankl, goes one step further. It requires you to try deliberately having the obsessional thoughts and even embellishing them, thereby giving full vent to them. The effect is eventually to deflate the impulse behind the thoughts and provide a sense of control over them. As a result, they become less numerous and less frightening.

I encourage clients to take their obsessional daydreams as the signals that they are: a message from you to yourself about your feelings in that situation. Clients then become aware of the connections between their obsessional images and both their feelings and the circumstances that gave rise to them. Making these connections may be hard to do, because those who have obsessional daydreams often have limited awareness of their feelings. But by examining the obsessional daydreams and their feelings carefully, it is often possible over time to understand what the images mean—to break the code. At that point, they lose their scariness. They rejoin the ranks of normal daydream experiences and can serve the same functions as other daydreams: expressing how you feel and what you want, even when you might not otherwise have known what you really feel or want.

For example, Gary knew only that he had terrifying images of injuring himself, and he was afraid that he was going crazy. Having entered psychotherapy, he received reassurance that his images did not portend insanity. Eventually, Gary discovered that he had those self-mutilation daydreams mostly after suffering severe disappointments, usually in his relationships with women. He came to accept the imagery as a communication to himself of frustration over rejection, of anger at himself for not providing better for himself. His horror of his images was ample evidence that, on balance, he did not really mean to hurt himself. As he took this far more innocuous view of his self-mutilation daydreams, they became far less frightening; they became for him more like indicators of his feelings. With his psychotherapist's guidance, Gary began trying to voice those feelings to himself, to focus on them directly and express them, rather than to funnel them only through his images; and, as he did so, his self-mutilation daydreams began to fade away.

Recently, psychiatrists such as National Institute of Mental Health researchers Judith Rapoport and Henrietta Leonard have recommended treating obsessive-compulsive problems with a drug called chlomipramine hydrochloride, also known as Anafranil. This drug is an antidepressant, but its ability to relieve obsessional daydreams seems to be unrelated to its effect on depression. At this time, no one knows exactly why it works, but it does help many people with obsessions and compulsions.

The fact that drug therapy can be effective with obsessional daydreams does not necessarily contradict the psychological explanation. Both psychological treatment and drug therapy ultimately work through the human brain and may achieve the same favorable effect by different means. Judging from recent research, people eager to rid themselves of obsessive-compulsive problems, including obsessional daydreams, can benefit from either behaviorally oriented psychological techniques or drug therapy.

Because this specific drug therapy for obsessive-compulsive conditions is still so new, the long-term effects are still unclear. In other conditions, such as depression, both psychological treatment and drugs have been shown effective; but in recent research, psychologists Mark Evans and Steven Hollon found that depressed individuals relapse significantly less often following psychological treatment than following treatment with antidepressants. It is possible that therapy for obsessive-compulsive problems will show a similar pattern.

In any event, several avenues have now been shown effective for dealing with obsessional daydreams. This provides sufferers with a number of options for getting help.

CHAPTER 10

# The Hidden Benefits: What Daydreaming Can Do for You

*He who passes not his days in the realm of dreams is the slave of the days.*

—Kahlil Gibran

*Imagination is not a talent of some men but is the health of every man.*

—Ralph Waldo Emerson

Daydreaming is so much a natural part of being human that we tend to take it for granted, but it carries many specific benefits for us. Some of these benefits come to us from natural, everyday daydreaming; others come from harnessing our daydreaming ability and using it in a controlled fashion. Taken altogether, daydreaming can:

- make us feel more relaxed
- stimulate us
- help us keep our lives organized
- increase our understanding of ourselves
- help improve physical skills through mental practice
- help us become more effective in social and other situations through exploration and rehearsal

- provide a medium for growth and therapy
- move us toward making decisions
- foster finding creative solutions to problems
- help us to empathize better with other people
- perhaps help us develop desirable personality traits

Curiously, hardly anyone has set out to demonstrate these benefits. Knowledge about them has emerged from scientific investigations and clinical experiences that had initially been directed at other questions.

For example, during World War I the Dutch psychologist Julien Varendonck undertook an extensive examination of his own daydreams, hoping to contribute to the development of psychoanalytic theory. Many of his conclusions ran counter to his presuppositions. Near the end of his book on *The Psychology of Day-Dreams* he wrote of the "good number of instances of assistance which our conscious self gets from our affective thinking," using his term for the process behind daydreaming, saying that "it prepares . . . plans for the future, composes the text of letters to be written, devises means and arguments for prospective discussions, warns me that I am in the wrong train, that I should not miss an appointment, puts forgotten memories at my disposal at the very moment when I want them most. . . ." He had discovered pervasive benefits of daydreaming.

Sigmund Freud and many subsequent psychoanalysts sought ways to understand their patients, fixing for this purpose on dreams and "free association"—patients' reports of everything that goes through their minds during therapy sessions, including daydreams. Psychoanalysts thereby drew attention to the potential of daydreams for self-understanding.

Similarly, the most influential pioneer of guided-daydream therapy, German psychiatrist Hanscarl Leuner, discovered while substituting mental images for words in psychoanalysis that the guided daydreams themselves seemed to have a therapeutic effect. A range of people from physical educators to clinical psychologists tried having athletes and patients practice physical, logical, and social skills in their mental images. They discovered that this mental practice worked in improving skills, with little thought that they had in effect harnessed daydreaming and therefore demonstrated one of its potential benefits. Many different traditions, from Eastern meditative traditions to clinical psychiatry and psychology, contributed to the gradual realization that daydreamlike mental imagery could be harnessed to help people relax.

Psychologist and pioneer of modern daydream research Jerome L. Singer was convinced from personal experience that daydreams could be a source of stimulation and creativity. He remained alert to the benefits of daydreaming, and his subsequent studies broke new ground in showing the normality of daydreaming. His work also first revealed that small children's fanciful play, a probable forerunner of daydreaming in our individual development, is associated with desirable personality traits.

## DAYDREAMS AND RELAXATION

Whether daydreaming helps you to relax depends on how you do it. If you let your daydreams flow and they are largely about pleasant matters, they are likely to have a relaxing effect. If they are worried daydreams, you may be more relaxed after your worrying has run its course, although the initial effects may be to tense you up. You can also simply choose something pleasant to daydream about—an example of easily applied controlled daydreaming.

Although there has been little research on the relaxing effects of natural daydreaming, the ability of controlled daydreaming to relax us is by now well known and well documented. Pleasant images make people feel more relaxed, and physiological measurements—from brain waves and breathing to electrical skin conductance and muscle potentials—confirm this.

Controlled daydreaming is used as a relaxer in a variety

of contexts. At some point your dentist may have said to you, "Now sit back, close your eyes, relax, and imagine yourself on a beach. You are flopped on a beach chair, so relaxed, so pleasantly warm, and you can see the waves come in and hear the surf, one wave after the other, each breaking with a PSHHH, one after the other, peaceful, so relaxing."

Many people make use of daydreaming such as this to relax and soothe themselves. When they are feeling harried, they switch to a pleasant daydream and let it gradually calm their emotions and make them feel good. At night they may break through a chain of worrying and put themselves to sleep by plunging into an attractive daydream about anything from football to beachcombing to sex.

Daydreaming can also have a calming effect by letting you spontaneously work through problems until you get a sense of having a grasp of them. At that point, you are likely to feel less tense. As Louisiana communication researchers Zagacki, Edwards, and Honeycutt have shown, many people report that one of the outcomes for them of imagining interactions with other people is relief.

For example, suppose you have just had a row with a coworker that has left you upset. As you replay the incident in your mind, you notice things about it that you had not noticed in the heat of the moment—her expression of indignation, for instance, and the hurt look in her eye. You now wonder why, of all things, she felt indignant and hurt. As you spontaneously put yourself in her place, you realize that from her point of view you must have been intruding on her turf. To her, you now realize, it must also have felt like a betrayal.

You then begin to daydream about the next time you encounter your coworker. Still somewhat miffed, you imagine acting icy and superior, as though you were within your rights, and in your daydream you feel the tension in the air between you—the mounting anger, the rupture in your working relationship. You also begin to regret the hurt you caused her, which you realized only in the course of daydreaming about your row, and you begin daydreaming that next interaction with her all over again. "Let's talk," you imagine yourself saying to her, your own eyes a bit moist, some of your own hurt welling up. You share your feelings and your observations of your coworker's probable feelings, and in your daydream you see her sit down and say, "All right, let's talk." In your daydream the conversation becomes constructive, a negotiation that restores your working relationship. After a while, you have a sense of knowing the damage done by the argument and your options for damage control and conciliation. You know how to proceed. This allows you to turn your mind to other matters and your turmoil subsides.

## DAYDREAMING AS SELF-STIMULATION

People in boring jobs often plunge themselves into daydreaming not for relaxation but to keep their minds stimulated—sometimes even to keep themselves awake. For example, among a group of swimming-pool lifeguards, long-distance truck drivers, and tractor drivers my research group surveyed, most launch deliberately into daydreams. Nearly four out of ten reported doing so often, and about two-thirds were of the opinion that vivid daydreaming helped them to combat boredom, although most conceded that it also made them less alert.

Whatever it did to their alertness, daydreaming may have helped keep the participants awake. In an experiment by New York psychologist John S. Antrobus and Jerome L. Singer, people were asked to perform a very dull task for periods of an hour and a half. Besides performing the task, one group was asked to count repeatedly from one to nine, whereas the other group was asked to talk about whatever they wished, in the style of mindwandering. The two groups performed their tasks overall about equally well, but the first group became drowsier and sometimes fell asleep. Apparently, the daydreamlike talk helped keep the others awake.

This suggests that in boring situations, daydreaming might provide a trade-off. At the cost of absorbing some of your attention and therefore making you less attentive to things going on around you, daydreaming may keep you more aroused and therefore readier for action. For example, a daydreaming lifeguard might risk being slower to react to a swimmer in trouble but might be less likely to drowse off, which would briefly make her or him completely useless.

## DAYDREAMS AS ORGANIZERS

When our minds wander, they wander away from what we are doing but onto our other concerns. Unless you run your whole life by lists and schedules, you would have trouble keeping its many details in mind were it not for the fact that you keep coming back to them in the mindwandering and flashes of imagery that make up so much of our daydreams. This imagery and mindwandering have the effect of keeping your concerns before your eyes enough so that you do not forget about them.

In this way, daydreaming functions as a reminder mechanism, a kind of mental calendar pad—much less compact and organized than a real calendar pad—that helps you keep tabs on your life. And that in turn helps keep you organized in the pursuit of your goals. While you are driving your kids to a game with their Little League opponents, your mind may wander to the confrontation you expect in tomorrow's conference with a troublesome manager in your firm. As your daydream version of that conference unfolds in your mind, you may remember things you need to do to prepare for the real version. And the next day, while you are in that conference, your mind may briefly play over the morning argument with your teenager about borrowing your car, and this daydream may remind you of your need to work that conflict through.

**Worried Daydreams**

Some kinds of daydreams do nothing but parade our problems before us. Because of the emotions these daydreams stir up, they make us tense and anxious; they are part of worrying. We think of what we might have done wrong, what we might be called on to face or do, and the scenarios for upcoming events that put us under stress; and our bodies react almost as if these situations were here and now.

It is possible to lie in bed and feel as activated as if you were rushing around conducting business. That is the most common reason for having trouble falling asleep at night. It seems troublesome, a curse on our night's sleep.

But, up to a point, even this kind of daydreaming has a real function: it, too, helps us to keep our lives organized—to remind us of our agendas, to help us sort through the things we have experienced, and to prepare us for the challenges and opportunities ahead.

Much as we would often rather go to sleep, we often seem even more strongly to *desire* to worry. We worry about matters that are important to us, and these carry a strong emotional charge. The strong feelings that launch each daydream are impulses to do something about the matter. We *want* to do something, but here we are, in bed, with nothing to be done. So we think instead—spontaneously, daydream-style—reviewing the problem and rehearsing solutions for the moment when we *will* be able to act.

That is why the usual prescription for cutting off worry and getting to sleep—distracting yourself and going into deep relaxation—doesn't always work very well. The very same worrier who complains about losing sleep may feel reluctant to give up the worrying, because it is an emotional expression of the desire to act. At the very least, the worry keeps intruding on some worriers' consciousness until they feel worried out. Only then do they drop off to sleep.

As we saw earlier, Pennsylvania psychologist Thomas Borkovec has shown that many worriers might be better off to accept the need to worry and to plan accordingly—that setting aside time to worry actually seems to reduce overall worrying. This method is a tribute to the strong need to worry, and it suggests the importance to us of even worried daydreaming.

**Unhappy Daydreams: Working Through Grief and Sorrow**

Some of us are bothered by gloomy, unhappy daydreams. Contrary to what Freud has said, both happy and unhappy people daydream. But, as Steven Gold's research team found, the mentally healthiest daydreamers feel better after their daydreams, whereas the mentally least healthy feel worse. Given the way unhappy daydreams can deepen unhappiness, it is easy to see why.

Yet, even unhappy daydreams can be good for us. They can help us sort things out, and they are part of the process of working through our disappointments and fears. Chicago psychologist Rosalind Dymond Cartwright once studied the night dreams of women who went through divorce. For some of these women, the divorce and its aftermath figured heavily in their dreams; for others it did not. The group that dreamed more about their marital status reported less depression than the group that kept the divorce-related themes out of their dreams.

Cartwright did not study these women's daydreams, but if she had she would probably have found the same thing, because what people dream about at night is usually an extension of what they daydream about while awake. Cartwright's research was not set up to establish whether dreaming about divorce contributed to getting over it more quickly; nevertheless, insofar as dreaming is part of confronting a problem, that seems a likely explanation.

Conversely, happy daydreaming is not always a good thing. Our daydreams, as we have seen repeatedly in this book, are an extension of our personalities. Some of us ("repressors") react to serious threats to our well-being by ignoring them. Repressors put the best face on themselves and on the world and experience less fear and inner turmoil than the rest of us. But their bodies give them away: beneath the calm exteriors, their bodies are reacting even more strongly than those of people who fully experience their emotional agitation. Their daydreams may resemble those of truly happy daydreamers, but their happy daydreams are really a psychological cover-up. This kind of cover-up can be bad for your physical as well as your mental health.

Consider, for example, a group of women with breast cancer studied by Yale psychologist Mogens Jensen. Jensen gave them personality tests and then checked on them over a period averaging one-and-a-half years. The cancers progressed on the average faster in repressors during this period than in women who confronted their problems more fully; they also progressed somewhat faster in women with happier daydreams. Apparently, when your daydreaming ignores dire realities, you are less well-equipped to deal with them, even at a physical level.

## DAYDREAMING AS REHEARSAL

If you are an athlete, you will practice every move and every play many times before your first game or meet of the season. If you are a theatrical performer, your director will take you through numerous rehearsals to help you memorize and refine your performance. But in addition to these real-life physical kinds of practice, you can practice those same skills—whether they are physical, theatrical, social, or any other kind—in the arena of your mind. You can do that deliberately, but you are undoubtedly doing it spontaneously as well. As you daydream about the upcoming game or opening night, you are in effect rehearsing mentally. As you daydream about personal encounters you expect to have, you are rehearsing them willy-nilly.

There are conditions under which this kind of mental practice works best. You need to have at least a beginning acquaintance with the movements involved from actually having tried them; and your mental images during mental practice need to be of you actually performing the movements, rather than of you watching someone make them.

When you imagine moving your muscles, even though they are in fact not moving at all, a polygraph can still pick up electrical activity—so-called electromyographic (EMG) activity—in the muscles you imagine moving. As Pennsylvania sports psychologists Dorothy Harris and William Robinson have shown, these EMG signals are strongest when you imagine moving your own muscles in ways you have already practiced in reality. Therefore, if you are watching a videotape of someone modeling a skill, such as putting a golf ball, you would do well to shape your internal images of your own movements to the movements on the screen. Thus the daydream rehearsals best for golf would be those in which you daydream about yourself doing the putting, using the best form you know, rather than going through motions unlike any you have ever performed.

What is true for movements is true for behavior in general: mental practice can improve it. Behavior therapists have long used a technique called "covert rehearsal" to improve clients' coping skills, such as their ability to assert themselves. If you were in such a program, your therapist would, among other things, request you to imagine a social situation, such as asking the boss for a raise or inviting an acquaintance to dinner, and then to imagine yourself taking appropriate actions in those situations.

As Pennsylvania psychologist Alan Kazdin has shown, developing your own images of doing this, rather than using a script handed you by someone else, makes the mental rehearsal more effective in helping you to act assertively in the outside world. The more natural, daydreamlike mental rehearsals are more helpful than following a script. There have been no investigations yet to show whether daydream rehearsals are effective without the guidance of a therapist, but, if you know what kind of behavior would be most constructive in a situation and are convinced of its rightness for you, there is no reason to doubt that rehearsing it in your daydreams would have a similar beneficial effect on your later performance.

When psychologists talk about daydreaming being a kind of spontaneous rehearsal for real life, that is not just a metaphor. Our daydream images represent parts of the same brain mechanisms at work that generate our actions. When we give them a workout, the benefits of the practice rub off on our physical behavior the next time we have to act, making it more accurate, better coordinated, or faster.

Long before contemporary science could demonstrate the truth of that, people had known it and had harnessed mental imagery accordingly. Musicians had practiced mentally the music they were to perform later; athletes had mentally run through plays before the big game; and many others had "psyched themselves up" in part by rehearsing mentally their requests for a raise, their job interviews, and their marriage proposals.

Many investigations have by now shown that practicing physical skills mentally—for example, repeatedly imagining the act of shooting baskets—improves performance the next time you try them out in reality. This is true whether the skill is throwing baskets, typing, or laboratory tasks such as tracking a spot on a rotating disk. With a growing scientific base of knowledge, harnessing mental imagery has become something of a growth industry.

One growing company called SyberVision, for example, markets an extensive array of audio- and videotapes aimed at improving personal qualities that range from achievement to weight control and from foreign languages to golf. The company's strategy is to change behavior by developing their customers' mental images—in the case of sports, images of professionals in action. The company offers no specific evidence that their particular tapes work, but considerable basic research by others lends their claims credence.

## DAYDREAMS, PERSONAL GROWTH, AND PSYCHOTHERAPY

Our everyday daydreaming contributes to our personal growth in that it helps us to explore our options, to improve our understanding of ourselves, and to find creative ways of achieving our goals. In addition to these benefits of natural daydreaming, many kinds of therapists and counselors have used mental imagery in dozens of different ways to treat psychological difficulties.

These therapeutic uses range from having clients with phobias focus on static images of things they fear to having them build daydreams around specific kinds of scenarios, as in Beverly Hills psychologist Joseph Shorr's psychoimagination therapy. The scenarios in psychoimagination therapy might take such forms as two animals walking down a road together holding a conversation or the client climbing a great many steps. Clients then let their own daydream processes specify what kinds of animals they are picturing; what they look, sound, and act like; and what they say to each other. These images help both clients and therapists to understand the clients' feelings and their views of themselves and their worlds.

Although guided daydreams such as this help to improve self-understanding, some therapists go a step further. Instead of using guided daydreams mostly as an information source for understanding, they make them the focal point of treatment itself. Here, therapists do not consider clients' insights into themselves essential for therapeutic progress; rather, clients work their problems through in the course of the guided daydreams themselves. Much as you develop your abilities and your views of yourself and your surroundings through your experiences in the real world, you develop and learn better coping strategies through your experiences in guided daydreams. In your daydreams, as in the real world, you interact with people and animals, only they are figments of your imagination. As in the real world, you run into problems—the whole array of conceivable problems with other people, projects, inanimate objects, and natural disasters—and you cope with them. As you cope, you learn; and in the context of guided daydreams, you have the luxury of coping with the same issues repeatedly in different versions, with a therapist by your side to support, encourage, and guide you. In a sense, you have brought the whole universe into the therapy room, only in your own imaginary version.

One well-developed variant of this method is German psychiatrist Hanscarl Leuner's method of "guided affective imagery." At each session, the therapist and client decide on a starting scene for a guided daydream, such as a meadow, a house, or a lion. The client then lets a waking dream unfold, much as Lucille's first guided daydream began in a cow pasture and ended with a swim. A guided daydream such as this averages perhaps fifteen to twenty minutes in length.

The client keeps the therapist posted at all times about what is happening in the imagery, and the therapist asks questions and occasionally makes suggestions about what the client might try doing or avoid doing in the image. It is remarkable how robust these daydream images can be in the face of questions and discussions, as well as how much they can go in directions that surprise not only the therapist but also the client.

Guided affective imagery helps clients achieve their purposes for entering therapy, such as ridding themselves of anxiety and depression. Because images are part of the client her- or himself, therapeutic learning from images appears to carry over to the client's real world. Researchers have shown experimentally that therapy clients using guided daydreams improve significantly, whereas comparable clients on a waiting list do not.

The method may be suitable not only for those with many psychological problems but also for those of us with psychophysiological disorders, in which, as in ulcerative colitis—severe nervous bowel—psychological stress leads to bodily illness. In an investigation by German internist Eberhard Wilke, patients who suffered from ulcerative colitis all received standard medical care plus psychological treatment. For some, the psychological treatment was a standard, psychoanalytically oriented psychotherapy and for others it was guided affective imagery. It is not clear that the guided-imagery group did significantly better than the other group when considered statistically, but they clearly improved, and in absolute terms they did at least slightly better than the group who received standard psychotherapy. The group who underwent guided imagery treatment required on the average slightly fewer therapy sessions, were out of the hospital slightly sooner, and, in the years that followed, relapsed slightly less.

Research nurse Jeanne Achterberg describes how mental imagery has helped burn patients to withstand the extreme pain and misery of treatment. These patients had suffered burns over an average of 25 percent of their bodies, many over 50 percent. Treatment consisted, among other things, of removing devitalized skin over a period of many days, using a brush, tweezers, and water. Patients reported that it felt like being skinned alive. The imagery treatment consisted of relaxing and mentally rehearsing the treatment experience—a kind of regimented daydream. It focused on anticipating each step, including the pain it caused, and also practicing tolerating it and turning attention to other things: features of the situation that were not painful, the soothing quality of a cream, and the purpose of the treatment. As compared with groups that did not receive the imagery treatment, including a group that received relaxation training without imagery, the imagery group felt less agitated, experienced less tension in their muscles, and asked for fewer pain-killers or sedatives.

Guided mental imagery has been used to treat a great variety of physical disorders, from headaches to cancer. The evidence for its effectiveness in cancer and other such serious illnesses is at this time almost entirely anecdotal and weak.

There are numerous accounts of patients who have rallied during imagery treatments, probably because of the indirect effects of the imagery or because their faith in the treatment improved their body's ability to fight back; but there is at this point no properly controlled, direct scientific evidence that imagery-based treatments can cure cancer. Such a treatment should never replace valid medical treatment.

Nevertheless, we are beginning to see solid evidence that guided daydreaming can improve patients' emotional states, which can in turn affect the body's ability to deal with cancer. A team of British psychiatric researchers led by Linda Briggs recently studied a group of women with breast cancer who were receiving radiation treatment. They showed that women who spent at least fifteen minutes a day relaxing and daydreaming about a peaceful scene of their own choosing felt better than those who only relaxed: they felt less tense, depressed, tired, and angry.

In a study by New Mexico psychotherapist Stephen Feher and his research team, guided imagery helped nursing mothers of hospitalized premature infants produce milk for them. Some of the mothers used a twenty-minute audiocassette tape daily to help them relax and imagine "pleasant surroundings, milk flowing in the breasts, and the baby's warm skin against the mother," especially before pumping milk. As compared with a group that did not use the tape, they averaged 63 percent more milk, and the more often they used the imagery procedure, the more milk they averaged.

Just how our mental imagery influences our health has not yet been established. Perhaps it can affect our bodies directly, just as we know that images of moving our muscles affects those muscles and that imagining temperature changes can change the flow of blood to specific parts of our body. But another, very probable channel is through imagery's effects on emotion. Mental images carry emotions along with them, and emotions are tied into the full range of physical functions, from body chemistry and muscle tension to heart rate and the immune system. We already know with some confidence that emotional stress weakens the immune system and can bring on illness. Losing a spouse, for example, greatly increases the chances of dying during the following year. Insofar as mental images help regulate emotions, they indirectly influence bodily functioning. Because mental imagery is such a large part of daydreaming, what you daydream about and how you daydream about it probably also have an impact on your health. This affords us the hope that we will be able to harness daydreaming to help improve our health and fight disease.

## DAYDREAMING AND DECISION MAKING

Sometimes, when we face a difficult decision, we get stuck and seem unable to decide. When this happens, our natural daydreaming can probably help us explore the ramifications of deciding one way or the other and eventually move us toward a decision. There is no research evidence to show that natural daydreaming really provides this benefit. Now, however, we have evidence that at least a controlled form of daydreaming can help move us toward making a decision.

This was demonstrated when a group of women were asked by German psychologists Peter Gollwitzer, Heinz Heckhausen, and Heike Ratajczak to pick a difficult personal decision that they had been agonizing over and then to indicate how committed they were to the path they would most likely decide to take. The women faced such decisions as whether to break up with a boyfriend, whether to switch a field of study, and where to travel on their next vacation. A control group of these women then performed some arithmetic problems and went home, whereas two other groups spent some time in controlled daydreaming. One daydreaming group imagined in great detail the nicer benefits of one of the courses of action they had been deliberating, such as leaving their boyfriends. The second daydreaming group imagined in detail various things they would do to carry out that course of action, such as telling the boyfriend about their decision, moving out of their shared apartment, dividing common property, and spending a week with an old friend to take the edge off the separation. Just before they left the research session, all of the women indicated once more how committed they felt to the decision they had just entertained in their imagery. Three weeks later, they received a questionnaire that asked one last time about where they stood on their decision.

At that point, the women who had moved furthest toward making a firm decision were those who had imagined in detail the various things they would do to carry out that decision. Those who imagined only the good things that would come of their decisions felt more committed to that course of action right after the session than they had before, but three weeks later they had slid back to about their original level of indecision. The group who had done arithmetic problems—in whose decisions the experimenters had not intervened in any way—were further from a decision three weeks later than they had been at the beginning. This suggests that these women would not have moved closer to making their difficult decision during the three weeks without the extra daydreaming; but daydreaming about the actions involved in carrying out their decisions made them feel more committed to the courses of action they had daydreamed about.

This finding suggests that if you wish to make a decision, you might benefit from daydreaming in detail what you would do to carry it out. This will familiarize you with the steps you need to take, help you to identify potential problems, and make you feel more comfortable about deciding.

## DAYDREAMING AND CREATIVE THINKING

Truly great advances in the arts and sciences are the products of creative ideas that break the mold of conventional thinking and place problems in a new perspective. On a smaller scale, the challenges we face in our individual lives also often demand creative solutions. Therefore, as parents and employees, students and friends, our welfare depends partly on our ability to think flexibly and innovatively.

Surprisingly, daydreaming seems to facilitate creative thinking, at least for those already knowledgeable about a problem and highly motivated to solve it. This conclusion is drawn from the personal accounts of a large number of individuals who have made creative contributions, rather than from experimental evidence, but what these people report is fairly persuasive.

"When I examine myself and my methods of thought," physicist Albert Einstein once told his friend Janos Plesch, "I come close to the conclusion that the gift of fantasy has meant more to me than my talent for absorbing positive knowledge." He thereby gave credit to the wellspring of his scientific creativity, one credited by many other major contributors to the arts and sciences.

The history of creative ideas is replete with reports of their birth during casual, daydreamlike states. The mathematician Henri Poincaré described the origins of his work on Fuchsian functions: "For fifteen days I strove to prove that there could not be any functions like those . . . every day I seated myself at my work table, stayed an hour or two . . . and reached no results. One evening, contrary to my custom, I drank black coffee and could not sleep. Ideas rose in crowds; I felt them collide until pairs interlocked, so to speak, making a stable combination. By the next morning I had established the existence of a class of Fuchsian functions."

Poincaré then described a succession of other creative insights, all during some activity in which his mind was distracted with simple, routine actions, the kind of activity during which we often daydream: "The changes of travel made me forget my mathematical work. Having reached Coutances, we entered an omnibus to go some place or other. At the moment when I put my foot on the step the idea came to me, without anything in my former thoughts seeming to have paved the way for it, that the transformations I had used to define the Fuchsian functions were identical with those of non-Euclidean geometry. . . . Then I turned my attention to the study of some arithmetical questions apparently without much success. . . . Disgusted with my failure, I went to spend a few days at the seaside, and thought of something else. One morning, walking on the bluff, the idea came to me with just the same characteristics of brevity, suddenness and immediate certainty."

Daydreaming plays a major part in creative writing. For example, French playwright Jean Cocteau wrote that the play *The Knights of the Round Table* was a "visitation . . . I was sick and tired of writing, when one morning, after having slept poorly, I woke with a start and witnessed, as from a seat in a theater, three acts which brought to life an epoch and characters about which I had no documentary information and which I regarded moreover as forbidding."

Pulitzer-Prize-winning playwright August Wilson described to Minnesota journalist Bob Ehlert the way he developed the character called Memphis in his play *Two Trains Running*: "Wilson says he just heard him up there talking away in his mind. Now, whenever Memphis wants to talk, Wilson takes notes."

The four children of the Reverend Patrick Brontë spent much of their childhood during the 1820s in daydreams, both the usual individual kind and group productions in which all four produced a joint daydream. As told by biographer Jörg Drews, they soon began to record and embellish their daydreams in notebooks, and their evolving fantasy life gradually grew into adult authorship. Two of them went on to become distinguished novelists: Charlotte, the author of *Jane Eyre*, and Emily, the author of *Wuthering Heights*. Charlotte in particular recorded the hold of her vivid daydreams—near hallucinations—on her writing and the difficulty with which she eventually had to force her daydreams to change in the interests of literary value.

Many other creative writers and artists have left a record of their dependence on their own daydreams. For example, during nineteenth-century British novelist Anthony Trollope's childhood, as described by his biographer Andrew Wright, he was an avid daydreamer who learned to turn his daydreams into fiction. The great Russian novelist Leo Tolstoy, author of *War and Peace*, grew up fascinated by day- and night dreams. Two of his three autobiographical novels, *Boyhood* and *Youth*, each contain a whole chapter entitled "Daydreams," and he sprinkled his other novels and stories with the daydreams of his characters. Contemporary author Alois Vogel subtitled a book of his stories "Daydream Tales." And artist Gretchen Lanes writes, "Often when I paint I am in a state of daydreaming. When I start a painting, I may have chosen the subject matter, but the content and context of the subject are yet to be revealed."

Creative insights don't simply arise out of nowhere during one's meandering thoughts. The creative scientists and mathematicians I have quoted had worked hard in their fields, were thoroughly acquainted with the problem they needed to be creative about, and were highly motivated to create. But, from that background, daydreamlike states seem to foster creative ideas.

Perhaps the reason for this is that when we work hard and deliberately, our thinking is constrained by our preconceptions regarding which approaches and ideas *ought to* work. Those preconceptions are likely to be futile precisely with problems that call for creativity, because these problems do not yield to standard solutions. And since states of mind during daydreaming are less dominated by standard approaches and preconceptions, daydreaming may foster those unexpected solutions that we consider creative.

In fact, one feature of creative ideas is the element of surprise. As poet and novelist Robert Nathan told Jeffrey Elliot, ". . . the writing of a book is—for me—like the singing of a song. I don't always know how it's going to end, but it flows along by itself. In *One More Spring*, for instance, I had expected Elizabeth to end up with Mr. Rosenberg, but she ended up with Mr. Otkar instead."

It is probably this force with which daydreams follow their own directions, often quite contrary to the expectations of our conscious logic, that enable them to give birth to creative ideas. But whatever the reason, the testimony of so many creative individuals strongly suggests that daydreaming states of mind are conducive to having creative insights.

## DAYDREAMING AND EMPATHY WITH OTHERS

If you tap into your daydreams while listening to other people, you are probably somewhat more empathic than average. For example, your coffee-break partner is telling you how hurt she felt when her neighbor formed a PTA committee without including her. As she goes on, you let your mind form a daydream in which you spontaneously visualize your friend looking crestfallen as she reads about the committee. With that picture in your mind, you feel the lump in her throat and her sense of hurt, and you probably end up with a more detailed, more accurate sense of what her experience was like for her than you would have had without the bits of daydream.

Minnesota clinical psychologist Nancy Lawroski, a former student of mine, found this to be true when she beeped people while they listened to a tape recording of others telling about emotional episodes in their lives. When the listeners visualized the others' experiences most vividly, they felt closer to the others' experiences and had emotions slightly more like those the others had reported having. Listeners who were more empathic overall experienced the most empathy for the others at those times when their mental images were most spontaneous—most daydreamlike. Although Lawroski's study was not designed to determine whether the daydreaming *caused* the improved empathy, it showed that daydreamlike images are at least associated with our empathy for other people. Those bits of daydreaming very likely help us to empathize.

That our daydreaming is related to being empathic was

shown also by Israeli psychologists Aaron Rabinowitz and Lea Heinhorn. They asked high school students to listen to tape recordings of people describing their emotional experiences. Those listeners who generally reported more daydreaming reacted to the tape recordings with more empathic concern.

All this strongly suggests that our daydreaming plays a role in feeling what others feel. Most likely, our daydream depictions of the people we listen to make their experiences more lifelike for us. We gain a better sense of what it must be like to experience what happened to them, which helps deepen our understanding of them.

## IMAGINATIVE FANTASIZING AND PERSONALITY

It is beginning to look as if those of us with vivid, imaginative daydreams may also have some special personal strengths, and perhaps even as if fantasizing helps us to develop those qualities. We know that just because our daydreams are especially fanciful we are overall no worse off psychologically than others. Although we know surprising little so far about special benefits that fancifulness might bestow on adults, most psychologists seem to agree that our daydreaming has its roots in our childhood play, about which we do have some solid information.

For children, playing imaginatively appears to carry some very positive benefits. We have already seen that culturally deprived children grow intellectually—including in their ability to tell the possible from the impossible—by being immersed in fairy-tale fantasies. There are also a number of studies of children who already play more imaginatively than average when investigators reach them, and those studies show an impressive list of ways in which the more imaginative children stand out. Some of these are clearly positive. In one nursery school studied by psychologist Roni Beth Tower, for example, teachers rated their more imaginative pupils as on the average more:

- resourceful
- alert
- energetic
- able to concentrate
- assertive
- persistent
- composed in the face of frustration
- liked by the other children
- positive in their overall mood
- inclined to express anger

They were also less dependable and organized, which many would regard as less positive traits.

Overall, the picture is one of resourceful, self-confident, individualistic children who know what they want and set out to get it. Other studies, such as those by Yale psychologist Jerome L. Singer, show that imaginative children:

- are less aggressive
- can wait longer without getting upset
- display more control over their emotions and actions
- are more sensitive to the facial expressions of others
- have more empathy with other people

It is less clear which of these things are causes and which are effects. It is possible that playing imaginatively helps children develop the desirable personality traits described by Tower and Singer; but it is also possible that those personality traits help children to play imaginatively. There is also a third possibility: that the personality traits as well as imaginative play are all linked to some other factor, such as genes, that affect all of them. We do know that they are not linked to general intelligence, since imaginative children generally score no higher on intelligence measures than the others do.

Although not all the facts are known yet, imaginative play probably helps to develop the above-mentioned qualities of personality. As Singer and other psychologists have noted, when children play imaginative games, they practice controlling their emotional expressions and their actions in order to fit the roles required by their play. This gives them extra experience at self-control. They get practice at "pretending," which helps them keep fantasy firmly separated from reality and gives them experience with deliberately harnessing their imaginations. Finally, they also get a chance to try out and explore a wider range of situations and actions than they otherwise could, which equips them with a greater level of sophistication about the world and its possibilities. With increased self-control and knowledge, the children grow in self-confidence. And all of this makes them more interesting and attractive playmates.

While not all imaginative children may grow up to be fanciful daydreamers, there is good reason to believe that most do, because there is considerable continuity between play and daydreaming. The hard data are not yet in, but it is very likely that imaginativeness shows up in play during childhood and evolves into fanciful daydreaming during adolescence and adulthood. And it probably continues to confer some of the same benefits.

## A PERSONAL RESOURCE

Daydreaming—that bane of puritan taskmasters, that near-synonym for wasting time—turns out to be a fundamental human quality, a part of the brain's machinery for fostering human survival, and a major personal resource. Daydreaming, ironically enough, helps us to get the most mileage out of our brain power. It does it by fitting into the interstices of our consciousness, into the spaces left by our other activities; and in this way it does its work while piggybacking on other activities.

Those spaces would go to waste, except for the fact that our brains seem designed to fill them. Whenever our minds are not fully occupied, they cut out from whatever we are doing and spontaneously start working on other concerns, sometimes realistically, sometimes fancifully. This switch-over process seems to be automatic—involuntary and, under most circumstances, even irresistible. It assures that whenever we are not using our full brain capacity for the task at hand, we will be using it for something else. And what goes on in our minds under those circumstances—what our brain fills those spare spaces with—mostly qualifies as daydreaming.

This process of switching into daydreaming makes it possible for us to keep the important threads of our lives in view even while we are not actively occupied with them. While steeped in work, we think now and again about family issues and relationships; we remember that we need to call someone about a party, and we imagine making the call; we remember that we need to get the car fixed, and we catch a mental glimpse of the car or the repairman; we remember that Thursday is the last day for mailing our tax forms, and we see them and our files scattered about the desk and imagine the reading lamp lit late into the night as we labor to finish by the deadline. While eating dinner, we go over things that happened at work or that will be coming up tomorrow, and we play them through our minds, sometimes in brief flashes, at other times in whole scenarios.

Most likely, this switching process is a part of our capacity for interruption, without which we would never have made it into the twentieth century. If we attended simply to that which we have undertaken to do, our ancestors digging roots would have missed the sounds that betrayed a rhinoceros starting a charge, a boulder starting to roll, an enemy gang sneaking up, or a lover walking by. The capacity for interruption is a priceless asset. The switch into daydreaming is probably a specialization of that gift; but in daydreaming, instead of reacting only to cues outside us, we also react to those that well up inside us, and instead of them sending us into action, they send us into imagined action.

The switch into daydreaming is highly selective. Our minds gravitate toward daydream topics that stir our feelings, and those tend to be about things we value highly, consider accessible, have become committed to doing something about, and do not yet feel completely sure of. They may be things about which our feelings remain unresolved—that we have not finished scrutinizing or have not yet made our peace with.

What daydreaming does with these topics is to contemplate them—review those that lie in the past, which enables us to draw remaining insights and lessons from them, and rehearse those that lie in the future, which lets us assess prospects and dangers and try out different approaches while there is still time to reconsider goals and tactics. Looking at the past, we might try out different scenarios of what might have been, a kind of mental Monday-morning quarterbacking that lets us learn from mistakes and missed opportunities. We also assess how satisfying our experiences have been, which helps us in choosing objectives to pursue thereafter. Looking into the future—or into alternatives to our present lives—we explore the limits of reality, sometimes going far beyond them, as a way of probing possibilities, including possibilities for what we want or for circumstances more gratifying than our immediate realities. In effect, we are exploring alternative goals preliminary to setting them.

As a mental resource, daydreaming is a kind of inadvertent tool; and, like any tool, its purposes are specialized. Although it is clearly not the best way to solve problems that you know exactly how to solve, it provides a hospitable framework for coming up with solutions after you are stumped. It is also far from the best way to search your memory for simple facts about yourself, but it provides a leisurely exploration of your past and future through which you can discover new truths about yourself and envision for yourself a fitting future. Daydreaming is inherently a disorderly process, and yet it serves as a natural reminder system: by parading before us our many hopes and fears, our possibilities and commitments, it keeps them fresh in our minds and thereby helps us to keep our lives organized.

Our daydreams are no alien intrusions, nor are they Shakespeare's "airy nothing," ephemeral wisps unconnected to life. They are products of the same brain processes that would produce our perceptions of the things we imagine seeing, that would produce the movements we imagine making, and that would produce the emotions we imagine feeling if what was happening were real rather than imaginary.

Because our daydream images are part and parcel of ourselves, the lessons that we learn in our daydreams are learned just as surely as if we had learned them in real life. Therefore, we can carry over the knowledge and skills we learn in imagery to our actions, whether they be tenis strokes or invitations to dance. That is what makes mental practice feasible and makes psychotherapy using mental images effective.

Despite some ways in which daydreams can go awry, their costs are greatly outweighed by their benefits. They are in the main an essential personal resource for coping with life.

# Bibliography


Achterberg, J. 1985. *Imagery in healing: Shamanism and modern medicine.* Boston: New Science Library.

Antrobus, J. S., and Singer, J. L. 1964. Visual signal detection as a function of sequential variability of simultaneous speech. *Journal of Experimental Psychology* 68, 603–10.

Antrobus, J. S., Singer, J. L., and Greenberg, S. 1966. Studies in the stream of consciousness: Experimental enhancement and suppression of spontaneous cognitive processes. *Perceptual and Motor Skills* 23, 399–417.

Arndt, W. B., Jr., Foehl, J. C., and Good, F. E. 1985. Specific sexual fantasy themes: A multidimensional study. *Journal of Personality and Social Psychology* 48, 472–80.

Beckmann, J. 1988. *Kognitive und autonome Handlungskontrolle.* Habilitationsschrift, University of Mannheim.

Bentall, R. P. 1990. The illusion of reality: A review and integration of psychological research on hallucination. *Psychological Bulletin* 107, 82–95.

Bobey, S. T. 1981. The effects of imagery and EMG biofeedback on relaxation. Unpublished doctoral dissertation, California School of Professional Psychology.

Bock, M. 1988. Emotion, self, and memory. In K. Fiedler and J. Forgas (eds.), *Affect, cognition, and social behavior: New evidence and integrative attempts*, 120–37. Toronto: Hogrefe.

Bock, M., and Klinger, E. 1986. Interaction of emotion and cogniti word recall. *Psychological Research* 48, 99–106.

Borkovec, T. D. Dec. 1985. What's the use of worrying? *Psychology Today* 19, 58–60, 62–64.

Bridge, L. R., Benson, P., Pietroni, P. C., and Priest, R. G. 1989. Relaxation and imagery for breast cancer patients. *Advances* 6 (2), 28–30.

Brown, J. J., and Hart, D. H. 1977. Correlates of females' sexual fantasies. *Perceptual and Motor Skills* 45, 819–25.

Brusman, M. M. 1985. A comparison of EMG biofeedback and guided imagery upon anxiety reduction in high-risk college students. Unpublished doctoral dissertation, Northern Arizona University.

Campagna, A. F. 1985–86. Fantasy and sexual arousal in college men: Normative and functional aspects. *Imagination, Cognition and Personality* 5, 3–20.

Cartwright, R. D. 1984. Broken dreams: A study of the effects of divorce and depression on dream content. *Psychiatry* 47, 251–59.

Chapman, L. J., and Chapman, J. P. 1988. The genesis of delusions. In T. F. Oltmanns and B. A. Maher (eds.), *Delusional beliefs*, 167–83. New York: John Wiley.

Chick, D., and Gold, S. R. 1988. Correlates of college students' sexual fantasies. Abstract submitted to the Society for the Scientific Study of Sex.

Crastnopol, M. G. 1980. Separation-individuation in a woman's identity vis-a-vis mother. *Dissertation Abstracts International* 41 (1-B), 345.

Crastnopol, M. G., and Seeman, W. 1978. The land of make-believe: Androgeny and fantasy. Paper presented at the annual meeting of the American Psychological Association.

Crépault, C., Abraham, G., and Porto, R. 1978. L'imaginaire érotique de la femme. *Actes du IIIe Congrés International de Sexologie*, 71–119. Montreal: Presses de l'Université de Quebec.

Crépault, C., and Couture, M. 1978. Contribution empirique á l'étude de l'imaginaire érotique de l'homme. Unpublished manuscript.

Cronbach, L. 1963. *Educational psychology*. New York: Harcourt, Brace & World.

Del Pilar, J. A. 1985. The relationship of biculturalism and androgyny to daydreaming, cognitive flexibility, and rise. Unpublished doctoral dissertation, New York University.

Domino, G. 1976. Compensatory aspects of dreams: An empirical test of Jung's theory. *Journal of Personality and Social Psychology* 34, 658–62.

Drews, J. 1987. Blühende Pantastereien, Proto-Literatur. *Merkur* 41, 498–507.

Edwards, R., Honeycutt, J. M., and Zagacki, K. S. 1988. Imagined interaction as an element of social cognition. *Western Journal of Speech Communication* 52, 23–45.

Ehlert, B. 8 Jan. 1989. Listening to the voices. *Star Tribune Sunday Magazine*, 6–9.

Elliot, J. M. June 1985. Portrait of Nathan. *Writer's Digest*, 34–37.

Farah, M. J. 1988. Is visual imagery really visual? Overlooked evidence from neuropsychology. *Psychological Review* 95, 307–17.

Farah, M. J., Péronnet, F., Gonon, M. A., and Giard, M. H. 1988. Electrophysiological evidence for a shared representational medium for visual images and visual percepts. *Journal of Experimental Psychology: General* 117, 248–57.

Feher, S. D. K., Berger, L. R., Johnson, J. D., and Wilde, J. B. 1989. Increasing breast milk production for premature infants with relaxation and imagery. *Advances* 6 (2), 14–16.

Fehrman, C. 1980. *Poetic creation: Inspiration or craft.* Minneapolis: University of Minnesota Press.

Foulkes, D., and Fleisher, S. 1975. Mental activity in relaxed wakefulness. *Journal of Abnormal Psychology* 84, 66–75.

Fowler, R. D. Nov. 1986. The case of the multicolored personality. *Psychology Today* 20 (11), 38–40, 41, 46–47, 49.

Freud, S. 1953. The relation of the poet to day-dreaming. In *Collected papers* (Vol. 4). London: Hogarth. (Original work published 1908.)

Friday, N. 1973. *My secret garden: Women's sexual fantasies.* New York: Pocket Books.

Friday, N. 1975. *Forbidden flowers: More women's sexual fantasies.* New York: Pocket Books.

Friday, N. 1980. *Men in love: Men's sexual fantasies: The triumph of love over rage.* New York: Delacorte.

Ghiselin, B. 1952/1955. *The creative process.* New York: Mentor.

Giambra, L. M. 1974. Daydreaming across the life-span: Late adolescent to senior citizen. *International Journal of Aging and Human Development* 5, 115–40.

Giambra, L. M. 1980. A factor analysis of the items of the Imaginal Processes Inventory. *Journal of Clinical Psychology* 36, 383–409.

Giambra, L. M. 1981. Daydreaming, attentional processes, and curiosity in white Americans: Religious, educational, economic, and residency influences for a life span sample. *Journal of Clinical Psychology* 37, 262–75.

Giambra, L. M. 1982. Daydreaming: A black-white comparison for 17–34-year-olds. *Journal of Personality and Social Psychology* 42, 1146–56.

Giambra, L. M. In press. A circadian rhythm in the frequency of spontaneous task-unrelated images and thoughts. *Imagination, Cognition and Personality.*

Giambra, L. M. In press. Task-unrelated-thought frequency as a function of age: A laboratory study. *Psychology and Aging.*

Giambra, L. M., and Grodsky, A. 1988. Task-unrelated images and thoughts while reading. Paper presented at the annual meeting of the American Association for the Study of Mental Imagery, New Haven, Connecticut, June 18.

Giambra, L. M., and Martin, C. E. 1977. Sexual daydreams and quantitative aspects of sexual activity: Some relations for males across adulthood. *Archives of Sexual Behavior* 6, 497–505.

Giambra, L. M., and Stone, B. S. 1982–83. Australian-American differences in daydreaming, attentional processes, and curiosity: First findings based on retrospective reports. *Imagination, Cognition and Personality* 2, 23–35.

Giambra, L. M., and Traynor, T. D. 1978. Depression and daydreaming: An analysis based on self-ratings. *Journal of Clinical Psychology* 34, 14–25.

Glaister, B. 1985. A case of auditory hallucination treated by satiation. *Behavior Research and Therapy* 23, 213–15.

Gold, R., and Gold, S. 1982. Sex differences in actual daydream content. *Journal of Mental Imagery* 6 (2), 109–12.

Gold, S., and Minor, S. W. 1983–84. School related daydreams and test anxiety. *Imagination, Cognition and Personality* 3, 133–38.

Gold, S., and Reilly, J. P. III. 1985–86. Daydreaming, current concerns and personality. *Imagination, Cognition and Personality* 5, 117–25.

Gold, S. R., Andrews, J. C., and Minor, S. W. 1985–86. Daydreaming, self concept and academic performance. *Imagination, Cognition and Personality* 5, 239–47.

Gold, S. R., Gold, R., Milner, J. S., and Robertson, K. R. 1986–87. Daydreaming and mental health. *Imagination, Cognition and Personality* 6, 67–74.

Golding, J. M., and Singer, J. L. 1983. Patterns of inner experience: Daydreaming styles, depressive moods, and sex roles. *Journal of Personality and Social Psychology* 45, 663–75.

Gollwitzer, P. M., Heckhausen, H., and Ratajczak, H. 1987. From weighing to willing: Approaching a change decision through deliberative or implemental mentation. Research report. Munich: Max Planck Institute for Psychological Research.

Gosselin, C., and Wilson, G. 1980. *Sexual variations: Fetishism, sadomasochism and transvestism.* New York: Simon and Schuster.

Green, G. H. 1923. *The daydream: A study in development.* London: University of London Press.

Groth, A. N. 1979. *Men who rape: The psychology of the offender.* New Y[illegible] Plenum.

Hardin, K. N., and Gold, S. R. 1988–89. Relationship of sex, sex guilt, and experience to written sexual fantasies. *Imagination, Cognition and Personality* 8, 155–63.

Hariton, E. B., and Singer, J. L. 1974. Women's fantasies during sexual intercourse: Normative and theoretical implications. *Journal of Consulting and Clinical Psychology* 42, 313–22.

Harris, D. V., and Robinson, W. J. 1986. The effects of skill level on EMG activity during internal and external imagery. *Journal of Sports Psychology* 8, 105–11.

Henderson, B. B., and Gold, S. R. 1983. Intellectual styles: A comparison of factor structures in gifted and average children and adolescents. *Journal of Personality and Social Psychology* 45, 624–32.

Henry, W. E. 1956. *The analysis of fantasy*. New York: John Wiley.

Henry, W. E., and Farley, J. 1959. The validity of the Thematic Apperception Test in the study of adolescent personality. *Psychological Monographs* 73 (10).

Heuer, H. 1985. Wie wirkt mentale Übung? *Psychologische Rundschau* 36, 191–200.

Hoelscher, T. J., Klinger, E., and Barta, S. G. 1981. Incorporation of concern- and nonconcern-related stimuli into dream content. *Journal of Abnormal Psychology* 90, 88–91.

Hurlburt, R. T. 1990. *Sampling normal and schizophrenic inner experience.* New York: Plenum.

Isaacs, I. 1975. Self reports of daydreaming and mindwandering: A construct validation. Unpublished doctoral dissertation, City University of New York.

Jacobson, E. 1929–30. Electrical measurements of neuromuscular states during mental activities. I. Imagination of movement involving skeletal muscle. *American Journal of Physiology* 91, 567–608.

Jacobson, E. 1930. Electrical measurements of neuromuscular states during mental activities. II. Imagination and recollection of various muscular acts. *American Journal of Physiology* 94, 22–34.

Jacobson, E. 1932. The electrophysiology of mental activities. *American Journal of Psychology* 44, 677–94.

Jensen, M. R. 1987. Psychobiological factors predicting the course of breast cancer. *Journal of Personality* 55, 317–42.

Johnson, M. K. 1988. Discriminating the origin of information. In T. F. Oltmanns and B. A. Maher (eds.), *Delusional beliefs*, 34–65. New York: John Wiley.

Kazdin, A. E. 1979. Imagery elaboration and self-efficacy in the covert modeling treatment of unassertive behavior. *Journal of Counseling and Clinical Psychology* 47, 725–33.

Kelso, H. G. 1986. *The relationship between absorption capacity and electro-*

*myographic biofeedback relaxation training with a male clinical sample.* Nashville, Tenn.: Vanderbilt University.

Klinger, E. 1971. *Structure and functions of fantasy.* New York: John Wiley.

Klinger, E. 1974. Utterances to evaluate steps and control attention distinguish operant from respondent thought while thinking out loud. *Bulletin of the Psychonomic Society* 4, 44–46.

Klinger, E. 1977. *Meaning and void: Inner experience and the incentives in people's lives.* Minneapolis: University of Minnesota Press.

Klinger, E. 1978. Modes of normal conscious flow. In K. S. Pope and J. L. Singer (eds.), *The stream of consciousness: Scientific investigations into the flow of human experience,* 225–58. New York: Plenum.

Klinger, E. 1978–79. Dimensions of thought and imagery in normal waking states. *Journal of Altered States of Consciousness* 4, 97–113.

Klinger, E. 1981. The central place of imagery in human functioning. In E. Klinger (ed.), *Imagery: Concepts, results, and applications,* 3–16. New York: Plenum.

Klinger, E. 1987. Current concerns and disengagement from incentives. In F. Halisch and J. Kuhl (eds.), *Motivation, intention and volition,* 337–47. Berlin: Springer.

Klinger, E. Oct. 1987. The power of daydreams. *Psychology Today* 21 (10), 36–39, 42, 44.

Klinger, E. In press. Emotional mediation of motivational influences on cognitive processes. In F. Halisch and J. van den Bercken (eds.), *International perspectives on achievement and task motivation.* Amsterdam: Swets & Zeitlinger.

Klinger, E., Barta, S. G., and Maxeiner, M. E. 1980. Motivational correlates of thought content frequency and commitment. *Journal of Personality and Social Psychology* 39, 1222–37.

Klinger, E., and Cox, W. M. 1987–88. Dimensions of thought flow in everyday life. *Imagination, Cognition and Personality* 7, 105–28.

Kosslyn, S. M. 1975. Information representation in visual images. *Cognitive Psychology* 7, 341–70.

Kripke, D. F., and Sonnenschein, D. 1978. A biological rhythm in waking fantasy. In K. S. Pope and J. L. Singer (eds.), *The stream of consciousness: Scientific investigations into the flow of human experience,* 321–32. New York: Plenum.

Kunzendorf, R. 1985–86. Hypnotic hallucinations as "unmonitored" images: An empirical study. *Imagination, Cognition and Personality* 5, 255–70.

Kunzendorf, R. In press. Mind-brain identity theory: A materialistic foundation for the psychophysiology of mental imagery. In R. Kunzendorf & A. Sheikh (eds.), *The psychophysiology of mental imagery: Theory, research, and application.* Farmingdale, NY: Baywood.

Kunzendorf, R., Brown, C., and McGee, D. 1983. Hypnotizability: Correlations with daydreaming and sleeping. *Psychological Reports* 53, 406.

Lanes, G. 1982. Creative daydreaming. *Dreamworks* 2, 234–35.

Lang, P. J., Kozak, M. J., Miller, G. A., Levin, D. N., and McLean, A., Jr. 1980. Emotional imagery: Conceptual structure and pattern of somato-visceral response. *Psychophysiology* 17, 179–92.

Lawroski, N. A. 1989. Cognitive and emotional aspects of empathic process and their relation to personality traits and situational variables. Unpublished doctoral dissertation, University of Minnesota.

Lee, C. N. 1973. Dreams and daydreams in the early fiction of L. N. Tolstoj. In V. Terras (ed.), *American Contributions to the 7th International Congress of Slavists: Vol. 2. Literature and folklore*, 373–92. The Hague: Mouton.

Lentz, S. L., and Zeiss, A. M. 1983–84. Fantasy and sexual arousal in college women: An empirical investigation. *Imagination, Cognition and Personality* 3, 185–202.

Leonard, H. L. 1989. Drug treatment of obsessive-compulsive disorder. In J. L. Rapoport (ed.), *Obsessive-compulsive disorder in children and adolescents*, 217–36. Washington, D. C.: American Psychiatric Press.

Leslie, A. M. 1987. Pretense and representation: The origins of "theory of mind." *Psychological Review* 94, 412–26.

Libet, B., Gleason, C. A., Wright, E. W., and Pearl, D. K. 1983. Time of conscious intention to act in relation to onset of cerebral activity (readiness-potential): The unconscious initiation of a freely voluntary act. *Brain* 106, 623–42.

Likierman, H., and Rachman, S. 1982. Obsessions: an experimental investigation of thought-stopping and habituation. *Behavioural Psychotherapy* 10, 324–38.

Locke, E. A. 1968. Toward a theory of task motivation and incentives. *Organizational Behavior and Human Performance* 3, 157–89.

Loftus, E. F. 1979. *Eyewitness testimony*. Cambridge, MA: Harvard University Press.

Lynn, S. J., and Rhue, J. W. 1986. The fantasy-prone person: Hypnosis, imagination, and creativity. *Journal of Personality and Social Psychology* 51, 404–408.

Lynn, S. J., and Rhue, J. W. 1988. Fantasy proneness: Hypnosis, developmental antecedents, and psychopathology. *American Psychologist* 43, 35–44.

Maher, B. A. 1988. Anomalous experience and delusional thinking: The logic of explanations. In T. F. Oltmanns and B. A. Maher (eds.), *Delusional beliefs*, 15–33. New York: John Wiley.

Malamuth, N. M., and Check, J. V. P. 1980. Sexual arousal to rape and consenting depictions: The importance of the woman's arousal. *Journal of Abnormal Psychology* 89, 763–66.

Marcel, A. J. 1983. Conscious and unconscious perception: Experiments on visual masking and word recognition. *Cognitive Psychology* 15, 197–237.

Marks, I. 1976. Advances in the healing of psychopathology: Exposure treatment. In G. Serban (ed.), *Psychopathology of human adaptation*, 271–290. New York: Plenum, 1976.

Martin, L. L., and Tesser, A. 1989. Toward a motivational and structural theory of ruminative thought. In J. S. Uleman and J. A. Bargh (eds.), *Unintended thought*. New York: Guilford.

Masters, W. H., and Johnson, V. E. 1979. *Homosexuality in perspective*. Boston: Little, Brown.

McCauley, C., and Swann, C. P. 1978. Male-female differences in sexual fantasy. *Journal of Research in Personality* 12, 76–86.

McCauley, C., and Swann, C. P. 1980. Sex differences in the frequency and functions of fantasies during sexual activity. *Journal of Research in Personality* 14, 400–11.

McGuigan, F. J. 1970. Covert oral behavior during the silent performance of language tasks. *Psychological Bulletin* 74, 309–26.

Mednick, R. A. 1977. Gender-specific variances in sexual fantasy. *Journal of Personality Assessment* 41, 248–54.

Meek, L. R. 1987. *The effects of mental practice and guided imagery on skill acquisition and retention*. Unpublished manuscript.

Millar, K. U., Tesser, A., and Millar, M. In press. The effects of a threatening life event on behavior sequences and intrusive thought: A self disruption explanation. *Cognitive Therapy and Research*.

Mischel, W., Ebbesen, E. B., and Zeiss, A. R. 1972. Cognitive and attentional mechanisms in delay of gratification. *Journal of Personality and Social Psychology* 21, 204–18.

Moreault, D., and Follingstad, D. R. 1978. Sexual fantasies of females as a function of sex guilt and experimental response cues. *Journal of Consulting and Clinical Psychology* 46, 1385–93.

Morphy, R. 1980. An inner view of obsessional neurosis. *The Gestalt Journal* 3, 120–36.

Mosher, D. L., and Anderson, R. D. 1986. Macho personality, sexual aggression, and reactions to guided imagery of realistic rape. *Journal of Research in Personality* 20, 77–94.

Nielsen, T. I. 1963. Volition: A new experimental approach. *Scandinavian Journal of Psychology* 4, 225–30.

Perky, C. W. 1910. An experimental study of imagination. *American Journal of Psychology* 21, 422–52.

Posey, T. B., and Losch, M. E. 1983–84. Auditory hallucinations of hearing voices in 375 normal subjects. *Imagination, Cognition and Personality* 3, 99–113.

Pressey, S. L., Robinson, F. P., and Horrocks, J. E. 1959. *Psychology in education*. New York: Harper.

Qualls, P. J., and Sheehan, P. W. 1981. Imagery encouragement, absorption capacity, and relaxation during electromyograph biofeedback. *Journal of Personality and Social Psychology* 41, 370–79.

Rabinowitz, A., and Heinhorn, L. 1984–85. Empathy and imagination. *Imagination, Cognition and Personality* 4, 305–312.

Rapoport, J. L. 1989. *The boy who couldn't stop washing: The experience and treatment of obsessive-compulsive disorder.* New York: Dutton.

Rapoport, J. L. (ed.) 1989. *Obsessive-compulsive disorder in children and adolescents.* Washington, D. C.: American Psychiatric Press.

Rhue, J. W., and Lynn, J. L. 1987. Fantasy proneness and psychopathology. *Journal of Personality and Social Psychology* 53, 327–36.

Rhue, J. W., and Lynn, J. L. 1987. Fantasy proneness: Developmental antecedents. *Journal of Personality* 55, 121–37.

Roberson, L. 1984. Development and validation of the Work Concerns Inventory: A measure of employee work goals. Unpublished doctoral dissertation, University of Minnesota.

Roland, P. E., Larsen, B., Lassen, N. A., and Skinhøj, E. 1975. Supplementary motor area and other cortical areas in organization of voluntary movements in man. *Journal of Neurophysiology* 41, 118–36.

Romaniuk, M., and Romaniuk, J. G. 1982–83. Life events and reminiscence: A comparison of the memories of young and old adults. *Imagination, Cognition and Personality* 2, 125–36.

Rosenfeld, E., Huesmann, L. R., Eron, L. D., and Torney, J. V. 1982. Measuring patterns of fantasy behavior in children. *Journal of Personality and Social Psychology* 42, 347–66.

Rowe, R. R. 1963. Daydreaming under stress. Unpublished doctoral dissertation, Columbia University.

Rychlak, J. E. 1973. Time orientation in the positive and negative free phantasies of mildly abnormal versus normal high school males. *Journal of Consulting and Clinical Psychology* 41, 175–80.

Schneider, K., and Eckelt, D. 1975. Die Wirkungen von Erfolg und Misserfolg auf die Leistung bei einer einfachen Vigilanzaufgabe. *Zeitschrift für experimentelle und angewandte Psychologie* 22, 263–89.

Schneider, W. 1987. Ablenkung und Handlungskontrolle: Eine 'kognitiv-motivationale Perspektive' (Distraction and action control: A "cognitive-motivational perspective"). Unpublished diploma thesis, University of Bielefeld, West Germany.

Schwartz, M. F., and Masters, W. H. 1984. The Masters and Johnson treatment program for dissatisfied homosexual men. *American Journal of Psychiatry* 141, 173–81.

Segal, B., Huba, G. J., and Singer, J. L. 1980. *Drugs, daydreaming, and personality: A study of college youth.* Hillsdale, NJ: Erlbaum.

Segal, S. J., and Fusella, V. 1970. Influence of imaged pictures and sounds on detection of visual and auditory signals. *Journal of Experimental Psychology* 83, 458–64.

Shakespeare, W. 1600/1953. A midsummer night's dream. In T. M. Parrott (ed.), *Shakespeare: Twenty-three plays and the sonnets*, 135–61; quote from Act V, Scene 1, Line 16, p. 156. New York: Scribner's.

Sheehan, P. W., Ashton, R., and White, K. 1983. Assessment of mental imagery. In A. A. Sheikh (ed.), *Imagery: Current theory, research, and application*, 189–221. New York: John Wiley.

Silverman, L. H. 1966. A technique for the study of psychodynamic relationships: The effects of subliminally presented aggressive stimuli on the production of pathological thinking in a schizophrenic population. *Journal of Consulting Psychology* 30, 103–11.

Silverman, L. H. 1966. A study of the effects of subliminally presented aggressive stimuli on the production of pathologic thinking in a nonpsychiatric population. *Journal of Nervous and Mental Disease* 141, 443–55.

Silverman, L. H. 1985. Mommy and I are one: Implications for psychotherapy. *American Psychologist* 40, 1296–1308.

Silverman, L. H., and Silverman, D. K. 1964. A clinical-experimental approach to the study of subliminal stimulation: The effects of a drive-related stimulus upon Rorschach responses. *Journal of Abnormal and Social Psychology* 69, 158–72.

Singer, J. L. 1966. *Daydreaming*. New York: Random House.

Singer, J. L. 1973. *The child's world of make-believe*. New York: Academic Press.

Singer, J. L. 1975. *The inner world of daydreaming*. New York: Harper.

Singer, J. L., and Antrobus, J. S. 1972. Daydreaming, imaginal processes, and personality: A normative study. In P. W. Sheehan (ed.), *The function and nature of imagery*, 175–202. New York: Academic Press.

Song of Song excerpts are from the *Good News Bible*, 735–37. 1976. New York: American Bible Society.

Starker, S. 1984–85. Daydreams, nightmares, and insomnia: The relation of waking fantasy to sleep disturbances. *Imagination, Cognition and Personality* 4, 237–48.

Stavosky, J. M., and Borkovec, T. D. 1987. The phenomenon of worry: Theory, research, treatment and its implications for women. *Women and Therapy* 6, 77–95.

Stockton, W. 18 Feb. 1979. Celebrating Einstein. *New York Times Magazine*, 15–17, 46–52, 61, 64–65.

Sue, D. 1979. Erotic fantasies of college students during coitus. *Journal of Sex Research* 15, 299–305.

Tanaka, J. S., and Huba, G. J. 1985–86. Longitudinal stability of three second-order daydreaming factors. *Imagination, Cognition and Personality* 5, 231–38.

Tanaka, J. S., Panter, A. T., and Winborne, W. C. 1986–87. *Imagination, Cognition and Personality* 6, 159–66.

Tantillo, J. 1981. Patterns of reported sexual fantasy in male and female college students. Paper presented at the annual meeting of the American Psychological Association, Los Angeles.

Tower, R. B. 1983. Imagery: Its role in development. In A. A. Sheikh (ed.), *Imagery: Current theory, research, and application*, 222–251. New York: John Wiley.

Tower, R. B. 1984–85. Preschoolers' imaginativeness: Subtypes, correlates, and maladaptive extremes. *Imagination, Cognition and Personality* 4, 349–64.

Vogel, A. 1982. *Das Fischgericht. Tagtraumerzählungen*. Vienna: Verlag Jugend und Volk.

Wegner, D. M. 1989. *White bears and other unwanted thoughts: Suppression, obsession, and the psychology of mental control*. New York: Viking.

Wilson, G. 1978. *The secrets of sexual fantasy*. London: Dent. (Quote from page 42.)

Wilson, S. C., and Barber, T. X. 1983. The fantasy-prone personality: Implications for understanding imagery, hypnosis, and parapsychological phenomena. In A. A. Sheikh (ed.), *Imagery: Current theory, research, and application*, 340–87. New York: John Wiley.

Wright, A. 1983. *Anthony Trollope: Dream and art*. Chicago: University of Chicago Press.

Young, J. 1987. The role of selective attention in the attitude-behavior relationship. Doctoral dissertation, University of Minnesota.

Zagacki, K. S., Edwards, R., and Honeycutt, J. M. 1988. Imagined interaction, social cognition and intrapersonal communication: Elaboration or a theoretical construct. Article submitted for publication.

# Index

NAMES

## SUBJECTS